PRINTERS, PEDLARS, SAILORS, NUNS

Aspects of Street Literature

Printers, Pedlars, Sailors, Nuns

Aspects of Street Literature

Edited by
DAVID ATKINSON and STEVE ROUD

LONDON
THE BALLAD PARTNERS
2020

Published by
The Ballad Partners
19 Bedford Road
London N2 9DB
theballadpartners.co.uk

ISBN 978-1-9161424-2-8

Printed and bound by Biddles Books Ltd, Castle House, East Winch Road, Blackborough End, King's Lynn, Norfolk PE32 1SF.

The Ballad Partners is a not-for-profit cooperative venture established with the aims of:
• publishing, or facilitating the publication of, essays, conference proceedings, and other materials in the fields of folk and traditional song, music, dance, custom (the folk arts), street literature, and related areas
• raising awareness and encouraging the study of the folk arts via publication of suitable materials and their subsequent sale and distribution.
The Ballad Partners may also organize or support other activities, such as conferences, meetings, exhibitions, and displays, the purpose of which is to encourage research or to disseminate information in the subject areas listed above.
To become a subscriber please contact: info@theballadpartners.co.uk.

Cover design by Laura Smyth.

Contents

Abbreviations and Resources

• Abbreviations used in this volume

BBTI: British Book Trade Index http://bbti.bodleian.ox.ac.uk/
ESTC: English Short Title Catalogue http://estc.bl.uk/
ODNB: *Oxford Dictionary of National Biography* https://www.oxforddnb.com/
OED: *Oxford English Dictionary* https://www.oed.com/
SBTI: Scottish Book Trade Index https://www.nls.uk/catalogues/scottish-book-trade-index/
SND: *Scottish National Dictionary* https://dsl.ac.uk/
VWML: London, Vaughan Williams Memorial Library https://www.vwml.org/

• Resources for ballads and songs

Bodleian Library Broadside Ballads Online http://ballads.bodleian.ox.ac.uk/
English Broadside Ballad Archive (EBBA) http://ebba.english.ucsb.edu/
Madden Ballads, Cambridge University Library (microfilm copy at VWML)
Roud Folk Song and Broadside Indexes https://www.vwml.org/

• Pre-decimal British currency

twelve pence (12*d.*) = one shilling (1*s.*)
twenty shillings (20*s.*) = one pound (£1)

• Online citations accessed and verified 29 September 2020

Preface

The **Broadside Day** is a one-day conference, held in February each year, organized by the Traditional Song Forum (TSF) and the English Folk Dance and Song Society (EFDSS). It is the annual gathering for those with a shared interest in cheap print and street literature, and serves to bring together people from a variety of disciplines and fields. The meeting moves around the country and in recent years has been held in London, Manchester, Glasgow, Oxford, and Cambridge, usually partnering with another organization that has an interest in, or important holdings of, street literature and related materials. Details of the meetings are posted on relevant websites, in particular:

- https://www.vwml.org/.
- http://tradsong.org/.

There is also an online discussion list called Pedlar's Pack, which is free for anyone interested to join:

- https://groups.yahoo.com/neo/groups/Pedlars_Pack/info.

Street literature is the generic term used to describe cheap printed items such as broadsides, chapbooks, and illustrations in the form of woodcuts and engravings, produced for, and avidly bought by, ordinary folk from the early sixteenth to the early twentieth century. Literally cried and sung in urban streets and at rural fairs, available on market stalls and in back-street stationers' shops, carried in pedlars' packs from village to village and house to house, few places would have been so isolated that they were not exposed to the print culture of the time, and few people were so poor that they could not afford to share in this material.

This volume is the second in a series of publications that began with *Street Literature and the Circulation of Songs* in 2019, and most of the essays were presented in an earlier form at the Broadside Day held in London in February 2020. The TSF and EFDSS are grateful to the Ballad Partners for enabling their timely publication in a permanent form and thereby allowing those who could not attend the event also to be part of the discussion.

The 'sailors' of the title reference the nautical theme that runs through the contributions by Martin Graebe, Michael King Macdona, and Lydia G. Fash, while the Irish ballads discussed by Catherine Ann Cullen provide the 'nuns'. Colin Bargery's essay looks at the impact on street literature of the advent of steam power in the textile industry of north-west England. The remaining essays address facets of the trade in street literature – the woodblocks that were used to illustrate chapbooks (Leo John De Freitas), the presentation and sale of cheap print in the streets (David Atkinson), and the development of a market for children's literature (Elisa Marazzi) and for cheap publications that encouraged the plebeian classes to embrace a distinct version of early nineteenth-century modernity (Gary Kelly).

The 2020 Broadside Day also heard presentations on ballad printing in the Vale of Glamorgan and on siege songs on Flemish broadsides. Peter Wood gave a paper on broadsides in the transmission of broken-token songs, the substance of which is to be found in his article in the 2021 issue of *Folk Music Journal*. While the Broadside Days have provided the kernel for this series of publications, it is not the intention that they be restricted to papers that originated in that forum. The essay on Hawkie was written for a conference that was unable to take place due to the coronavirus pandemic. Also reprinted here is a newspaper article on '"griddling" tramps' from 1879, introduced by Steve Roud, which sheds light on ballad singing and selling not by professional ballad sellers but by vagrants and professional beggars.

Contributors

David Atkinson is the author of *The English Traditional Ballad* (2002), *The Anglo-Scottish Ballad and its Imaginary Contexts* (2014), and *The Ballad and its Pasts: Literary Histories and the Play of Memory* (2018). With Steve Roud, he has co-edited *Street Ballads in Nineteenth-Century Britain, Ireland, and North America* (2014), *Street Literature of the Long Nineteenth Century* (2017), *Cheap Print and the People: European Perspectives on Popular Literature* (2019), and *Street Literature and the Circulation of Songs* (The Ballad Partners, 2019). He has published articles on cheap print in *The Library*, *Publishing History*, *Papers of the Bibliographical Society of America*, and the *Journal of the Edinburgh Bibliographical Society*. He is the editor of *Folk Music Journal*, Honorary Research Fellow at the Elphinstone Institute, University of Aberdeen, and Executive Secretary of the Kommission für Volksdichtung (Ballad Commission).

Colin Bargery has been singing folk songs for forty years. In the 1980s he was asked to write a history with songs about the navvies who dug the canals. This prompted an enduring interest in songs about the Industrial Revolution. Since retiring from his role as a risk manager in the NHS he has been researching these songs and curating a website called Songs from the Age of Steam which gathers together songs about the social impact of steam power and puts them into their historical context: http://songsfromtheageofsteam.uk/. He has given several papers at EFDSS Broadside Days and conferences organized by the National Railway Museum and the British Commission for Maritime History. He has contributed to *Street Literature of the Long Nineteenth Century* (2017) and *Street Literature and the Circulation of Songs* (2019), both edited by David Atkinson and Steve Roud.

Catherine Ann Cullen is the inaugural Poet in Residence at Poetry Ireland. She is an award-winning poet, children's writer, and songwriter, and a recipient of the Patrick and Katherine Kavanagh Fellowship for Poetry (2018). From 2016 to 2019 she was Writer in Residence at St Joseph's School, East Wall, Dublin, for which she won the Business to Arts Award for Best Use of Creativity in the Community. Her poetry collections include *The Magical, Mystical,*

Marvelous Coat (2001), *The Other Now: New and Selected Poems* (2016), and *All Better!* (2019), poems for children about illness and recovery reimagined from a Latvian book. She was the winner of the Camac Song Contest (2018) and the Francis Ledwidge Poetry Award (2009 and 2016), and joint winner of the Joyce-Cycle Poetry Prize (2019). She has worked on songwriting projects for children across Ireland and is a former producer with RTÉ Radio 1.

Leo John De Freitas is a graduate of the Royal College of Art where he researched commercial engraving on wood, 1700–1918. He has lectured and written extensively on the history of British illustration. He has published *The Banbury Chapbooks* (2004), and a study of the illustration of the *Alice* books by John Tenniel and the commercial engravers the Dalziel Brothers (1988). He has organized competitions and exhibitions on British graphic art and ran his own touring exhibition company, Graphicus Touring (1994–2020). He is currently engaged in studies of printing houses at the time of the Great Fire of London and eighteenth-century woodcut illustrations to *Robinson Crusoe*. As a sign of the scant attention the academy has given to that most ubiquitous art, popular illustration, practically all of his research has been without institutional support.

Lydia G. Fash is an assistant professor of English Literature at Simmons University in Boston, Massachusetts, where she runs the humanities internship programme and teaches US and transatlantic literature, creative writing, and all things pirate. She is the author of peer-reviewed articles in journals including *Narrative*, *New England Quarterly*, *Symbiosis: A Journal of Transatlantic and Literary Cultural Relations*, and *Transformations: The Journal of Inclusive Scholarship and Pedagogy*. Her monograph *The Sketch, the Tale, and the Beginnings of American Literature*, which argues that US authors used short fiction to theorize who counted as American before the Civil War, was published in 2020. She is currently working on Popular Pirates, a project about the ubiquity and meaning of piratical characters in Atlantic basin literature.

Martin Graebe is an independent researcher, writer, and singer, who has studied and written about a number of aspects of traditional song. His book *As I Walked Out: Sabine Baring-Gould and the Search for the Folk Songs of Devon and Cornwall* (2017) received both the Folklore Society's Katharine Briggs Award and the W. G. Hoskins Prize. He has been the Secretary of the Traditional Song Forum since its inception.

Martin and his wife, Shan, sing traditional songs together, with a repertoire based mainly on the traditional songs of southern England and in particular those collected by Sabine Baring-Gould.

Gary Kelly teaches English and Comparative Literature at the University of Alberta in Canada. Most of his research and publication has been in fiction, popular literature, women's writing, and print culture in Romantic-era Britain. He is general editor of the *Oxford History of Popular Print Culture*, with three volumes published so far. Current projects include a book on 'modern fun' (the collision and entangling of cultures of fun and of modernity since the mid-eighteenth century), and another on 'cheap Romanticism' (mainly Alex Hogg, Thomas Kelly, John Fairburn, and George Nicholson, and the sixpenny number and pamphlet trade).

Michael King Macdona is a retired solicitor, married with one daughter and living in Bedford. He has a long-standing interest in folk song, dating from the mid-1960s, especially shanties and sea songs. Michael Palin's book *Erebus: The Story of a Ship* sparked a particular interest in Sir John Franklin's ill-fated attempt to find the North-West Passage and the songs associated with it.

Elisa Marazzi is Marie Skłodowska Curie Research Associate at Newcastle University. Her current research on Children and Transnational Popular Print in Europe, 1700–1900, bridges her interests in the publishing history of ephemera and books for children, focusing on transnational encounters between children and cheap print across Europe. She has published a monograph, *Sotto il segno di Barbanera* (Milan, 2018), on an Italian almanac with a three-century tradition, as well as numerous articles on Italian juvenile publications. Her dissertation on the educational book trade in nineteenth-century Italy was published in 2014.

Steve Roud is a retired Local Studies librarian and now a freelance writer, researcher, and indexer specializing in the history of traditional song and street literature. He is the compiler of the online Folk Song Index and Broadside Index databases and his most recent book is *Folk Song in England* (2017). With David Atkinson, he has co-edited *Street Ballads in Nineteenth-Century Britain, Ireland, and North America* (2014), *Street Literature of the Long Nineteenth Century* (2017), *Cheap Print and the People: European Perspectives on Popular Literature* (2019), and *Street Literature and the Circulation of Songs* (The Ballad Partners, 2019).

The *Chesapeake* and the *Shannon*: A Battle and its Broadsides

Martin Graebe

Few today know that in 1812 Britain was at war with the USA, over issues of 'free trade and sailors' rights'. While the British and the French were engaged in their much larger conflict each sought to prevent neutral countries trading with the other, which placed intolerable pressure on the Americans. Another reason for American rage was the arrogant behaviour of Royal Navy captains who, when they stopped American ships, took off any sailors whom they suspected of being British. The war was fought on land and at sea, and while the land war produced reverses for each side, the fledgling US Navy did remarkably well in the early stages of the war and their large, well-armed frigates sank or captured a number of Royal Navy vessels. Then, on 1 June 1813, HMS *Shannon* captured the American frigate USS *Chesapeake* in a short but violent battle and at last the Royal Navy had something to be proud of. But it was not until Napoleon was defeated that the Royal Navy could redeploy its ships to deal effectively with the upstart Americans.

The battle between the *Shannon* and the *Chesapeake* caught the public imagination and was memorialized in songs, which appeared first in print. A few of them survived among traditional singers to be collected a century later. In this paper I will look at some of these songs, but before doing so it would be as well to say something about the background to the war and about the ships and the men who took part in the engagement.

The naval war

The naval action in the war of 1812 was largely conducted between frigates, rather than the great ships of the line, most of which were blockading the French fleet in their ports in Europe. The United States had a relatively small fleet, the pride of which was their eight frigates. Three of them, USS *United States*, USS *Constitution*, and USS *President*, could be regarded as super-frigates. They were the creation of the master shipbuilder Joshua Humphreys and were considerably more powerful than any other frigates then afloat. Some of the key events leading up to the battle between the frigates HMS *Shannon* and USS *Chesapeake* are listed in *Table 1*.

22 June 1807	USS *Chesapeake* boarded by HMS *Leopard* and several British deserters captured.
16 May 1811	HMS *Little Belt* attacked by USS *President*, believing her to be HMS *Guerriere*.
18 June 1812	United States of America declares war on Britain.
13 August 1812	HMS *Alert* taken by USS *Essex*.
19 August 1812	HMS *Guerriere* sunk by USS *Constitution*.
17 October 1812	HMS *Frolic* taken by USS *Wasp*, both ships then captured by HMS *Poictiers*.
25 October 1812	HMS *Macedonian* taken by USS *United States*.
29 December 1812	HMS *Java* sunk by USS *Constitution*.
23 February 1813	HMS *Peacock* sunk by USS *Hornet*.
1 June 1813	USS *Chesapeake* taken by HMS *Shannon*.

Table 1. Key naval events in the period before 1 June 1813.

USS *Chesapeake* appears early in the story and it was particularly grievous to the Americans when she was intercepted and boarded by HMS *Leopard* in 1807. Though smaller than the three super-frigates, the *Chesapeake* was still a formidable opponent, but she was just out of harbour and was caught unprepared. When her captain, James Barron, refused to allow his ship to be inspected, the *Leopard* fired on the *Chesapeake*, which returned only one shot before she was boarded. Three of her sailors were killed and seventeen wounded, including Barron. Four more sailors were taken from the American vessel and tried for desertion from the Royal Navy.

During the Napoleonic wars the Royal Navy was always short of men and sought to impress men from ships of other nations. Ships of the large American merchant fleet were frequently targeted. At that time Britain did not recognize the foreign naturalization of British citizens, and the concept of 'inalienable allegiance' held that any British-born man was liable to serve the crown. In any case, the process of naturalization was frequently fraudulent and a 'protection' document could be bought for just a few dollars.[1]

---

[1] Anthony Price, *The Eyes of the Fleet: A Popular History of Frigates and Frigate Captains, 1793–1815* (London: Hutchinson, 1990), p. 235, reports that an estimated 12,000 bogus citizenship papers were issued each year in New York, at a cost of $2 each.

It was less common for Royal Navy captains to stop American naval vessels and when they did so they were usually on the lookout for deserters. Of the four seamen taken from the *Chesapeake*, three were Americans who had been impressed on board HMS *Melampus* and had deserted. They were flogged and imprisoned, while the fourth man, Jenkyn Ratford, was found to be of British birth and was hanged for desertion. The Admiralty did not condone the actions of British captains who overstepped the mark and boarded American naval vessels, however, and Captain Humphries of the *Leopard* was relieved of his command. Nonetheless, on the far side of the Atlantic, Royal Navy captains continued to stop and search American merchant vessels and privateers, to impress men, and occasionally to 'forget' the admonishment to leave US naval vessels alone.

In May 1811 the sloop USS *Spitfire* was stopped by HMS *Guerriere* and another sailor was taken off. A fortnight later, Captain Rodgers of the American frigate USS *President* spotted a ship that he thought was the *Guerriere* and sought revenge for this action. He pursued the British vessel and engaged it as darkness fell. It was, in fact, the sloop HMS *Little Belt*, of twenty-two guns, no match for the *President* with twice that number of cannon.[2] The outcome was inevitable and bloody, but once the Americans recognized their error they offered assistance. Captain Bingham refused their help and took his badly damaged ship back to Halifax, Nova Scotia, with eleven dead and twenty-one wounded out of a complement of 121 men. This action was celebrated in a broadside printed by Nathaniel Coverly of Boston titled *Rodgers & Victory, Tit for Tat*.[3] The first half of the ballad is given over to the *Chesapeake's* encounter with the *Leopard* (stanza 3):

---

[2] The sloop *Lillebælt* had been captured by the British at the Second Battle of Copenhagen in 1807. She was named after the strait between the island of Funen and the Jutland peninsula in Denmark and *Little Belt* was the anglicized version of her name.

[3] *Rodgers & Victory, Tit for Tat; or, The Chesapeake Paid for in British Blood!!!* (printed and sold by Nathaniel Coverly, corner of Theatre Alley) [Worcester, MA, American Antiquarian Society, Isaiah Thomas Broadside Ballad Collection (hereafter ITBC)]. Nathaniel Coverly, Jr., was a prolific printer of broadsides in Boston between 1810 and 1824. Fortunately, the antiquarian Isaiah Thomas visited Coverly's shop in June 1814 and carried away a bundle of more than three hundred broadsides, printed by Coverly and others, which he had bound into three volumes, now held by the American Antiquarian Society. See further Kate van Winkle Keller, 'Nathaniel Coverly and Son, Printers, 1767–1825', *Proceedings of the American Antiquarian Society*, 117 (2007), 211–52. The ballads and accompanying metadata can be accessed online at the Isaiah Thomas Broadside Project https://www.americanantiquarian.org/thomasballads/.

You all remember well, I guess,
The Chesapeake disaster,
When Britons dar'd to kill and press,
To please their royal master.
> That day did murder'd freemen fall,
> Their graves are cold and sandy;
> Their funeral dirge was sung by all
> Not yankee doodle dandy.

The actual action begins with Rodgers spying a sail and chasing after the British vessel he believes to be the *Guerriere*, leading to the ballad's unapologetic conclusion (stanzas 9–11):

'Where are you from?' bold Rodgers cried –
Which made the British wonder –
Then with a gun they quick replied,
Which made a noise like thunder.
> Like lightening [*sic*] we return'd the joke,
> Our matches were so handy,
> The Yankee bull-dog nobly spoke,
> The tune of doodle dandy.

A brilliant action then began,
Our fire so briskly burn'd sir,
While blood from British scuppers ran,
Like *seventy-six* returned sir.
> Our cannon roar'd, our men huzza'd,
> And fir'd away so handy,
> Till Bingham struck, he was so scar'd,
> At hearing doodle dandy.

Then having thus chastis'd the foe,
And wounded thirty British,
We gave the rascals leave to go,
They felt so deuced skittish.
> Now toast our Commodore so brave,
> In toddy, flip, or brandy,
> And strike aloud the merry stave
> Of yankee doodle dandy.

The *Constitution* and the *Guerriere*

Diplomatic efforts to find a peaceful solution to the disputes continued until President Madison lost patience and declared war on Britain in June 1812. Ten weeks later, USS *Constitution*, under Captain Isaac Hull, chanced upon HMS *Guerriere* near Sable Island, off the coast of Nova Scotia. Captain Dacres took the *Guerriere* into battle with the words 'Not the *Little Belt*' painted on his foretopsail. Though both were classed as frigates, the American ship was larger, stronger, and carried forty-four guns to the *Guerriere*'s thirty-three. Captain Hull held his fire as the *Guerriere* approached him firing ineffective broadsides until, at a distance of just twenty-five yards, Hull ordered, 'Now, boys, pour it into them!' The British ship surrendered after it had been dismasted and so badly damaged that it had to be blown up. It is said that Hull got so excited that he split his trousers.[4]

This was the greatest success of the US Navy to date and Hull's victory was celebrated in print. Coverly printed several broadsides, of which *The American Constitution Frigate's Engagement with the British Frigate Guerriere* is an example:

> Come jolly lads, ye hearts of gold,
> Come fill your cans and glasses,
> Be fun the order of the day,
> A health to all our lasses.
>> Yankee doodle keep it up,
>> Yankee doodle dandy,
>> As hot as British folks can sup,
>> We'll give it to 'em handy.[5]

None of Coverly's ballads about the engagement seems to have been adopted by singers. There is, however, a song called 'The *Constitution* and the *Guerriere*' (Roud 626) which became popular with traditional singers. The text, often with the tune 'The Landlady of France', has appeared in many books of American songs and there are a number of collected versions. Unsurprisingly, there is no record from any British singer. Although it is one of the best-known songs from the War of 1812, the only broadside I have discovered is *The Constitution & Guerriere*, printed by John Lane of New York:

> We often have been told
> Of how British Sailors bold,
> How they whip't the tars of France so neat and handy O,
>> But they never found their match
>> 'Till the Yankees did them catch,
> For the Yankee tars for fighting are the dandy O.

---

[4] Ronald D. Utt, *Ships of Oak, Guns of Iron: The War of 1812 and the Forging of the American Navy* (Washington, DC: Regnery History, 2012), p. 56.
[5] *The American Constitution Frigate's Engagement with the British Frigate Guerriere* [ITBC].

The Guerriere so bold.
O'er the foaming ocean roll'd,
Was commanded by proud Dacres the Grandee O;
 With his saucy British crew,
 As his armour ever drew,
They could whip the Frenchmen two to one quite handy O.

 When his frigate hove in view,
 Says bold Hull to his crew,
'Come clear the ship for action and be handy O;
 The weather gage boys get her,
 And we very soon will let her
Know the Yankee tars for fighting are the dandy O.'

 The first Broadside we pour'd
 [Brought] her main-mast by the board
Which made this lofty frigate look quite dandy O,
 Then Dacres slip't aside
 To his officers he cried,
'God I never thought the Yankee's [*sic*] were so handy O.'

 Our shot it flew so well
 That her fore and mizen fell,
Which brought her royal ensign down right handy O;
 Then Dacres says 'I'm done'
 And he fir'd his lee gun
Then our drummer struck up Yankee doodle dandy O.

 When Dacres came on board
 To deliver up his sword
The Yankee's [*sic*] they all look'd so neat and handy O;
 'You may keep it' says bold Hull,
 'For it makes you look so dull
Come cheer up and let us have a glass of brandy O.'

 Come fill up your glasses full
 Drink a health to valiant Hull
And so merrily we'll push about the brandy O;
 Johnny Bull may boast his f[i]ll
 Let the world say what they will
For our Yankee tars for fighting are the dandy O.[6]

The text is similar to versions published by, for example, Joanna Colcord and Charles Harding Firth.[7]

---

[6] *The Constitution & Guerriere* (printed and sold by John Lane, No. 17, Chatham Street; where a variety of naval songs may be had) [Washington, DC, Library of Congress, Portfolio 113, Folder 15a https://www.loc.gov/resource/rbpe.1130150a/].

The loss of the *Guerriere* to the *Constitution* was the first of many setbacks for the Royal Navy over the coming months. Like Dacres, other British frigate captains failed to accept that an engagement with one of the American super-frigates was unlikely to end well. Captain John Carden of HMS *Macedonian* discovered this in just seventeen minutes on 25 October 1812 when he met USS *United States* and surrendered his ship after having lost 40 per cent of his crew. Another of Coverly's broadsides, titled *Brilliant Victory*, exclaimed:

Let Jonny Bull no longer boast,
He lords it o'er the seas,
We'll make his blood-hounds leave the coast
When they our cannons see.[8]

Then, on 29 December, HMS *Java* under Captain Henry Lambert met USS *Constitution*, now under the command of the veteran William Bainbridge. Lambert was killed in an action in which, at one point, he had had the upper hand. In the end, however, the *Java* was so badly damaged that, like the *Guerriere*, she had to be sunk:

Only in one short hour, and fifty-five minutes,
The Java and her crew gave up with us disputes,
    Her scuppers ran with British blood,
    As if it was a purple flood,
    We real Yankee tricks them show'd,
                        As true Yankee boys.[9]

Small ship actions

Not all of the significant naval actions involved the frigates. In October 1812 there was a more even match between the sloops USS *Wasp* and HMS *Frolic*. Although the American vessel took the *Frolic*, the following morning, while they were being repaired, both ships were captured by the 74-gun ship of the line HMS *Poictiers*. The *Wasp*'s brief triumph was celebrated by Coverly in a broadside which made a point of the large number of British sailors killed in the action:

[7] Joanna C. Colcord, *Songs of American Sailormen*, rev. edn (New York: W. W. Norton; London: Putnam, 1938), pp. 126–28, C. H. Firth, *Naval Songs and Ballads* ([London]: Navy Records Society, 1908), pp. 309–11. At stanza 2, line 5, Colcord and Firth have 'As a rammer ever drew'.
[8] *Brilliant Victory, Obtained by Commodore Decatur, of the United States Frigate, over the British Frigate Macedonian* [ITBC].
[9] *Naval Victory, by the United States Frigate Constitution, and the English Frigate Java* [ITBC].

From the deck of the Wasp, five seamen so brave,
With sorrow were launched to a watery grave,
But their comrads so bold, had the pleasure to know,
That sixty poor Britons went with them below.
Then fill up your glasses, let's laugh, drink and sing,
And toast the brave Wasp, which the British did sting.

The Frolick was mann'd and ordered for port,
'Having seen full enough of true yankee sport;
But the devil of it was, that the very next day,
Both Frolick and Wasp had to steer 'tother way.
Then fill up your glasses, let's laugh, drink and sing,
And toast the brave Wasp, which the British did sting.

A huge seventy-four with them chanc'd to meet,
And no chance was now left to make good a retreat,
To give up, the bold crew were compell'd rather loth,
And the Poictiers, the Wasp, and the Frolick took both.
Then fill up your glasses, let's laugh, drink and sing,
And toast the brave Wasp, which the British did sting.

But no honor was lost to the American name,
And the Wasp long shall shine on the records of fame,
And we hope e'er the war we're engaged in is o'er,
That our Navy will have a few Frolicks more.
Then fill up your glasses, let's laugh, drink and sing,
And toast the brave Wasp, which the British did sting.[10]

To ensure that the *Wasp*'s name did not live on the Royal Navy took her into its service and changed her name, initially to HMS *Loup Cervier* and then, in 1813, to HMS *Peacock*.

The reason for this second name change was that in February 1813 the previous HMS *Peacock* had encountered USS *Hornet*, under the command of Captain James Lawrence, whom we will meet again shortly. Both ships were eighteen-gun sloops, but the *Peacock* only had 24-pound carronades, while the *Hornet* carried 32-pound guns. The *Peacock*, commanded by Lieutenant William Peake, was known to be 'one of those shining spick-and-span British Warships whose gunnery and fighting quality did not match her appearance'.[11] Lawrence's superior tactics and gunnery reduced the *Peacock* to a wreck within fifteen minutes and she sank with a number of hands still on board, as well as some American sailors who were trying to save them.

---

[10] *Wasp Stinging Frolick; or, Engagement between the American Sloop of War Wasp, of 18 Guns, and the British Sloop of War, of 20 Guns* (printed by Nathaniel Coverly, jun'r.) [ITBC].
[11] Price, *Eyes of the Fleet*, pp. 261–62.

Coverly's broadside *The Peacock Stung by the Hornet* loudly trumpeted Lawrence's fame:

> Long may Columbia's Eagle soar,
> And o'er Britannia's Lion cower, [*sic*]
> And long shall gallant Lawrence's name,
> Rank high upon the page of Fame.
> *For every true Columbian tar,*
> *Will hail him Hero of the War.*[12]

The *Chesapeake* and the *Shannon*

In May 1813, USS *Chesapeake* was in Boston naval dockyard. Following a refit, she was ready to go to sea with her newly appointed captain, James Lawrence, fresh from the triumph of the *Hornet* over the *Peacock* three months earlier. Meanwhile, HMS *Shannon*, with her captain Philip Bowes Vere Broke, had been prowling around Boston Bay, hoping for an opportunity to meet the *Chesapeake* in battle. The *Shannon* had been there for fifty-six days and needed to return to Halifax to replenish her stores. Unable to wait any longer, Captain Broke sent a challenge to Captain Lawrence to come out and meet him, but before it was delivered the *Chesapeake* had hoisted her sails and was on her way to meet the *Shannon*.

The citizens of Boston crowded the hills overlooking the bay and many small boats followed the two ships as they prepared for action. Among them was a private schooner carrying the American captains Hull and Bainbridge, who wanted to see their younger colleague in action.[13] A banquet had been planned for that evening to celebrate Lawrence's victory, and Broke was to be invited.

Of the two frigates, the *Chesapeake*, though not the size of the super-frigates, was slightly bigger and carried a larger crew. However, the British captain was a master of gunnery and, unusually for the Royal Navy of the time, had drilled his crew daily on the big guns, for which he had devised a system of sights that rendered them deadly. He was also the better tactician and leader, with a crew that was well trained and who liked their captain.[14] The battle lasted twelve minutes.

---

[12] *The Peacock Stung by the Hornet; or, Engagement between the United States Ship Hornet, Captain Lawrence, of 16 Guns, and his Britannic Majestys Brig Peacock, Captain Peake, of 19 Guns* (printed by Nathaniel Coverly, corner Theatre Alley, Milk Street, Boston) [ITBC].

[13] Utt, *Ships of Oak, Guns of Iron*, p. 208.

[14] These were not qualities to be found in the three captains who had already lost their ships to the Americans. As an example, Captain Lambert of HMS *Java*, with a crew of

Captain Broke's report to the Admiralty said fifteen minutes, because otherwise he did not think he would be believed.

When the two ships collided, Captain Broke led a boarding party on board the *Chesapeake*, where, at the moment of surrender, he was struck down by a group of English deserters, who were in turn killed by his men. Captain Lawrence, who had been wounded early in the battle, had been carried below. The citizens of Boston looked on in anguish as the *Chesapeake* limped away in the wake of the *Shannon* and they cancelled their grand dinner.

Isiah Whyte, *Battle of Boston Harbor, USS Chesapeake and HMS Shannon* (public domain).

With her captain seriously wounded and her first lieutenant dead, the *Shannon* was under the command of her 21-year-old second lieutenant, Provo Wallis, for the six-day voyage to Halifax, where they were greeted by enthusiastic crowds rejoicing at a long-overdue victory. Lawrence died on the voyage and Broke was in a critical condition. He survived, however, and in October 1813 returned on

---

newly impressed men, convicts, and boys, had exercised his guns only once on the voyage from Britain, and that was not a live firing (Utt, *Ships of Oak, Guns of Iron*, p. 126).

board the *Shannon* to England, where he received a knighthood. His wound left him unable to continue in the service and he retired to his home, Broke Hall, in Suffolk, where he died in 1841.

Songs about the battle

I have found seven different ballads based on the action (*Table 2*). Their titles show little imagination and it is necessary to look at the texts in order to identify them. For the broadsides the first line is usually sufficient, but with the collected versions a more thorough examination is needed.

The Shannon and Chesapeak (Roud 963) 'On board the Shannon frigate in the merry month of May'. Printed on several broadsides.

Chesapeake & Shannon (Roud 1583) 'Now the Chesapeake so bold, out of Boston I am told'. Printed in song books, but only two broadsides identified.

Shannon & Chesapeak; or, She Comes in Glorious Style (Roud V9697) 'She comes, she comes in glorious style'. Printed in several songbooks and on broadsides.

At Boston One Day (Roud V44407) 'At Boston one day as the Chesapeake lay'. Printed in a few songbooks, including *The Vocal Library*.

The Shannon and Chesapeake (Roud V43924) 'Come all you gallant seamen, landsmen listen unto me'. Printed in Scottish chapbooks.

The Battle between the Chesapeake and Shannon (Roud V50816) ''Twas in the morning, the first day of June'. Printed by Nathaniel Coverly in Boston.

The Chesapeake and the Shannon (Roud 1891) ''Twas on the glorious fourth of June'. Collected by Helen Creighton and Doreen Senior in Nova Scotia, not previously printed.

Table 2. Songs in print about the *Chesapeake* and the *Shannon*.

The Shannon and Chesapeak (Roud 963) is the version most frequently found on broadsides and, as we will see shortly, it is also the song that has been collected most frequently from singers. The following is the text of a broadside printed by H. P. Such, reproduced in full as a demonstration of how the ballad writer has rendered the action:

> On board the Shannon frigate, in the merry month of May
> To watch the bold Americans, off Boston lights we lay:
> The Chesapeak lay in harbour, a frigate stout and fine;
> Four hundred and 40 men she had – her guns were 49.

'Twas Captain Brooke command'd us, a challenge he did write
To the captain of the Chesapeak, to bring her out to fight:
Our captain says, 'Brave Lawrence 'tis not from enmity,
But 'tis to prove to all the world that we rule on the sea.'

'Don't think, my noble captain because you've had success,
That British tars are humbled – not even in distress;
No; – we will fight like heroes, our glory to maintain,
In defiance of superior size, & the number of your men.'

The challenge was accepted, the American came down;
A finer frigate ne'er belonged unto the British crown;
They brought her into action on the true British plan,
Nor fired a gun till within hail, then they the fight began.

Broadside for broadside then did yield a most tremendous roar
Like thunder it re-sounded, re-echoed from each shore;
This dreadful firing lasted near a quarter of an hour,
When the enemy's ship drove right aboard & lock'd her yards were in
    ours.

Our captain went to the ship's side to see how she did lie,
And soon perceived the enemy's men, who from their guns did fly;
'All hands for boarding now,' he cried, 'the victory is sure,
'Come bear a hand, my gallant boys, our prize we'll soon secure.'

Like lions then we rushed on board, & fought them hand to hand,
And tho' they overnumber'd us, they could not us withstand,
They fought in desperation, disorder, and dismay,
And in a few minutes' time were forced to give way.

Their captain and 5 lieutenants, with 70 of the crew,
Were killed in this action, and a 100 wounded too;
The ship was taken to Halifax – the captain buried there,
And the remainder of the crew as his chief mourners were.

Have courage then all British seamen, & never be dismay'd,
But push the can of grog about, and drink success to trade;
A health to Captain Brooke so brave, & all his valiant crew,
Who beat the bold Americans and brought their courage to.[15]

Chesapeake & Shannon (Roud 1583) is rare on broadsides. A slip held in the Bodleian Library is in poor condition.[16] The ballad text is better preserved, however, in a broadside of later date, issued by the Poet's Box in Glasgow in 1869:

---

[15] *Battle of the Shannon and Chesapeak* (London: printed by H. Such, 123, Union Street, Borough, S.E.) [Oxford, Bodleian Library, Firth c.12(51), Harding B 11(3475)].
[16] *Shanon* [*sic*] *& Chesapeak* [Oxford, Bodleian Library, 2806 c.17(383)].

The Chesapeake so bold,
From Boston we are told,
Came out to fight a frigate neat and handy, O,
    And the people of the port
    Came out to see the sport,
Their music playing 'Yankee Doodle Dandy, O'.

The British frigate's name,
That was there at the time,
For cooling Yankee courage neat and handy, O,
    Was the Shannon, Captain Brook,
    His crew were hearts of oak,
And for fighting were known to be the dandy, O.

Before they began the fight,
Said the Yankees with delight,
'We'll tow her into Boston neat and handy, O,
    And afterwards we'll dine,
    With our girls we'll drink their wine,
And we'll dance and sing, Yankee Doodle Dandy, O.'

He no sooner gave the word
Than we all jumped on board,
'Haul down the Yankee colours neat and handy, O.'
    And, notwithstanding all the brag,
    Our glorious British flag
At the Yankees' mizzen-peak hung quite the dandy, O.

Here's to the true blue,
The officers and crew,
Who fought the Shannon frigate neat and handy, O,
    And may they ever prove,
    That in fighting, as in love,
The tars of Old England are the dandy, O.[17]

This is evidently a triumphalist reworking of *The Constitution & Guerriere*, quoted above. Some writers have questioned the order in which the songs were written, but it is logical that the American song, concerning the earlier engagement, should have come first.[18]

Shannon & Chesapeak; or, She Comes in Glorious Style (Roud V9697) appeared on several broadsides and in songsters, but has rarely been anthologized and apparently never collected from singers:

[17] *Chesapeake & Shannon* (Poet's Box, 80, London Street, Glasgow, 24 April 1869).
[18] Firth, *Naval Songs and Ballads*, pp. 309–12, 361–62. Another text is included in William Logan, *A Pedlar's Pack of Ballads and Songs* (Edinburgh: William Paterson, 1869), pp. 69–72.

She comes, she comes in glorious style,
To quarters fly ye hearts of oak;
Success shall soon reward our toil,
Exclaimed the gallant captain Brook.
Three cheers, my brave boys, let your ardour bespeak,
And give them a round from your cannon;
And soon shall they find that the proud Chesapeake
Shall lower a flag to the Shannon.

Lawrence, Columbia's pride and boast,
Of conquest counted sure as fate;
He thus addressed his haughty host,
With form erect and heart elate:
Three cheers, my brave men, let your courage bespeak,
And give them a taste of your cannon;
And soon shall they know that the proud Chesapeake
Shall ne'er lower a flag to the Shannon.

Silent as death each foe drew nigh,
While locked in hostile close embrace,
Brave Brook, with a British seaman's eye
The signs of terror soon could trace.
He exclaimed, whilst his looks did ardour bespeak,
Brave boys they all flinch from their cannon;
Board, board, my brave mesmates [sic], the proud Chesapeake
Shall soon be a prize to the Shannon.

Swift flew the word, Britannia's sons,
Spread death and terror where they came;
The trembling foe forsook their guns,
And called aloud on mercy's name.
Brave Brook led the way, but fell wounded and weak,
Yet exclaimed they are fled from their cannon,
Three cheers my brave seamen, the proud Chesapeake
Has lower'd a flag to the Shannon.

The day was won, but Lawrence fell
He closed his eyes in endless night;
And oft Columbia's sons will tell,
Of hopes all blighted in that fight.
[B]rave Captain Brook, though yet wounded and weak,
Survives to again play his cannon;
His name from the shores of the wide Chesapeake,
Shall resound to the banks of the Shannon.[19]

---

[19] *Shannon & Chesapeak; or, She Comes in Glorious Style* (J. Catnach, printer, 2 and 3, Monmouth Court, Seven Dials) [Oxford, Bodleian Library, Firth b.25(109), Harding B 11(3474), Johnson Ballads 272]. This broadside is not alone in giving the captain's

At Boston One Day (Roud V44407) is comparatively rare but appears in a few songbooks, including *The Vocal Library*, subtitled 'the largest collection of English, Scottish, and Irish songs ever printed in a single volume', which survives in multiple editions issued by several different publishers:

At Boston one day as the Chesapeake lay,
The captain his crew thus began on –
See that ship out at sea! she our prize soon shall be;
'Tis the tight little frigate the Shannon.
    Oh 'twill be a good joke,
    To take Commodore Broke,
And add to our navy the Shannon.

Then he made a great bluster, calling all hands to muster,
And said, now, boys, stand firm to your cannon;
Let us get under weigh [*sic*], without further delay,
And capture the insolent Shannon.
We soon shall bear down on the Shannon,
The Chesapeake's prize is the Shannon,
    Within two hour's space,
    We'll return to this place,
And bring into harbour the Shannon.

Now alongside they range, and broadsides they exchange;
But the Yankees soon flinch from their cannon,
When the captain and crew without further ado,
Are attack'd sword-in-hand from the Shannon,
By the tight little tars of the Shannon;
The brave Commodore of the Shannon,
    Fir'd a friendly salute,
    Just to end the dispute,
And the Chesapeake struck to the Shannon.

Let America know the respect she should show
To our national flag and our cannon;
And let her take heed, that the Thames and the Tweed,
Give us tars just as brave as the Shannon.
Here's to Commodore Broke of the Shannon,
    May the olive of peace,

---

name as 'Brook'. The correct spelling was certainly 'Broke', but some confusion arises over the pronunciation. 'Broke' gave the balladeers the opportunity to rhyme with 'joke' etc., but here the author fails to rhyme 'Brook' with 'oak'. The name of his former home, Broke Hall, is pronounced 'brook', and in the absence of contemporary guidance I think this gives a strong indication of his own preference.

Soon bid enmity cease,
From the Chesapeake shore to the Shannon.[20]

The Shannon and Chesapeake (Roud V43924) is found in a chapbook
printed by M. Randall in Stirling. That it is not better known is a pity,
because it is quite well written and includes some nice details about
the outward voyage of the *Shannon* that are not in other broadsides.

Come all you gallant seamen
landsmen listen unto me,
Whilst I relate a bloody fight,
was lately fought at sea.

So fierce and hot upon each side,
as plainly will appear,
There's not been such a battle fought,
no not this many a year.

The eighteenth day of May, brave boys,
from Halifax we set sail
And up the American coast we did steer,
with a sweet and pleasant gale.

And standing off New York river,
on the twenty second day,
A sloop of war round Sandy Hook,
a man from our mast head did spy.

We gave to her three broadsides,
her colours soon came down,
We sent on board our Master's mate,
with a number of our men.

Standing further to the northward,
being ordered for to go;
And cruising off Boston Bay,
our captain commanded so.

On the twenty-eighth day of May
off Boston Bay we lay,
We sent a challenge to the Chesapeake,
to engage us in the bay.

And on the first of June, my boys,
the weather being clear,

[20] *The Vocal Library, Being the Largest Collection of English, Scottish, and Irish Songs Ever Printed in a Single Volume* (London: John Souter, 1818), p. 482 (no. 1297). It is a nice coincidence that I bought my own copy of this collection in Boston.

Bold Lawrence, he soon hove in sight,
As plainly you shall hear.

Our commander of the Shannon,
gallant Brook was his name,
Cheer up your hearts my seamen bold
for now she's bearing down.

And in the space of twenty one minutes,
the action hot began,
And after two or three broadsides,
foul of yard and yard we came.

Being broadside to broadside,
our cannon loud did roar,
While ninety five seamen and marines
lay bleeding in their gore.

Which causes many a widow
in Scotia for to mourn,
And many disconsolate mothers,
Lamenting the first of June.

For the space of fifteen minutes,
this action it did hold,
All on the brimy [*sic*] ocean,
men never fought more bold.

The Americans we must confess,
they did their valor shew,
But, the remainder of our ship's company,
soon brought their colours low.

Great rejoicings were made in Boston
their bells did loudly ring,
Expecting our commander and crew
prisoners to be brought in.

But unto their misfortune,
we soon did let them know,
That the Chesapeake to the Shannon,
her colours had laid low.

So now my song is ended,
I hope each tar will smile,
And as we have obtain'd a peace,
may plenty crown our isle.

Hoping Columbia's sons will never
oppose our future joy,

Or if they do, may we courage find
our enemy to annoy.[21]

The reference to 'many a widow / in Scotia' suggests it was written for the Scottish market. There is another copy in a chapbook printed in Kilmarnock, where the song is structured as eight-line stanzas.[22] That copy does not have the final two stanzas of the Stirling version, which refer to the coming of peace, suggesting they were composed after hostilities had ended.

The Battle between the Chesapeake and Shannon (Roud V50816) is an example of a broadside from the American side of the conflict.[23] While not excusing the defeat of the *Chesapeake*, it does declare: 'Tars, the British as yet, nothing have won, / Three frigates they've lost, and only took one.' Nathaniel Coverly in Boston printed one broadside that listed the killed and wounded, along with a set of memorial verses.[24] Another Coverly broadside, composed by one James Campbell of the USS *Constitution*, lamented the loss of Captain Lawrence of the *Chesapeake*.[25]

Songs collected from singers

The battle between the *Chesapeake* and the *Shannon* made a lasting impression on the British public. It has been the subject of a number of books, including biographies of the major figures involved; public houses were named after the battle, some of them surviving to the present day; and some of the songs were collected from singers, right up until near the end of the twentieth century.

Versions of 'The Battle of the Chesapeake and the Shannon' (Roud 963) and (somewhat less frequently) 'Chesapeake and Shannon' (Roud 1583) have been collected in England, and also in Nova Scotia (*Table 3*).

---

[21] *Gloomy Winter's Now Awa'; to which are added, The Shannon and Chesapeake; The Fourteenth of April; and Let Ambition Fire thy Mind* (Stirling: printed and sold by M. Randall) [Edinburgh, National Library of Scotland, L.C.2870(6)].

[22] *Four Songs: The Braes of Gleniffer; Shannon and Chesapeake; Fourteenth of April; Fly Not Yet* (Kilmarnock: printed for the booksellers) [University of Toronto Library, Thomas Fisher Chapbook Collection 178].

[23] *The Battle between the Chesapeake and the Shannon* [ITBC].

[24] *Chesapeake and Shannon: A List of the Killed and Wounded on Board the Chesapeake, Furnished by Lieut. Chew, Late Purser of the Chesapeake* (printed by Nathaniel Coverly, jun., Milk Street, corner Theatre Alley, Boston) [ITBC].

[25] *Written and Corrected by James Campbell, Late of the Constitution, in Behalf of the Brave Capt. James Lawrence, and Lieut. C. Ludlow, of the Chesapeake; together with Lines on the Death of Lt. Ludlow* (N. Coverly, Jr., printer, Milk Street, Boston) [ITBC].

'Captain Brooks and his Gallant Crew' (Roud 963) 'On the twenty-ninth of May, my boys, off Boston lights we lay'. Collected by Alfred Williams from Edward Williams, Siddington, Gloucestershire.

'The Chesapeake and the Shannon' (Roud 963) 'Oh the Chesapeake laid in harbour'. Collected by Ewan MacColl and Peggy Seeger from Sam Larner (one stanza).

'The Shannon Frigate' (Roud 963) 'Whilst on board the Shannon frigate'. Collected by Mike Yates from Jack Goodban, St Margaret's at Cliffe, Kent.

'The Chesapeake and the Shannon' (Roud 963) ''Twas of the Shannon Frigate in the merry month of May'. Collected by W. Roy Mackenzie from Peter Hines, Tatamagouche, Nova Scotia.

'The Shannon and the Chesapeake' (Roud 1583) ''Twas Captain Brook commanded us'. Collected by D. Hume from Mrs Read, Bournemouth, and sent to George B. Gardiner.

'The Shannon and the Chesapeake' (Roud 1583) 'The Chesapeake so bold, out of Boston, I am told'. Collected by Alfred Williams from Henry Harvey, Cricklade, Wiltshire (one stanza and chorus).[26]

'The Chesapeake and Shannon' (Roud 1583) 'The Chesapeake so bold out of Boston she was towed'. Collected by Cecil Sharp from Captain Lewis, Minehead, Somerset.

'The Chesapeake and Shannon' (Roud 1583) 'The Chesapeake so bold / Out of Boston as we're told'. Collected by W. Roy Mackenzie from Alexander Murphy, Cape John, Nova Scotia.

'Chesapeake and Shannon' (Roud 1891) ''Twas on the Glorious fourth of June'. Collected by Helen Creighton and Doreen Senior from Catherine Gallagher, Chebucto Head, Nova Scotia.

Table 3. Collected songs about the *Chesapeake* and the *Shannon*.

The War of 1812 was (and indeed still is) regarded by Canadians as of much greater significance than it was by the British, as it was a major step on their journey from being a colony to nationhood. Halifax, Nova Scotia, was the base for the Royal Navy in North America and the destination of the *Shannon* and the *Chesapeake* after the battle. W. Roy Mackenzie was the first folk song collector in Nova Scotia and one of the singers whom he met on his first collecting trip, in 1909, was the octogenarian Robert Langille, known as 'Old Bob', who lived in Tatamagouche, who told him:

---

[26] For the identification of this song and singer, see https://history.wiltshire.gov.uk/community/getfolk.php?id=1195.

'Onct I sung a song fer a Yankee sailor about the Chesapeake and the Shannon,' he announced. 'It was a good song too, an' it told about the British beatin' the Yankees like they deserved.' 'He was a younger man than I was,' he added gleefully, 'an' he'd a' licked me fer it if they hadn't been too many Britishers around fer him.'[27]

Despite his being descended from Swiss-French Huguenots, Mackenzie described Old Bob as 'a Britisher of intense and blazing patriotism'. Mackenzie published two songs he collected about the battle in his *Ballads and Sea Songs from Nova Scotia*.[28] It is worth noting that another singer, John Henderson, also of Tatamagouche, told Mackenzie that when his parents came to Nova Scotia from Scotland around 1820 they brought with them a much-prized collection of broadside ballads, and that the settlers were constantly receiving new ballads from Scotland.[29]

On 8 August 1939, Helen Creighton and Doreen Senior heard a unique ballad describing the fight between the two ships from Catherine Gallagher, the wife of the lighthouse keeper at Chebucto Head, at the mouth of Halifax harbour and overlooking the tideway that the *Shannon* and *Chesapeake* would have sailed up more than a hundred years earlier. Creighton reports that Mrs Gallagher recalled further parts of the song over subsequent visits but that two stanzas proved elusive, one dealing with the wounding of Captain Broke, and the final stanza describing the arrival of the two ships in Halifax.[30] Creighton went back to see Mrs Gallagher in 1943 with a tape recorder and recorded this song (along with several others):

'Twas on the glorious fourth of June
At ten o'clock in the fore-noon
That we sailed out of Boston Bay,
That we sailed out of Boston Bay
For to fight the Chesapeake boys.

The Chesapeake mounted forty-nine guns
With four hundred and twenty of Columbia's picked sons,
The Yankees thought they would never run,

[27] W. Roy Mackenzie, *The Quest of the Ballad* (Princeton: Princeton University Press, 1919), p. 44.

[28] W. Roy Mackenzie, *Ballads and Sea Songs from Nova Scotia* (Cambridge, MA: Harvard University Press, 1928), pp. 208–10.

[29] W. Roy Mackenzie, 'Ballad-Singing in Nova Scotia', *Journal of American Folklore*, 22 (1909), 327–31 (p. 328).

[30] Helen Creighton and Doreen Senior, *Traditional Songs from Nova Scotia* (Toronto: Ryerson Press, 1960), pp. 266–67.

The Yankees thought they would never run
They being all picked Yankee heroes.

The Shannon mounted guns the same
With less men, but of better fame,
To beat those Yankees it was their aim,
To beat those Yankees it was their aim
To show them, Rule Britannia.

Up spoke our gallant Captain Broke,
To beat those Yanks it is no joke,
Your guns sponge well and make them tell,
For Yankees they don't like the smell
Of British balls and powder.

Bold Wallis being next in command,
So boldly on the deck did stand,
Saying, 'Fire on brave boys, the day's our own,
Since Bunker Hill brought forth a groan,
The Chesapeake is falling.'

But ten minutes work we had to do
While Yankee bullets around us flew,
We boarded her down, her colours drew,
We boarded her down, her colours drew
And stuck her to the Shannon.[31]

* * *

Time has moved on and although historians on both sides of the Atlantic continue to argue about the tactics of the two captains, the battle between the *Chesapeake* and the *Shannon* has become a footnote in British history. This is less true on the other side of the Atlantic. I have mentioned that Canadians still recognize the War of 1812 as an important step on their path to nationhood and in the United States, too, there is increasing recognition of the significance of what they sometimes call the Second War of Independence. In an address to the annual meeting of the American Historical Association in 1912 the historian Charles Francis Adams proposed that the exact moment at which the United States became a world power was 6.30 p.m. on 19 August 1812 when HMS *Guerriere* lowered its flag to USS *Constitution*.[32]

The pride that Americans took in the achievements of their small navy was reflected in the exuberant broadsides issued by Nathaniel

---

[31] Part of the recording is at https://www.helencreighton.org/collection/Shannon/.
[32] Utt, *Ships of Oak, Guns of Iron*, pp. xxxi–xxxii.

Coverly in Boston. The delight felt by the British at HMS *Shannon*'s victory over USS *Chesapeake* was likewise reflected in the cheap literature of the time. Although some of the more grandiloquent of those effusions apparently held only passing interest, a few passed into the repertoire of singers.

Relics of the conflict are rare, but the American billionaire Bill Koch, a descendant of Captain James Lawrence, bought up most of what was available from both sides of the conflict. There is one thing, however, that he has not yet been able to buy, and that is the *Chesapeake* herself. Surprisingly, the ship survives, albeit in rather strange fashion. After she had been repaired in Halifax she was taken into service in the Royal Navy. She never fought another action and following a visit to South Africa she returned to Britain to be used as a store ship, before being broken up at Portsmouth in 1819. Her shot-holed and bloodstained timbers were bought by a miller from Wickham in Hampshire, who used them in the construction of his new flour mill. The building still stands, although it is now an antique centre and tea shop. The name of the ship lives on as 'Chesapeake Mill'.

Sir John Franklin in Broadside and Oral Tradition

Michael King Macdona

Many readers may know the ballad 'Lord Franklin' recorded in 1955 by A. L. Lloyd, and subsequently by Martin Carthy, Pentangle, and others.[1] The purpose of this paper is to examine the broadside from which the ballad derives, as well as two others relating to Sir John Franklin's ill-fated attempt to find the North-West Passage (the long-sought route to China and the East across the northern coast of North America), to place them in their historical context, and to consider the extent to which they transferred into the oral folk song tradition.

To understand the broadsides fully it is necessary to go into some history. On 19 May 1845, Captain Sir John Franklin, Arctic explorer and lately lieutenant governor of Van Diemen's Land (Tasmania), sailed from Greenhithe with two ships, HMS *Erebus* and HMS *Terror*, and a complement of 134 officers and men in search of the North-West Passage (*Figures 1 and 4*).[2] Before the expedition was fully under way five crewmen were sent back on health and other grounds, leaving 129 to continue the expedition. Those five may have been disappointed to be excluded from the enterprise, but they were the lucky ones. The ships were seen by two whalers in Baffin Bay in late July and then sailed into Lancaster Sound and disappeared.

Franklin was expected to spend at least one winter in the Arctic and had provisions for three years, so news of the progress of the expedition was not expected for several months. However, when 1847 passed with no word having been received, anxiety arose and the following year two search expeditions were launched, the first of many over the coming years. In addition, the Admiralty offered substantial

---

[1] A. L. Lloyd and Ewan MacColl, *The Singing Sailor*, 12-inch LP (Topic TRL3, 1955). A recording of A. L. Lloyd's 'Lord Franklin' can be heard at https://www.youtube.com/watch?v=wtRdhdQ02T4.

[2] See further B. A. Riffenburgh, 'Franklin, Sir John (1786–1847)', *ODNB* https://doi.org/10.1093/ref:odnb/10090; Dorothy Middleton, 'Franklin [*née* Griffin], Jane, Lady Franklin (1792–1875)', *ODNB* https://doi.org/10.1093/ref:odnb/10089.

rewards to anyone who could discover, relieve, or provide information concerning the fate of Franklin's expedition (*Figure 2*).

Figure 1. Sir John Franklin in 1845 (public domain).

In 1850 the site of Franklin's first wintering on Beechey Island was found, along with the graves of three crewmen who had died during that first winter, and then nothing. Consequently, on 19 January 1854 the Admiralty issued a notice to the effect that, if positive news of the expedition was not received by 31 March, Franklin and his men would be considered to have died in the service of the Crown and arrears of pay up to that date would be paid to the men's families.[3] This also meant that officers' wives would be eligible for widows' pensions. Franklin's wife, Jane, was outraged and wrote at length to the Admiralty protesting that the decision was premature and stating that she would not be claiming the pension.

Later that year more definite news was received. Dr John Rae had been surveying the west coast of the Boothia Peninsula for the Hudson's Bay Company and had asked Inuit whom he had encountered if they knew if any white men had been seen in the

---

[3] *London Gazette*, 20 January 1854, p. 174.

region. From information obtained, as he put it, 'at various times and from various sources', he compiled a report that was hurried to the

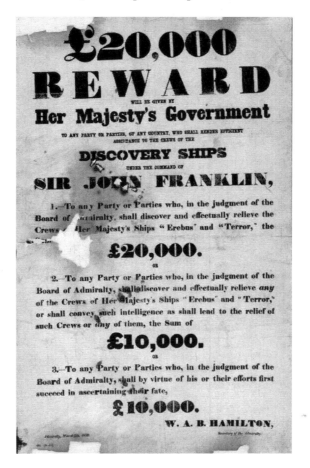

Figure 2. Broadside dated 7 March 1850 offering rewards for help with finding Franklin's expedition (Library and Archives Canada, public domain).

Admiralty immediately upon his return to England on 22 October 1854 and published in *The Times* the following day.[4] This stated that in the spring of 1850 a party of Inuit hunting seals on the coast of King William Island had encountered about forty white men travelling southwards over the ice and dragging a boat. None of them could speak the Inuit language intelligibly but they indicated by signs that

---

[4] 'The Arctic Expedition', *The Times*, 23 October 1854, p. 7.

their ship or ships had been crushed by ice and that they were going to where they expected to find deer to shoot. All except one officer appeared thin and it was assumed that they were running short of provisions. Later that same season, another party of Inuit discovered the bodies of some thirty-five men, some under the shelter of an upturned boat. From this and from various articles purchased from the Inuit, Rae concluded that a portion, if not all, of the surviving members of Franklin's party had died from starvation. However, there was more to come. To quote Dr Rae: 'From the mutilated state of many of the corpses and the contents of the kettles, it is evident that our wretched countrymen had been driven to the last resource – cannibalism – as a means of prolonging existence.'

This suggestion was greeted with horror and disbelief. Charles Dickens wrote a lengthy, two-part article in his magazine *Household Words* denouncing the notion that such men as constituted Franklin's party could ever, even under the direst of circumstances, have resorted to such an extremity.[5] It was only many years later that bones were found bearing marks of butchery which vindicated the report of cannibalism. Nevertheless, cannibalism apart, Dickens accepted that Dr Rae's evidence demonstrated that Franklin and his companions had perished, and even Lady Franklin came to accept this as well.

Further expeditions were sent out to try to establish what had happened. In 1859 a cairn erected by Franklin's men on the north-west coast of King William Island was found containing a document now known as the Victory Point Record (*Figure 3*). This document contained (*inter alia*) a message dated 25 April 1848 stating that the ships had been trapped in the ice north-north-west of the island since September 1846, that to the date of the message nine officers and fifteen men had died, that Franklin himself had died on 11 June 1847, and that the remaining 105 men had deserted the ships and were leaving the next day for Back's Fish River to the south of the island. However, it appears that at least some of the crews returned to the ships, since Inuit testimony suggests that they were manned after 1848, possibly as late as 1850, and that they were seen and had sunk considerably further south than the position mentioned in the Victory Point Record. This has been confirmed by the recent discovery of the wrecks in the area indicated by the Inuit testimony, *Erebus* in 2014 west of the Adelaide Peninsula, and *Terror* in 2016 in the coincidentally named Terror Bay.

---

[5] 'The Lost Arctic Voyagers', *Household Words*, 10 (1854), 361–65, 385–93.

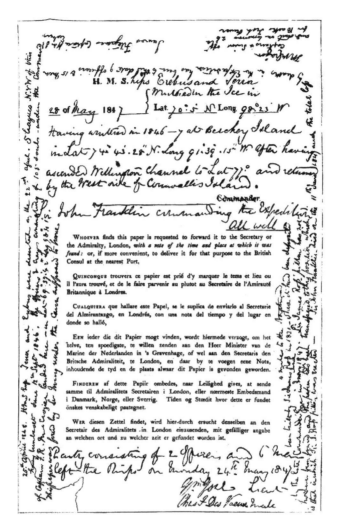

Figure 3. Facsimile of the Victory Point Record (*Illustrated London News*, 1 October 1859).

The fate of Franklin's expedition excited interest on both sides of the Atlantic from the 1850s onwards. Jules Verne included a chapter on it in his 1864 novel *The Adventures of Captain Hatteras*, poems were written in America and Britain, and the broadside balladeers were at work. Three broadsides are known and are transcribed in the Appendix to this paper. Chronologically, the first in the sequence, which can be dated to 1851, is entitled *Lady Franklin's Lament* and begins 'My Franklin dear long has been gone' (*Appendix* Text A).[6] It portrays Lady Franklin lamenting the absence of her husband and praying for his return, and for dating purposes it contains a reference to 'The brave and good Lieutenant Pim'. This was Lieutenant Bedford Clapperton Trevelyan Pim, a young naval officer who had conceived the theory that Franklin, having negotiated the North-West Passage, had become trapped north of the Bering Strait which divides Alaska from Siberia and had been unable to penetrate into the Pacific as his instructions from the Admiralty required. He therefore proposed to lead a small expedition across Siberia to search for traces of Franklin's ships along the Siberian coast. The idea attracted support, particularly from the Royal Geographical Society; funds were raised, including £300 from Lady Franklin; and the Admiralty, while declining to adopt it officially, granted Pim indefinite leave to pursue his scheme on his own account.

Pim left London on 18 November 1851 and having crossed the Channel proceeded via Berlin to St Petersburg, arriving on 5 December. He was cordially received, granted an audience with the tsar, and met other members of the imperial family. However, the Russian authorities had taken the advice of those familiar with the region, who pronounced the plan to be impractical, and accordingly declined to support the expedition on the grounds that the tsar could not consent to allow the life of a British officer to be imperilled in vain. Without Russian support Pim could proceed no further, as was reported in a letter from the president of the Royal Geographical Society to *The Times*, published on 6 January 1852.[7] Pim had returned to England by early February, refunded Lady Franklin's £300, paid the balance of the money raised into a fund to finance further search expeditions, and volunteered to go on the next one himself. The broadside, therefore, can be dated between 18 November 1851 and 6 January 1852, and from its wording probably to the early part of that period. It may be no coincidence that it was printed in Bideford since Lieutenant Pim had been born there and there is a memorial to him in the Church of St Mary, Bideford.

The third broadside in the chronological sequence is of a very different character. It reads as a summary of news concerning Franklin's expedition as it emerged in 1854. Entitled *A Lament on the Fate of Sir J. Franklin and his Crews*, it begins 'You tender Christians I

---

[6] *Lady Franklin's Lament* (Wilson, printer, Bideford) [Oxford, Bodleian Library, Firth c.12(81)].

[7] 'Sir John Franklin's Expedition and Lieutenant Pim', *The Times*, 6 January 1852, p. 5.

pray attend' (*Appendix* Text C).[8] The broadside states that Franklin and his companions had perished and that nine years had elapsed since their departure. It goes on to say that 'in this present year' the government had granted a pension to their families and that Lady Franklin had refused it. It reports that at length news had come that all were dead and that their ships had been crushed by ice, and also refers to the forty or so men referred to in Dr Rae's report.

Unlike Charles Dickens, the ballad writer did not shrink from the allegation of cannibalism and, if anything, enlarged upon the evidence ('Their limbs and bodies lay scattered round. / The flesh knawed off from every bone'). It would seem, therefore, that this broadside was written in the last months of 1854, after the publication of Dr Rae's report on 23 October. Later, it was printed again by H. P. Such, with the time since Franklin's departure altered to fifteen years, but remaining otherwise almost identical to the earlier version, including the by-now anachronistic detail that the government had granted pensions to the families 'in this present year'.[9]

Neither *Lady Franklin's Lament* nor *A Lament on the Fate of Sir J. Franklin and his Crews* is known to have made any impression upon oral tradition, but the same cannot be said of the second broadside in the chronological sequence. This is entitled *Lady Franklin's Lament for her Husband* (sometimes confusingly abbreviated to *Lady Franklin's Lament*) and begins 'You seamen bold, that have oft withstood' (*Appendix* Text B).[10] The names of those who went to search for Franklin provide a significant detail in this broadside. 'Captain Ross' is either Captain Sir James Clark Ross or his uncle Sir John Ross, both of whom led expeditions in search of Franklin. 'Penny' is William

---

[8] *A Lament on the Fate of Sir J. Franklin and his Crews* [Oxford, Bodleian Library, Firth c.12(438), Harding B 15(292b)]; *Lament on the Fate of Sir J. Franklin and his Crews* ([Harkness, printer, Preston]) [Oxford, Bodleian Library, Harding B 11(4292)].

[9] *Lament on the Fate of Sir J. Franklin and his Crews* (London: H. Such, machine printer & publisher, 177, Union Street, Boro', S.E.) [Glasgow, Mitchell Library, Frank Kidson Broadside Collection, vol. 5, p. 129 (VWML Digital Archive, FK/13/125/2); London, British Library, L.R.271.a.2/5.(216.), 11621.h.11/5.(74.); Oxford, Bodleian Library, Firth c.12(82), Harding B 11(3546)].

[10] *Lady Franklin's Lament for her Husband* (Stewart, printer, Carlisle) [Madden Ballads 17.72]; *Lady Franklin's Lament for her Husband* (Harkness, printer, 121 Church Street, Preston) [Madden Ballads 18.1283]; *Lady Franklin's Lament for her Husband* [Glasgow University Library, Sp Coll Mu23-y.1 (48)]; *Lady Franklin's Lament for her Husband* [Oxford, Bodleian Library, 2806 c.13(212)]; *Lady Franklin's Lament for her Husband* (J. Scott, Pittenweem; sold by J. Wood, 49, North Richmond Street, Edinburgh) [Oxford, Bodleian Library, Firth c.12(83)]. Readers familiar with A. L. Lloyd's version will recognize parts of the text, though not necessarily in the same order.

Penny, a Scottish whaler captain heavily engaged in the search. No 'Granville' was involved, but this name is most likely to be a mistaken reference to John Gravill, a whaler captain from Hull in whose ship, the *Abram*, Lady Franklin purchased a quarter share in order to enable him to engage in the search. 'Captain Austen' is taken to be Captain Horatio Austin, RN. The spelling of his surname is different and he has no known connection with Scarborough, but no other Austin of any spelling was involved in the search and we must assume that the ballad writer had his own reasons for including the Scarborough reference. All of these men were involved in searches before 1852.

Lady Franklin's offer of a reward of ten thousand pounds is something of a mystery. It is also mentioned in the later broadside *A Lament on the Fate of Sir J. Franklin and his Crews*, which perhaps supports its authenticity, but I can find no evidence for it. Lady Franklin did, however, expend considerably more than that sum in commissioning search expeditions, and she offered £3,000 to any whalers who might search for and discover Franklin outside of their usual fishing grounds. Perhaps it was merely the ballad writer's way of emphasizing the value she placed upon the discovery of her husband (approximately one million pounds at present-day values).

Lady Franklin's Lament for her Husband entered the sailors' repertoire of songs. I am beginning to suspect that this applies particularly to the northern whalers. A version was inscribed in the logbook of the barque *Morning Light* of New Bedford for the years 1859–62.[11] One stanza is included in an article on shanties in the magazine *Once a Week* for 1 August 1868 as an example of songs sung by sailors in their leisure hours.[12] It is said to be the opening stanza, but is in fact a combination of the fifth and eighth stanzas of the broadside. A version comprising nine stanzas, seven deriving from the broadside and two of uncertain origin, appears in the book *Eighteen Months on a Greenland Whaler* by Joseph P. Faulkner, published in New York in 1878, under the title 'The Sailor's Dream'.[13] In 1938, Joanna Colcord published a seven-stanza version with the title 'Franklin's Crew' in her *Songs of American Sailormen*.[14]

---

[11] Martha's Vineyard Museum, Logbook of the Bark *Morning Light*, master Hervey E. Luce, 1859–1862, pp. 220–21 https://archive.org/details/logbookofmorning1859 morn/page/n215/mode/2up.
[12] 'On Shanties', *Once a Week*, n.s. 2 (no. 31) (1868), 92–93 (p. 93).
[13] Joseph P. Faulkner, *Eighteen Months on a Greenland Whaler* (New York: published for the author, 1878), pp. 73–74.
[14] Joanna C. Colcord, *Songs of American Sailormen*, rev. edn (New York: W. W. Norton; London: Putnam, 1938), pp. 157–59.

Many versions have been collected in the field, mainly in Scotland, northern England, and in particular the maritime regions of eastern Canada. Newfoundland has been a particularly rich source. None is complete in the sense that it reproduces all twelve stanzas of the broadside (the longest has ten stanzas), and some are merely fragments. Naturally, there are variations: words and names are changed, stanzas omitted or transposed, new stanzas created by combining elements from other stanzas, and sometimes singers compensate for lapses of memory by substituting words of their own. Nevertheless, virtually every version can be seen to derive from the broadside of 1852.

I say 'virtually', for I know of two Franklin songs collected in the field that originated elsewhere than on the 1852 broadside. The first is a fragment of two stanzas collected in 1929 by Elisabeth Greenleaf and Grace Mansfield.[15] Although they collected other versions deriving from *Lady Franklin's Lament for her Husband*, Greenleaf wrote that this one 'belongs to another song which I have not found'. In fact, its origin can be found in a poem by Elizabeth Doten entitled 'A Song of the North' which appeared in *The Lily of the Valley for 1854*, an anthology of prose and poetry published in Boston early that year.[16] Greenleaf and Mansfield did not collect a tune, but were apparently satisfied that it was a song and not a partial recitation from a poem.

The second exception was collected by Cecil Sharp and the Rev. Charles Marson from Captain James Vickery at Minehead on 18 August 1905.[17] Again, it is only a fragment. What is evidently the full version of this song was printed in a Tasmanian newspaper, the *Hobarton Guardian*, on 15 October 1853, although it may have been written the previous year since it refers to Franklin and his crew roaming on the ice for seven years.[18] It is entitled 'The Arctic Voyagers; or, Lady Franklin's Lament for her Husband', but despite

---

[15] Elisabeth Bristol Greenleaf (ed.), *Ballads and Sea Songs of Newfoundland*, music recorded by Grace Yarrow Mansfield (Cambridge, MA: Harvard University Press, 1933), p. 310 (C).

[16] Elizabeth Doten (ed.), *The Lily of the Valley for 1854* (Boston: James M. Usher, 1854), pp. 109–13.

[17] VWML, Cecil Sharp Manuscript Collection, Field Notebook Words 1905 (2), Field Notebook Tunes 1905 (3a) (VWML Digital Archive, CJS1/9/1/1905/2, CJS1/9/2/1905/3a); fair copies at Cambridge, Archive of Clare College, ACC1987/25, Cecil J. Sharp MSS, Folk Words 647, Folk Tunes 571 (VWML Digital Archive, CJS2/9/647, CJS2/10/571). I am grateful to David Sutcliffe for identifying Marson's handwriting in Field Notebook Words 1905(2).

[18] *Hobarton Guardian; or, True Friend of Tasmania*, 15 October 1853, p. 3 https://trove.nla.gov.au/newspaper/page/20204394.

the alternative title it bears no relation to the 1852 broadside *Lady Franklin's Lament for her Husband* other than that it, too, involves a seashore encounter with the grieving Lady Franklin. It has a chorus, indicating that it is a song rather than a poem and, unlike the Canadian example, it was certainly sung, for Sharp and Marson collected a tune as well as words from Captain Vickery. Unfortunately, the newspaper does not give a provenance for it, although it appears in a section with the heading 'Late English News'. I cannot say whether it originated in an English newspaper or magazine, or whether it was printed on another broadside that has so far eluded discovery.

Appendix: Broadside texts

Note: Texts are given in chronological order. Some evident typographical errors have been silently corrected.

Text A: *Lady Franklin's Lament* (Wilson, printer, Bideford) [Oxford, Bodleian Library, Firth c.12(81)], dated to 1851.

My Franklin dear long has been gone,
To explore the Northern Seas,
I wonder if my faithful John
Is still battling with the breeze;
Or, if he ever will return again –
To these fond arms once more,
To heal the wounds of his dearest Jane,
Whose heart is griev'd full sore.

Chorus:
My Franklin dear, though long thy stay,
Yet still my prayer shall be,
That Providence may choose a way,
To guide thee safe to me.

My Franklin dear where dost thou dwell?
What part of the Frozen Sea?
Oh, how I wish that I could tell,
I'd quickly haste to thee;
With my goodly Ship in motion,
No longer here I'd stay,
But athwart the rolling ocean,
For thee I'd bear away.

My Franklin dear, I can but mourn,
At thy long protracted stay,

Oh, would to God, thou could'st return,
How bless'd would be that day;
The hearts of merry England,
Would swell with joy once more,
To welcome my lost husband,
To his dear native shore.

The brave and good Lieutenant Pim,
Is now gone off to sea,
May heaven's blessing go to [*sic*] with him,
And guide my love to me,
And if again he should return
To this fond heart once more,
We shall not cause his friends to mourn,
Nor again his loss deplore.

My Franklin dear once more safe home,
Upon Britannia's shore;
To the northern seas no more shall steer,
Where the cruel icebergs roar,
But once safe in his native home,
Bless'd by wife and children dear,
With bears and wolves no more to roam,
He'll be free and happy here.

My Franklin dear may be laid low,
Amidst the icebergs drear;
The sad thought fills my heart with woe,
Yet one ray of hope is near,
That if I never meet him more,
In this world of hope and fears.
Yet we may meet on a happy shore
And wipe away my tears.

Text B. *Lady Franklin's Lament for her Husband* (J. Scott, Pittenweem; sold by J. Wood, 49, North Richmond Street, Edinburgh) [Oxford, Bodleian Library, Firth c.12(83)], dated to 1852.

You seamen bold, that have oft withstood,
Wild storms of Neptune's briny flood,
Attend to these few lines which I now will name,
And put you in mind of a sailor's dream.

As homeward bound one night on the deep,
Slung in my hammock I fell asleep,
I dream't a dream which I thought was true,
Concerning Franklin and his brave crew.

I thought as we near'd to the Humber shore,
I heard a female that did deplore,
She wept aloud and seem'd to say,
Alas! my Franklin is long away.

Her mind it seem'd in sad distress,
She cried aloud, I can take no rest,
Ten thousand pounds I would freely give,
To say on earth that my husband lives.

Long time it is since two ships of fame,
Did bear my husband across the Main,
With one hundred Seamen of courage stout,
To find a North Western passage out.

With one hundred Seamen with hearts so bold,
I fear have perish'd in frost and cold,
Alas! she cried, all my life I'll mourn,
Since Franklin seems never to return.

For since that time seven years are past,
And many a keen and bitter blast,
Blows o'er the grave where poor Seamen fell,
Whose dreadful sufferings no tongue can tell.

To find a passage by the North Pole,
Where tempests rave and wild thunders roll,
Is more than any mortal man can do,
With hearts undaunted and courage true.

There's Captain Austen of Scarboro' town,
Brave Granville and Penny of much renown,
With Captain Ross, and so many more,
Have long been searching the Arctic shore.

They sailed east, and they sailed west,
Round Greenland's coast they knew the best,
In hardships drear they have vainly strove,
On mountains of ice their ships were drove.

At Baffin's Bay where the whale fish blows,
The fate of Franklin nobody knows,
Which cause many wife and child to mourn,
In grievous sorrow for their return.

These sad forebodings they give me pain,
For the long lost Franklin across the Main,
Likewise the fate of so many before,
Who have left their home to return no more.

Text C. *A Lament on the Fate of Sir J. Franklin and his Crews* [Oxford, Bodleian Library, Firth c.12(438)], dated to late 1854.

You tender Christians I pray attend,
To these few lines that I have now penn'd,
Of Sir John Franklin and his brave band,
Who've perished far from their native land.

    So listen now while I tell to you
    The fate of Franklin and his brave crew.

It's now nine years since they first set sail,
With joyous hearts and a pleasant gale,
In frozen regions to cruise about
The North-west passage to find out.

There was many a sad and an aching heart
As from their friends these brave men did part
To plough their way o'er the raging main
For fear they should ne'er return again.

When six dreary years they had been away
Some other vessels without delay
Were sent to search for the missing crews
But alas of them they could hear no news.

A gloomy mystery for nine long years,
Their wives and children has kept in tears;
In deepest anguish they did await
The ships sent out to learn their fate.

Poor Lady Franklin in great despair
In anguish wild she tore her hair;
Saying ten thousand pounds I'd give for news
Of my loving Franklin and his brave crews.

The government in this present year
Did pensions give to their families dear;
But Lady Franklin refused the grant
Crying give me my husband I no money want.

At length sad tidings of this brave band
Has reached the shores of their native land,
By which we hear that they are all dead,
Though suffering much ere their souls had fled.

As through the frozen seas they pushed
Their ships by blocks of ice were crushed,
And offering prayers for their babes and wives
Many brave souls did lose their lives.

Forty poor creatures from a watery grave
With one of the boats their lives did save,
And over the ice they now took their way
To reach in safety the Hudson's Bay.

What horrid sufferings of pain and want –
These frozen regions no food did grant;
At length oh horrid for want of meat
Their dying comrades they had to eat.

How horrid was the sight when found
Their limbs and bodies lay scattered round.
The flesh knawed off from every bone,
Oh may their souls to heaven have gone.

Now for to finish and to make an end,
May God their families from want defend,
And while their loss we sadly deplore,
We hope such horrors to hear no more.

Figure 4. HMS *Erebus* and HMS *Terror* (*Illustrated London News*, 24 May 1845).

The Dying Words of Captain Robert Kidd: A Ballad for the Common Sailor

Lydia G. Fash

The notorious pirate Captain William Kidd was hanged at London's Execution Dock on 23 May 1701. Immediately, at least five broadsides about his life and death appeared: two concerning his behaviour on the scaffold, penned by the Newgate chaplain, and three about his piratical career more generally. Of the last three, only *Captain Kid's Farewel to the Seas; or, The Famous Pirate's Lament* would survive and, in the United States, thrive (*Figure 1*).[1] While this English ballad is the origin of the version Nathaniel Coverly, Jr., would print more than a hundred years later in Boston, Massachusetts, there are notable differences between Coverly's *c*.1814 broadside, *The Dying Words of Captain Robert Kidd*, and *Captain Kid's Farewel to the Seas*. Most obviously, the historical William Kidd of the original British ballad became 'Robert Kidd' in the US tradition. 'Robert Kidd' was a thoroughly American creation, which came to speak quite directly to the frustrations of US sailors.

This paper argues that *The Dying Words of Captain Robert Kidd* offers the rare opportunity of re-creating a profile of those who read and helped form what became a beloved US ballad. Capturing the practice of reading is a difficult scholarly task. Most obviously, reading, in its contemporary form, often happens in silent and undocumented ways. While earlier reading practices were more likely to be voiced and social, that does not mean that they were any better recorded.[2] Moreover, tracking reading requires defining literacy, a notoriously tricky thing to do, since the skill exists on a spectrum rather than as an absolute. Further complicating the matter is the fact that scholars have tended to correlate the skills of reading and writing, and yet reading has not historically always been conjoined with writing. Women in eighteenth-century Puritan communities, for example, enjoyed high

---

[1] Willard Hallam Bonner, 'The Ballad of Captain Kidd', *American Literature*, 15 (1944), 362–80 (p. 362).
[2] Roger Chartier, 'Texts, Printing, Reading', in *The New Cultural History*, ed. Lynn Hunt (Berkeley: University of California Press, 1989), pp. 154–75 (p. 159).

rates of literacy in order to read the Bible, but were not all able to write, a skill more likely to be taught to men.

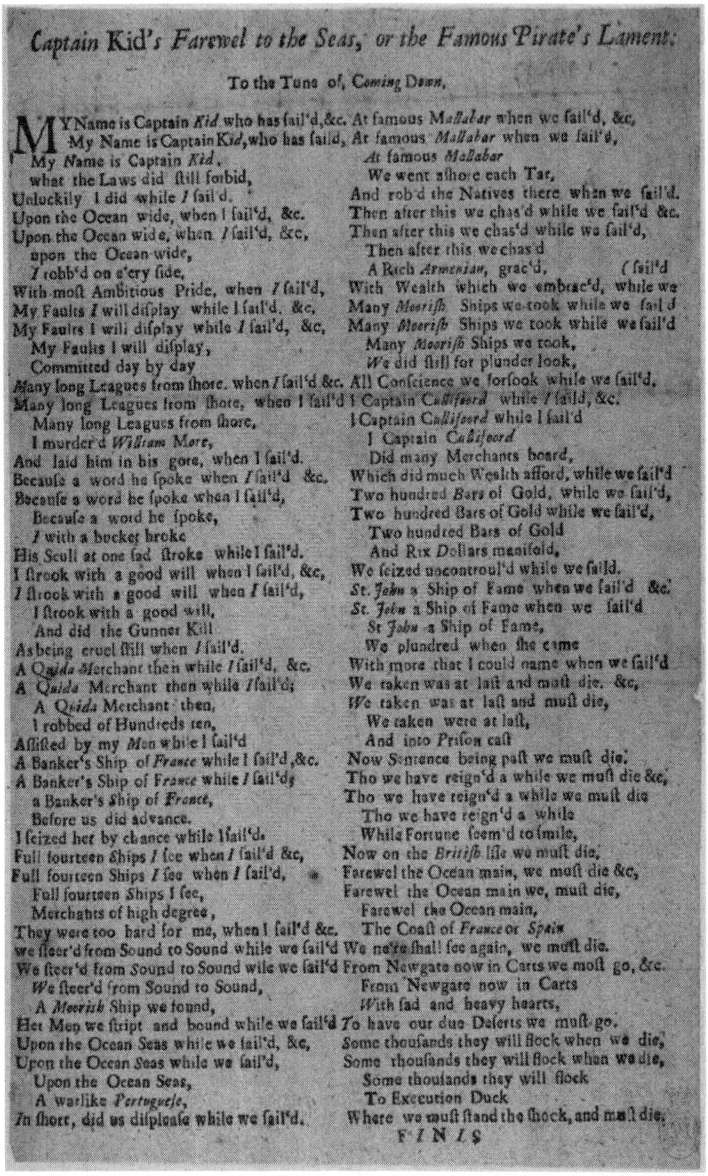

Captain Kid's *Farewel to the Seas, or the Famous Pirate's Lament:*

To the Tune of, *Coming Down*,

MY Name is Captain *Kid* who has ſail'd, &c.
My Name is Captain Kid, who has ſaild,
My *Name* is Captain *Kid*,
what the Laws did ſtill forbid,
Unluckily I did while *I* ſail'd.
Upon the Ocean wide, when I ſail'd, &c.
Upon the Ocean wide, when *I* ſail'd, &c,
upon the Ocean wide,
I robb'd on e'ery ſide,
With moſt Ambitious Pride, when *I* ſail'd,
My Faults *I* will diſplay while I ſail'd, &c,
My Faults I will diſplay while *I* ſail'd, &c,
My Faults I will diſplay,
Committed day by day
Many long Leagues from ſhore. when *I* ſail'd &c.
Many long Leagues from ſhore, when I ſail'd
Many long Leagues from ſhore,
I murder'd *William More*,
And laid him in his gore, when I ſail'd.
Becauſe a word he ſpoke when *I* ſail'd &c.
Becauſe a word he ſpoke when I ſail'd,
Becauſe a word he ſpoke,
I with a bucket broke
His Scull at one ſad ſtroke while I ſail'd.
I ſtrook with a good will when I ſail'd, &c,
I ſtrook with a good will when *I* ſail'd,
I ſtrook with a good will,
And did the Gunner Kill
As being cruel ſtill when *I* ſail'd.
A *Quida Merchant* then while *I* ſail'd, &c.
A *Quida* Merchant then while *I* ſail'd;
A *Quida* Merchant then,
I robbed of Hundreds ten,
Aſſiſted by my *Men* while I ſail'd
A Banker's Ship of *France* while I ſail'd, &c.
A Banker's Ship of *France* while *I* ſail'd,
a Banker's Ship of *France*,
Before us did advance.
I ſeized her by chance while I ſail'd.
Full fourteen Ships *I* ſee when *I* ſail'd &c,
Full fourteen Ships *I* ſee when *I* ſail'd,
Full fourteen Ships I ſee,
Merchants of high degree,
They were too hard for me, when I ſail'd &c.
we ſteer'd from Sound to Sound while we ſail'd
We ſteer'd from *Sound* to Sound wile we ſail'd
We ſteer'd from Sound to Sound,
A *Moorish* Ship we found,
Her Men we ſtript and bound while we ſail'd
Upon the Ocean Seas while we ſail'd, &c,
Upon the Ocean *Seas* while we ſail'd,
Upon the Ocean Seas,
A warlike *Portugueſe*,
In ſhort, did us diſpleaſe while we ſail'd.

At famous M*allabar* when we ſail'd, &c,
At famous *Mallabar* when we ſail'd,
At famous *Mallabar*
We went aſhore each Tar,
And rob'd the Natives there when we ſail'd.
Then after this we chas'd while we ſail'd &c.
Then after this we chas'd while we ſail'd,
Then after this we chas'd
A Rich *Armenian*, grac'd,
With Wealth which we embrac'd, while we (ſail'd
Many *Moorish* Ships we took while we ſail'd
Many *Moorish* Ships we took while we ſail'd
Many *Moorish* Ships we took,
We did ſtill for plunder look,
All Conſcience we forſook while we ſail'd,
I Captain C*alliford* while *I* ſaild, &c.
I Captain C*alliford* while I ſail'd
I Captain C*alliford*
Did many Merchants board,
Which did much Wealth afford, while we ſail'd
Two hundred *Bars* of Gold, while we ſail'd,
Two hundred Bars of Gold while we ſail'd,
Two hundred Bars of Gold
And Rix *D*ollars manifold,
We ſeized uncontroul'd while we ſaild.
St. John a Ship of Fame when we ſail'd &c.
St. John a Ship of Fame when we ſail'd
St *John* a Ship of Fame,
We plundred when ſhe came
With more that I could name when we ſail'd
We taken was at laſt and muſt die. &c,
We taken was at laſt and muſt die,
We taken were at laſt,
And into *Priſon* caſt
Now Sentence being paſt we muſt die.
Tho we have reign'd a while we muſt die &c,
Tho we have reign'd a while we muſt die
Tho we have reign'd a while
While Fortune ſeem'd to ſmile,
Now on the *Britiſh* Iſle we muſt die,
Farewel the Ocean main, we muſt die &c,
Farewel the Ocean main we, muſt die,
Farewel the Ocean main,
The Coaſt of *France* or *Spain*
We ne're ſhall ſee again, we muſt die.
From Newgate now in Carts we muſt go, &c.
From Newgate now in Carts
With ſad and heavy hearts,
To have our due Deſerts we muſt go.
Some thouſands they will flock when we die,
Some thouſands they will flock when we die,
Some thouſands they will flock
To Execution Duck
Where we muſt ſtand the ſhock, and muſt die,

F *I* N *I* S

Figure 1. Captain Kid's Farewel to the Seas; or, The Famous Pirate's Lament [ESTC R170787]. Reproduced with permission from materials on loan to the National Library of Scotland by the Balcarres Trust.

Class, too, plays an important role in the records we have. Phenomena such as marginalia (as in President John Adams's splendid library of books), letters, reading lists, logs, diaries, and, later, subscriptions to reading clubs and magazines were disproportionally created by people of some means, and their perceived status dictated the preservation of their documents. In the maritime world, the privileged classes of people would include the supercargo (the representative of the ship's owner on board a ship), passengers, and officers. James Osborn, for example, the 26-year-old second mate of the *Charles W. Morgan*, a mid-nineteenth-century whaling ship, recorded each book he read between 1841 and 1845 in a logbook now held in the G. W. Blunt White Library, Mystic Seaport, Mystic, Connecticut.[3] I have yet to find such a diary or logbook from a pre-1814 fo'c'sle hand.[4] Nevertheless, I look to these fo'c'sle hands and seek to explore the 'sparse and multiple traces' of their reading through *The Dying Words of Captain Robert Kidd*.[5]

Sailor balladeers

Two extant copies of the ballad printed by Nathaniel Coverly, Jr., will help me assemble a profile of who was buying and reading *The Dying Words of Captain Robert Kidd*, though I ultimately want to make an argument not just about who was purchasing the broadsides but also about who influenced the textual changes in the ballad, and why. First, I want to present some evidence that the audience for Coverly's broadsides was largely seamen. Gary Nash notes that eighteenth-century maritime and dock workers were 'perhaps the most elusive social group in early American history because they moved from port to port with greater frequency than other urban dwellers, shifted occupations, died young, and, as the poorest members of the free white community, least often left behind traces of their lives on the tax lists or in land or probate records'.[6] Still, we believe that sailors as a group had high rates of literacy for the working class; estimates put literacy at between 75 and 90 per cent by the beginning of the

---

[3] Hester Blum, *The View from the Masthead: Maritime Imagination and Antebellum American Sea Narratives* (Chapel Hill: University of North Carolina Press, 2008), p. 24 (fig. 1.1).

[4] The forecastle, or fo'c'sle, was the forward part of a ship, before the mainmast, where the common sailors lived and was close, dark, dank, and subject to the ship's pitching motion.

[5] Chartier, 'Texts, Printing, Reading', p. 157.

[6] Quoted in Marcus Rediker, *Between the Devil and the Deep Blue Sea: Merchant Seamen, Pirates, and the Anglo-American Maritime World, 1700–1750* (New York: Cambridge University Press, 1987), p. 5.

nineteenth century.[7] Scholars have used various methods to arrive at these figures. Historians understand signatures on wills, ships' registers, and other documents to indicate some level of literacy. So, too, they assume that ownership of books, as indicated by probate records, correlates with literacy. By the early nineteenth century the religious and temperance societies which distributed Bibles and other tracts to sailors sometimes took note of the rate of literacy within a ship's crew as a way of documenting the success of their missions. Naval records, which are more complete than those from merchant vessels, indicate the extent of shipboard libraries, which serve as another, albeit less certain, marker of shipboard reading, especially as we move further into the nineteenth century.[8] In addition, anecdotes support the idea of a high level of literacy among sailors. An anonymous naval memoir of 1841 includes a poem about an argument within the 'book-learned crew' over the literary merit of the popular maritime novelist Frederick Marryat.[9] Richard Henry Dana, Jr., who wrote the best-selling US maritime autobiography of the nineteenth century, even mentions the literacy of the black cook on the *Pilgrim*, whom Dana cites as reading the Bible every Sunday in his galley.[10] Dana also recounts moments of relaxation when the more educated (like Dana himself, who had been to Harvard) taught their fellow sailors 'letters and numbers'.[11]

While a literacy rate of 75–90 per cent was high, it made professional sense.[12] By the eighteenth century ships' officers needed to be able to read and write in order to keep logbooks, to reference charts and tables, and to perform navigational calculations. Before reliable and seaworthy chronometers, sailors would calculate latitude

---

[7] Blum, *View from the Masthead*, pp. 5, 27. See also Harry Robert Skallerup, *Books Afloat & Ashore: A History of Books, Libraries, and Reading among Seamen during the Age of Sail* (Hamden, CT: Archon Books, 1974), pp. 22–23; Rediker, *Between the Devil and the Deep Blue Sea*, p. 158.

[8] Blum, *View from the Masthead*, pp. 26–27.

[9] Quoted in Blum, *View from the Masthead*, p. 20.

[10] Richard Henry Dana, Jr., *Two Years Before the Mast* (Harmondsworth: Penguin, 1981), p. 78.

[11] Dana, *Two Years Before the Mast*, p. 208. Another sailor, George Little, wrote: 'On one side of the forecastle might be seen some engaged in painting vessels, landscapes, &c.; on the other were a group writing their journals; while a third set were learning navigation, taught by a young shipmate who had graduated at Cambridge' (quoted in Blum, *View from the Masthead*, p. 5).

[12] Also, by 1850 New England had a near 100 per cent literacy rate, and the majority of the sailors under discussion would have come from non-slave states, including many from New England. In New England white male literacy had been at 90 per cent at least fifty years earlier (Skallerup, *Books Afloat & Ashore*, p. 29).

with a quadrant or sextant. Longitude, however, required dead reckoning, an estimate of the distance travelled (taking into account speed and duration) from a known longitudinal point. With complications of drift and currents this method was often wildly inaccurate, but whatever accuracy it achieved relied on meticulous records kept by officers. By the nineteenth century Nathaniel Bowditch's *The New American Practical Navigator* (1799) was an essential companion for the US sailor. Not only did the book, which was colloquially known as the *Bowditch*, teach navigational concepts in ways easy for men before the mast to understand, but it included more accurate charts and became so indispensable that the US government eventually purchased rights to it. Literacy, which gave access to the *Bowditch* and the skills of record-keeping, offered a sailor a path up through the ranks.[13]

High rates of literacy also made sense because reading was a valuable way both of passing the time and of building community on board a ship. While there was daily work to be done to keep a vessel shipshape, the Sabbath was usually a time of rest. As Dana noted, fo'c'sle hands would then 'employ themselves in reading, talking, smoking, and mending their clothes'.[14] Longer voyages frequently had periods of being becalmed, or of less work, as when a vessel was in the doldrums or when whalers were searching for a whale. Slave ships (before the moratorium on the transatlantic slave trade in 1808) would have spent weeks or months off the shore of West Africa waiting for a full complement of slaves to be assembled. Reading helped sailors get through these periods of boredom. Even those who were not literate could interact with writing when one person read aloud to a group. In addition to retelling the time when he held much of the crew in thrall 'nearly all day' with his reading of 'descriptions of the Puritans, and the sermons and harangues of the Round-head soldiers', Dana recalls the communal joy when his ship received letters after being at sea for more than a year – 'when, at last, they were brought out, they all got round any one who had a letter, and expected to have it read aloud, and have it all in common'.[15] Although Dana was the earliest successful recorder of life before the mast, he details what were surely long-standing practices. Sailing had remained largely

---

[13] Dana reports having taken the *Bowditch* to sea with him; desperate for reading material at one point, 'I took hold of Bowditch's Navigator, which I had always with me. I had been through the greater part of it, and now went carefully through it, from beginning to end working out most of the examples' (*Two Years Before the Mast*, p. 225).
[14] Dana, *Two Years Before the Mast*, p. 58.
[15] Dana, *Two Years Before the Mast*, pp. 339, 338, 330.

unchanged from the sixteenth century to the first half of the nineteenth century and shipboard culture, with its high value on stories, can be imagined to have remained fairly consistent over that period. The phrase 'spinning a yarn', a metaphor for putting together a tale as a sailor would weave together a type of rope known as 'spun-yarn', shows that sailors were invested in reading and hearing narratives long before advances in print technology ushered in a spate of maritime autobiographies in the 1840s.[16]

Moreover, we should think of broadside ballads as attractive not just to those who could read but to those who wanted to be able to read. By following the words of a familiar ballad on a broadside copy, a sailor could learn the rudiments of reading. We know that readers in various historical moments did as much with a number of forms of cheap literature. Roger Chartier notes that 'rudimentary' French readers between 1700 and 1800 would 'memorize' the chapbooks of the *bibliothèque bleue* during social readings and then, 'when actually faced with the books, [they] recognized them more than they discovered them'.[17] This constituted a form of 'preknowledge' which less skilled readers 'mobilized to produce comprehension of what was read'.[18] Broadside ballads were part of the landscape of inexpensive reading material in the eighteenth- and early nineteenth-century United States. Sarah Josepha Hale, born in New Hampshire in 1788, recalled that 'innumerable were the ballads, songs and stories' with which her mother 'amused and instructed her children', because the books to which she had access 'were few, very few'.[19] Having gained her reading and writing skills in this manner, Hale went on to be the single most influential nineteenth-century literary editor in the United States. In an 1834 magazine she included a letter to the editor that described how one illiterate woman taught both herself and her children to read: using a hymn book, she directed the children to sound out passages, which she would then check by counting the words of the hymns, all of which she had memorized.[20] (Note that hymns and ballads can be metrically quite similar, and *The Dying Words of Captain Robert Kidd* became a popular fixture in church concerts.)

---

[16] Paul A. Gilje, *To Swear Like a Sailor: Maritime Culture in America, 1750–1850* (New York: Cambridge University Press, 2016), p. 107.

[17] Chartier, 'Texts, Printing, Reading', p. 165.

[18] Chartier, 'Texts, Printing, Reading', p. 165.

[19] 'Sarah Josepha Hale', in *The Ladies' Wreath: A Selection from the Female Poetic Writers of England and America* (Boston: Marsh, Capen & Lyon, 1837), pp. 383–88 (p. 384).

[20] Sarah Josepha Buell Hale, 'What Can Women Do?', *American Ladies' Magazine*, May 1834, pp. 215–16 (p. 216).

Familiarity and accessibility created opportunities for self-taught literacy, and broadside ballads fitted that description perfectly. Coverly charged a penny or two for most broadside ballads, whereas a volume of *A Narrative of the Captivity, Sufferings and Removes of Mrs. Mary Rowlandson*, printed by Coverly's father in 1771, cost six shillings.

Of course, a broadside ballad like *The Dying Words of Captain Robert Kidd* is not just a piece of writing, it is also a song, and sailors liked to sing. Timothy Connor, who shipped on board a privateer during the American Revolution, was subsequently captured and held in Forton Prison, near Portsmouth, where he kept a journal and wrote out a manuscript of songs, including verses copied from broadside ballads.[21] There are plenty more nautical logs and journals that include songs.[22] Herman Melville, who himself went to sea, made Billy Budd, the eponymous hero of his final unfinished novella, 'an illiterate nightingale', which made Billy beloved by his shipmates.[23] As Melville would have known, talented singers were esteemed by their fellows because good singing, like masterful storytelling, was a form of currency at sea.[24] Samuel Leech, a British sailor, recalled how when one skilled sailor-singer came on deck, 'every voice was hushed, all work was brought to a stand still', on account of his 'unequaled performances'.[25] Beyond their value as entertainment, tunes were also useful for regulating and coordinating shipboard tasks in the age before steam. The rhythm of a song kept sailors hauling lines in time so sails set evenly or the anchor came up smoothly. Sailors, Dana wrote, 'can't pull in time, or pull with a will', without a tune, and continued, 'Many a time, when a thing goes heavy, with one fellow yo-ho-ing, a lively song, like "Heave, to the girls!" "Nancy oh!" "Jack Crosstree," &c., has put life and strength into every arm.'[26]

In the seventeenth century printers started producing broadsides of songs about sailors. Because their work took them away from home for long periods of time, sailors were obvious characters for ballad stories that told of lovers leaving or yearning for their sweethearts.[27] Sailors were also directly and indirectly the heroes of

---

[21] Timothy Connor, *A Sailor's Songbag: An American Rebel in an English Prison, 1777–1779*, ed. George G. Carey (Amherst: University of Massachusetts Press, 1976), p. 14.

[22] Gilje, *To Swear Like a Sailor*, p. 307 n. 3.

[23] Herman Melville, *Billy Budd, Sailor*, in *Melville's Short Novels: Authoritative Texts, Contexts, Criticism*, ed. Dan McCall (New York: Norton, 2002), pp. 103–70 (p. 110).

[24] Gilje, *To Swear Like a Sailor*, p. 134.

[25] Quoted in Gilje, *To Swear Like a Sailor*, p. 134.

[26] Dana, *Two Years Before the Mast*, pp. 342–43.

[27] Gilje, *To Swear Like a Sailor*, p. 137.

the pirate and naval ballads that appeared later. Many of these ballads, such as the one about Captain Kidd, and a later ballad that the young Benjamin Franklin wrote about Blackbeard, provided contemporary news for those who did not have access to newspapers.[28] On the other hand, romantic, adventurous, and bawdy ballads about sailors relied on their entertainment value or novelty to promote sales. Whether fact or fiction, the words allowed the singer to express something important, be it sexual innuendo, romance, nationalism, or frustration with the maritime command structure.[29] Then, as now, people bought what they liked, and they liked what had meaning for them.

Besides their stories and didactic potential, broadside ballads attracted customers with their images. It is true that broadsides often have just one or two small woodcuts, and that woodcuts are reused from broadside to broadside, meaning that the images sometimes have only a loose thematic relevance to the content. Still, before more sophisticated pictures became widely available, the broadside provided an accessible form of visual culture.[30] Broadsides were pasted up on the walls of public houses and domestic dwellings.[31] Foc's'le sailors would have frequented alehouses, may well have grown up in houses decorated with broadsides, and may even have used ballads to decorate their own belongings. Seamen's chests, although built from simple pine, were sometimes gussied up with knotted string, paint, or carving,[32] and some, like a nineteenth-century example at the National Maritime Museum, Greenwich, also had paper decorations glued inside the lid.[33]

What reinforces conjecture about this particular ballad's use as a poster decoration is the remarkable popularity of *The Dying Words of*

---

[28] The ballads of the War of 1812 that Martin Graebe writes about elsewhere in this volume are prime examples, a number of which were printed as broadsides by Coverly.

[29] Gilje, *To Swear Like a Sailor*, pp. 134–48.

[30] Carleton Sprague Smith, 'Broadsides and their Music in Colonial America', in *Music in Colonial Massachusetts, 1630–1820: A Conference Held by the Colonial Society of Massachusetts, May 17 and 18, 1973*, ed. Colonial Society of Massachusetts (Boston: Colonial Society of Massachusetts, 1980), pp. 157–366 (p. 157).

[31] Izaak Walton wrote in *The Compleat Angler* (chapter 2): 'I'll now lead you to an honest ale-house, where we shall find a cleanly room, lavender in the windows, and twenty ballads stuck about the wall.'

[32] Lon Schleining, *Treasure Chests: The Legacy of Extraordinary Boxes* (Newtown, CT: Taunton Press, 2003), p. 112.

[33] Greenwich, National Maritime Museum, AAA3328 https://collections.rmg.co.uk/collections/objects/3302.html.

Captain Robert Kidd. Multiple copies from multiple printings have survived. A copy at the Houghton Library has creases from where it was folded in half lengthwise and then into quarters, just the right size for a pocket, indicating that it was carried around by at least one owner.[34] Many other copies must have been carried from place to place, since records show the ballad was sung across English-speaking North America, from Mississippi to Nova Scotia, and from the American West to US ships.[35] The ballad was sufficiently well known to be parodied in a newspaper in 1797 and remarked upon as a common tune in a book of US history in 1844.[36] As the nineteenth century wore on, it was incorporated into church revivals, Christian concerts, and song collections.[37] Harriet Beecher Stowe even interpolated it into her short story *Captain Kidd's Money*, about Kidd's buried treasure, which was published in the *Atlantic* in 1870. Put simply, the ballad became a fixture in US culture, through both oral and print renditions.

Sailors would have been instrumental to the spread of the ballad. From the beginning of English colonization the eastern seaboard had looked towards Europe, exporting goods such as tobacco and cotton, and importing textiles and other manufactured items. Urban areas were clustered along the coast at good ports (like Boston and New York City), and until a reliable rail network came into being in the mid-nineteenth century trade between the various colonies (and later states) was conducted predominantly by sea and river. From Columbus's first voyage to the Americas until after the publication of Coverly's ballads, sailors connected (what became) the USA with itself and with the outside world. They would have carried the news of Kidd's execution, either by reporting it to other colonists or bringing written material from London to printers in colonial ports. After that, sailors would have been central to the development, dissemination, and long-standing popularity of *The Dying Words of Captain Robert Kidd*. Cotton Mather complained in 1713 of the reach of 'foolish Songs and

[34] *The Dying Words of Capt. Robert Kidd* [Cambridge, MA, Houghton Library, American Broadsides 58].
[35] Bonner, 'Ballad of Captain Kidd', p. 374, records wide distribution: '"The Dying Words of Captain Robert Kidd", or more simply "Captain Kidd" or "Kidd's Lament", has been (and in some places still is) sung from Mississippi to Nova Scotia, in Boston, New York, and Philadelphia, in the woods of Maine and the highlands of Carolina, in the fo'castle of ships, on the lone prairie, in the southern peninsula of Michigan, and in Pennsylvania camp meetings. Well into the twentieth century it has been heard on the lips of old seamen, and of Negroes on the Mississippi.'
[36] Bonner, 'Ballad of Captain Kidd', p. 375.
[37] Bonner, 'Ballad of Captain Kidd', p. 379.

Ballads, which the Hawkers and Pedlars carry into all parts of the Countrey'.[38] Given the extent of printing in the colonies at that date, local presses (even Thomas Fleet's) could not have produced so many broadsides. Rather, sailors must have transported printed ballads from London.[39]

The frustrations of sailors

Two versions of *The Dying Words of Captain Robert Kidd* are part of the Isaiah Thomas Broadside Collection, a sheaf of broadsides assembled by patriot-printer Isaiah Thomas and given to the American Antiquarian Society in 1814 (*Figures 2 and 3* and *Appendix*).[40] When donating the items Thomas stated that he had purchased them from 'a Ballad Printer and Seller in Boston [. . .] to shew what articles of this kind are in vogue with the Vulgar'. That printer and seller was Nathaniel Coverly, Jr., 'the main provider of broadside ballad sheets in Boston from 1810 to 1815'.[41] According to a helpful, though unidentified, newspaper clipping at the American Antiquarian Society, 'juveniles', prostitutes and their clients, and 'sailors' were Coverly's main customers.[42] Despite being firmly planted on the ground, Nathaniel Coverly was thus connected to the sea. Both his grandfather and great-grandfather had been ships' captains. Like his fellow Massachusetts citizens, he relied on sea and river for information and trade, and he sold directly to sailors.

None of the claims I have made about sailors' literacy and inclinations or Coverly's customer base makes it certain that sailors were the primary audience for *The Dying Words of Captain Robert Kidd*. Still, of the broadsides that we have with Coverly's imprint, 20 per cent deal with maritime subjects or persons, as indicated by their titles, a tally that increases to 25 per cent when *The Dying Words of Captain Robert Kidd* and many other ballads without imprint (titles such as *Jolly*

---

[38] Cotton Mather, *Diary of Cotton Mather, 1681–1724*, ed. Worthington C. Ford (Boston: Massachusetts Historical Society, 1911), p. 242.

[39] Smith, 'Broadsides and their Music in Colonial America', p. 163.

[40] Worcester, MA, American Antiquarian Society, Isaiah Thomas Broadside Ballad Collection https://www.americanantiquarian.org/thomasballads/. Neither version carries an imprint, but both use woodcuts that are found on other broadsides with Coverly's imprint.

[41] Kate Van Winkle Keller, 'Nathaniel Coverly and Son, Printers, 1767–1825', *Proceedings of the American Antiquarian Society*, 117 (2007), 211–52 (p. 213).

[42] Quoted in Daniel A. Cohen, 'Introduction', in *The Female Marine and Related Works: Narratives of Cross-Dressing and Urban Vice in America's Early Republic*, ed. Daniel A. Cohen (Amherst: University of Massachusetts Press, 1997), pp. 1–45 (p. 5).

Sailor!) identified as being probably from Coverly's press are included.[43] Other patriotic songs and scandalous stories would no doubt have attracted the interest of sailors. Almost all of the materials that we have from Coverly from between 1800 and 1815 are broadsides or pamphlets of fewer than twenty pages – inexpensive publications for popular consumption. Coverly targeted consumers without much disposable income, both at his shop and through a

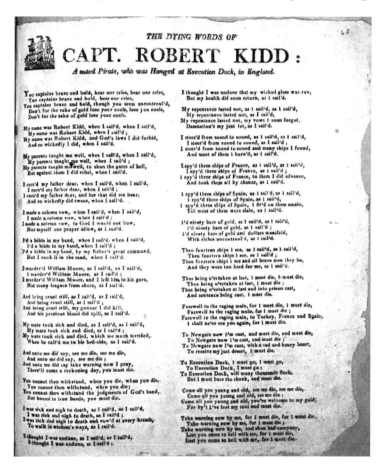

Figure 2. The Dying Words of Capt. Robert Kidd. Courtesy of the American Antiquarian Society.

---

[43] Figures derived from Kate Van Winkle Keller, 'Checklist of the Publications of Nathaniel Coverly and Son, 1767–1825,' *Proceedings of the American Antiquarian Society*, 117 (2007), 451–69.

network of ballad sellers who purchased in bulk at a discount. Given all this evidence, I would like us to accept the likelihood that sailors were buying and reading the Captain Kidd ballad, and to consider how that knowledge provides access to the imaginative world of the fo'c'sle hand and insights into why the ballad changed over time.

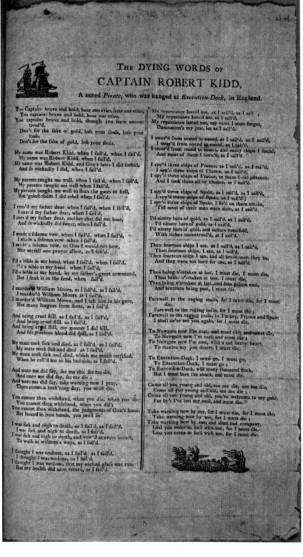

Figure 3. The Dying Words of Captain Robert Kidd. Courtesy of the American Antiquarian Society.

The words did change considerably between the first publication in London in 1701 and the two Coverly imprints of *c*.1814. The alterations demonstrate that the ballad lived not just in written form on broadsides but through an oral tradition of singing.[44] Nevertheless, by the time Nathaniel Coverly's father started printing in the 1770s, a *Captain Kid* broadside was already in circulation, with the same words as the Coverly broadsides.[45] We can speculate that sailors not only transmitted the changed words, but also that over the course of the eighteenth century they were instrumental in altering the words of the ballad to reflect their own worldview. The US ballad, sung in a 'plaintive' tone and usually in a minor key, allowed them to channel their frustrations with the strictures and inequities of life on the sea.[46]

Unlike the original English ballad which begins, 'My Name is Captain *Kid* who has sail'd', the US ballad begins, 'You captains brave and bold, hear our cries, hear our cries'. From this opening line, twice repeated, *The Dying Words of Captain Robert Kidd* aligns the singer with the working sailor and against the maritime command structure. The singer pleads with these 'uncontroul'd' captains, 'Don't for the sake of gold lose your souls', another line twice repeated. While the first line of each stanza is repeated throughout the entire printed ballad, the last line of the stanza is printed twice only in the opening and final stanzas: 'Don't for the sake of gold lose your souls', 'Lest you come to hell with me, for I must die', respectively. This repetition anchors the beginning and end of the song in print, rather like the thicker paper or board covers of a book. And like a book's covers, these repeated lines highlight the central concern of the ballad: the consequences of greed among the officer class. A number of critics, pointing to the song's later popularity in Christian circles, have read this ballad as a simple moral story.[47] Kidd buries his Bible and sacks ships, so he is a bad

[44] Unlike the 1701 ballad, Coverly published his broadsides without a tune direction (identified as 'Coming Down' on the English broadside). The American ballad was not printed with accompanying music until *The Western Minstrel* (1831), although Whittier Perkins in his collection of dancing tunes, marches, and song tunes, begun in Massachusetts *c*.1790, refers to a tune called 'Captain Kid'. For an overview, see the Isaiah Thomas Broadside Ballads Project https://www.americanantiquarian.org/thomasballads/items/show/97.
[45] *Captain Kid, a Noted Pirate, Who Was Hanged at Execution-Dock, in England* [ESTC W6960].
[46] Bonner, 'Ballad of Captain Kidd', p. 375.
[47] For example, Smith, 'Broadsides and their Music in Colonial America', p. 357 ('The amoral, mocking tone of the British imprint [*Captain Kid's Farwel to the Seas*] is in direct contrast to the moral, confessional tone of the North American version [*The Dying Words of Captain Robert Kidd*]'); Bonner, 'Ballad of Captain Kidd', p. 373 ('additions

man. But the ballad's opening, emphasized both by placement and repetition, clearly targets not just avarice but avarice among ships' captains.[48]

The opening of the ballad thus fits nicely with Marcus Rediker's contention that many sailors turned pirate because of the dreadful treatment of fo'c'sle hands. Various testimonies support this argument. William Fly, a pirate hanged in Boston in 1726, forewent the usual begging for forgiveness to issue a final caution to 'all Masters of Vessels' that they 'might take Warning by the Fate of the Captain', whom Fly had murdered, and be sure 'to pay Sailors their Wages when due, and to treat them better; saying, that their Barbarity to them made so many turn Pyrates'.[49] John Archer, another pirate, said before his execution in 1724, 'I could wish that Masters of Vessels would not use their Men with so much Severity.'[50] John Gow, convicted of mutiny and murder, cried out on the gallows that 'the captain's inhumanity had produced the consequences which had happened'.[51] These eighteenth-century complaints, and many others, registered the absolute authority that ships' captains exercised over their vessels.[52] Notably, instead of flipping between 'I' and 'we', as does the English ballad, the US version consistently employs the first-person voice of Captain Kidd. This means that the US ballad positions the singer-speaker as a frustrated Captain Kidd, who like William Fly, John Archer, and John Gow expresses his deep anger towards those who have wronged him.

Impressment, a matter serious enough that it constituted one of the causes of the War of 1812, was a dramatic example of the abusive authority of the officer class.[53] When the Royal Navy required more sailors it exercised its legal right to force any fo'c'sle hands they came across to serve the Crown. According to the letter of the law, only

---

both at the beginning and end [of the American version] gave it the moral dying-confession and dance-macabre touch [...] suitable always to the temperament of simple evangelical piety').

[48] Bonner, 'Ballad of Captain Kidd', p. 373.

[49] Marcus Rediker, *Villains of All Nations: Atlantic Pirates in the Golden Age* (Boston: Beacon Press, 2004), p. 2.

[50] Rediker, *Villains of All Nations*, p. 93.

[51] Rediker, *Villains of All Nations*, p. 93.

[52] William Murrell, in an account of brutal naval discipline quoted in Myra C. Glenn, *Jack Tar's Story: The Autobiographies and Memoirs of Sailors in Antebellum America* (New York: Cambridge University Press, 2010), p. 45, contends that landlubbers 'would not credit the various scenes of cruelty and tyrannic oppression' on board the USS *Columbia*.

[53] See Martin Graebe's contribution to this volume.

Britons could legally be impressed, but US sailors were regularly subject to impressment after the Revolution. The surge in the practice during the Napoleonic Wars angered the public and Congress, but it was already established well before the nineteenth century. Indeed, the historical Captain William Kidd suffered from it, not because he himself was impressed but because, having outfitted as a privateer in order to capture pirates menacing the American colonies, he found his entire carefully chosen crew impressed into the Royal Navy.[54] The rest of Kidd's story is subject to debate. Either he purposely turned pirate, or he was forced to seize a ship by his mutinous crew, or he honestly mistook a ship that was flying false French colours for a genuine French ship. Whatever the actual events surrounding the capture of the *Quedagh Merchant*, his most valuable prize, Kidd's political patron, Lord Bellomont, governor of New York and Massachusetts Bay, saw more benefit in selling Kidd out than in supporting him when he returned to port. Despite having given him a promise of safe conduct, Bellomont had Kidd arrested and thrown into Boston Gaol, where he languished for a year before he was shipped to London for a show trial. Even as a famed pirate captain, Kidd shared the central condition of fo'c'sle life, unfair judgement and punishment.

In the navy or out of it, eighteenth- and nineteenth-century sailors were regularly tied up and flogged with the cat-o'-nine-tails, until, after mid-century sea narratives such as Dana's had shocked readers, Congress tried to reign in the practice.[55] In 1847, Joshua Last was hooking up a gantline as a safety harness to slush the mainmast (that is, cover it with grease to minimize wear on the sail's fittings) during a heavy wind; when the mate chastised him for not finishing the job fast enough Last grumbled and things quickly escalated; the captain insisted that Last had shown insubordination and gave him a good lashing.[56] In 1807, James Durand deserted the *Constitution* after having received twelve lashes for a minor transgression; he lost over $350 in pay.[57] In 1841, Roland Gould received nine lashes for having a dirty hammock.[58] While lashings were a common punishment, officers also enjoyed wide latitude to hit and kick men as the mood took them. According to a court case from the 1840s, when one sailor was slow

---

[54] Robert C. Ritchie, 'Kidd, William (*c*.1645–1701)', *ODNB* https://doi.org/10.1093/ref:odnb/15515. Kidd's career is also summarized in Bonner, 'Ballad of Captain Kidd', pp. 362–63.

[55] Glenn, *Jack Tar's Story*, pp. 112–43.

[56] Gilje, *To Swear Like a Sailor*, p. 13.

[57] Glenn, *Jack Tar's Story*, p. 136.

[58] Glenn, *Jack Tar's Story*, p. 137.

to answer a call to duty the captain hit him over the head three times and clapped him in irons.[59] When John Dunford, the cooper on the whale-ship *Brooklyn*, refused to let his captain borrow a tool, he called Dunford 'a damned liar' and then assaulted him, pulling fistfuls of his beard from his face.[60] James M'Lean, who was impressed no fewer than three times (he kept escaping), once had a lieutenant knock out two of his teeth when he disapproved of how M'Lean was hauling a buoy rope.[61]

An enlisted sailor could even be legally executed following a trial in which high-ranking naval officers acted as prosecutor, judge, and jury. Following an on-deck court martial an enlisted man would be hauled up to the yardarm and hanged. This is what happens to Melville's Billy Budd. Although his captain knows it is an unfair decision, Billy is convicted in a drumhead court martial, and a shipmate memorializes the injustice in a ballad: 'O, 'tis me, not the sentence they'll suspend.' Usually all hands would be called on deck to witness a fellow sailor's flogging or hanging, so the event served as both punishment and deterrent. Having broken away from Great Britain in pursuit of liberty and freedom, US sailors must have been particularly sensitive to the paradox of (in Hester Blum's words) the 'terrific mobility and repressive confinement' of their lives at sea.[62] In his memoir the sailor Ben-Ezra Stiles Ely claimed that seamen endured 'as horrible slavery at sea, as any of the children of Africa in any part of the world'.[63] As Myra Glenn points out, maritime autobiographies of the 1840s repeatedly link floggings with existential emasculation. These punishments, sailors felt, transformed them from US citizens into feminized slaves.[64]

While some Golden Age pirate ships may have functioned as democratic heterotopias, piratical abuse certainly existed. Blackbeard was infamous for his brutality, once taking a pistol and shooting it under the table into a crewmate's knee just for the fun of it. William Kidd was charged with and found guilty not just of piracy but of murder, the most extreme form of mistreatment of a member of a ship's crew. While other specifics fell away from the US ballad, Kidd's murdering of his gunner, William Moore, remained a central part of the story. So Captain Robert Kidd brazenly declares, 'I murder'd

---

[59] Gilje, *To Swear Like a Sailor*, p. 13.

[60] Gilje, *To Swear Like a Sailor*, p. 13.

[61] Glenn, *Jack Tar's Story*, p. 51.

[62] Blum, *View from the Masthead*, p. 47.

[63] Quoted in Glenn, *Jack Tar's Story*, p. 124.

[64] Glenn, *Jack Tar's Story*, pp. 50–83.

William Moore, and I left him in his gore, / Not many leagues from shore', and in the following stanza, 'And being cruel still, my gunner I did kill, / And his precious blood did spill'. The murder of William Moore is such a key part of the US ballad that it is split over two stanzas; the historic William Moore *was* Kidd's gunner, but the effect in the ballad is also to make of him something of an everyman figure, standing for all brutalized fo'c'sle hands. Whereas the original English ballad uses 'we' and includes Kidd's entire crew in the act, in the US ballad Kidd acts alone and with malice. Through this ballad – through buying it, gifting it, teaching it, and singing it – sailors could condemn the acts of captains like Kidd and express their own frustration at the physical abuse rife within their profession.

As the first stanza of the ballad states – 'Don't for the sake of gold, lose your souls' – common sailors could resent officers for economic reasons, too. William Ray speaks with disgust of how his mess officer stole rum rations and how other officers aboard the USS *Philadelphia* tricked men out of their wages. More generally, he describes the naval command structure in 1801 as unequal and unjust, filled with well-connected but unqualified boy officers.[65] In circumstances such as whaling, sailors earned a share of the voyage's profit, meaning that they could work for many months but receive, on an unsuccessful trip, next to nothing. Sailors who jumped ship to escape their working conditions forfeited all of their wages. Financial insecurity drove the explosion of antebellum maritime autobiographies – unable to continue sailing and destitute, former seamen told their life stories for money. More generally, the eighteenth and early nineteenth century were periods of deep economic uncertainty in the United States and the lower classes were more susceptible to, and vulnerable in, economic downturns. Banking was volatile and uninsured; there were bubbles in land and stocks, embargos and shifts in trade policy, panics (1792, 1796, 1809, 1819, and 1837), recessions (1802, 1812, 1822, and 1825), and depressions (1807 and 1815).

Except during short windows when bankruptcy was allowed, debtors were thrown into prison. New York finally banned debtors' jails in 1831, but by 1849 only eleven other states had passed similar laws. Hence, despite the brutality of shipboard life, the sea remained an attractive alternative for many dogged by debt. The poverty-stricken William Ray enlisted in the US Navy in 1803 because he saw his only other option as suicide. In 1841, Herman Melville, whose

---

[65] William Ray, *Horrors of Slavery; or, The American Tars in Tripoli*, ed. Hester Blum (New Brunswick, NJ: Rutgers University Press, 2008), p. 47.

father took his own life after going bankrupt, went to sea for economic reasons. Nathaniel Coverly, too, experienced the same economic insecurity as his customers. In 1797 he was fined for not paying a school tax of two shillings, and in September of that year an attachment was filed on his goods or estate 'to the value of eighty Dollars'.[66] Eventually, Coverly moved to Salem, Massachusetts, a port city north of Boston, where he first started printing broadsides. Later, in Boston, he declared bankruptcy and in January 1803 the court seized his property, consisting of '74 pamphlets, 300 songs & one account book'.[67] These goods did not even cover the court charges, but bankruptcy (under the short-lived Bankruptcy Act of 1800) gave Coverly a debt-free new start with which he scaled up his business model, printing numerous broadside ballads.

Within *The Dying Words of Captain Robert Kidd*, mention of Captain Kidd's wealth – we hear of his seizing three Spanish and three French ships, and having 'ninety bars of gold and dollars manifold' – aligns with a critique of officer-class avarice. But these references would also have been attractive to common sailors dreaming about gold. The first-person ballad allows the singer to inhabit the persona of Robert Kidd, experiencing the pleasure of gaining wealth and the thrill of meting out arbitrary punishment. Even while a sailor would have felt anger at the murder of William Moore, he could also enjoy the way in which, in Kidd's voice, the powerless became powerful. Through the song, the fo'c'sle hand defies his parents, buries his Bible, seizes ships, gains riches, and kills a man. Through the song, he threatens shipboard officers with insubordination, mutiny, and piracy. The captains invoked at the ballad's beginning need to hear their sailors' cries and to recognize the dangerous power held by their crewmen.

Ultimately, though, once sentence has been passed Kidd bids 'Farewell to the raging main'. He is taken first to Newgate and then to 'Execution Dock, where many thousands flock'. His death provides both spectacle – 'Come all ye young and old, see me die, see me die' – and catharsis – 'Take warning now by me, for I must die, for I must die.' The price of not heeding the moral of his life story is that the singers, too, will 'come to hell' with Kidd. In the end, then, the threat of the ballad is contained. It permits the sailor to express his frustration, to contest his impotence, before bowing before the powerful structures that arrested and hanged – twice, since the rope broke on the first attempt – Captain Kidd.

---

[66] Van Winkle Keller, 'Nathaniel Coverly and Son', p. 230.
[67] Van Winkle Keller, 'Nathaniel Coverly and Son', p. 237.

Recovering traces of reading and readers is always difficult, even more so when they may have been semi-literate and incapable of writing. But all the evidence indicates that US sailors repeatedly bought, read, and sang *The Dying Words of Captain Robert Kidd*. Supporting shipboard fellowship, the ballad allowed them to express frustration with the conditions of sailing before the mast, and both to embrace and to censure Captain Kidd, a pirate who, having spent time in the old Boston Gaol, was in some sense one of their own. Over the decades of singing, Captain Kidd's story became Jack Tar's tale, until advances in printing technology – wood-pulp paper, steam-driven presses, stereotyping, and improved distribution systems – allowed common sailors to publish prose versions of their lives.

Appendix

The Dying Words of Captain Robert Kidd, a Noted Pirate, Who Was Hanged at Execution-Dock, in England

You Captains brave and bold, hear our cries, hear our cries,
You captains brave and bold, hear our cries,
You captains brave and bold, though you seem uncontroul'd,
Don't for the sake of gold, lose your souls, lose your souls,
Don't for the sake of gold, lose your souls.

My name was Robert Kidd, when I sail'd, when I sail'd,
My name was Robert Kidd, when I sail'd,
My name was Robert Kidd, and God's laws I did forbid,
And so wickedly I did, when I sail'd.

My parents taught me well, when I sail'd, when I sail'd,
My parents taught me well[,] when I sail'd,
My parents taught me well to shun the gates of hell,
But 'gainst them I did rebel when I sail'd.

I curs'd my father dear[,] when I sail'd, when I sail'd,
I curs d my father dear, when I sail'd,
I curs'd my father dear, and her that did me bear,
And so wickedly did swear, when I sail'd.

I made a solemn vow, when I sail'd, when I sail'd,
I made a solemn vow[,] when I sail'd,
I made a solemn vow, to God I would not bow,
Nor myself one prayer allow, as I sail'd.

I'd a bible in my hand, when I sail'd, when I sail'd,
I'd a bible in my hand[,] when I sail'd,

I'd a bible in my hand, by my father's great command,
But I sunk it in the sand, when [I] sail'd.

I murder'd William Moore, as I sail'd, as I sail'd,
I murder'd William Moore as I sail'd,
I murder'd William Moore, and I left him in his gore,
Not many leagues from shore, as I sail'd.

And being cruel still, as I sail'd, as I sail'd,
And being cruel still, as I sail'd,
And being cruel still, my gunner I did kill,
And his precious blood did spill, as I sail'd.

My mate took sick and died, as I sail'd, as I sail'd,
My mate took sick and died[,] as I sail'd,
My mate took sick and died, which me much terrified,
When he call'd me to his bed-side, as I sail'd.

And unto me did say, see me die, see me die,
And unto me did say, see me die;
And unto me did say, take warning now I pray,
There comes a reck'ning day, you must die.

You cannot then withstand, when you die, when you die[,]
You cannot then withstand, when you die;
You cannot then withstand, the judgments of God's hand,
But bound in iron bands, you must lie.

I was sick and nigh to death, as I sail'd, as I sail'd,
I was sick and nigh to death, as I sail'd,
I was sick and nigh to death, and vow'd at every breath,
To walk in wisdom's ways, as I sail'd.

I thought I was undone, as I sail'd, as I sail'd,
I thought I was undone, as I sail'd,
I thought I was undone, that my wicked glass was run,
But my health did soon return, as I sail'd.

My repentance lasted not, as I sail'd, as I sail'[d],
My repentance lasted not, as I sail'd,
My repentance lasted not, my vows I soon forgot,
Damnation's my just lot, as I sail'd.

I steer'd from sound to sound, as I sail'd, as I sail'd,
I steer'd from sound to sound, as I sail'd,
I steer'd from sound to sound, and many ships I found,
And most of them I burn'd, as I sail'd.

I spy'd three ships of France, as I sail'd, as I sail'd,
I spy'd three ships of France, as I sail'd,

I spy'd three ships of France, to them I did advance,
And I took them all by chance, as I sail'd.

I spy'd three ships of Spain, as I sail'd, as I sail'd,
I spy'd three ships of Spain, as I sail'd;
I spy'd three ships of Spain, I fir'd on them amain,
'Till most of their men were slain, as I sail'd.

I'd ninety bars of gold, as I sail'd, as I sail'd,
I'd ninety bars of gold, as I sail'd,
I'd ninety bars of gold, and dollars manifold,
With riches uncontroul'd, as I sail'd.

Then fourteen ships I see, as I sail'd, as I sail'd,
Then fourteen ships I see, as I sail'd,
Then fourteen ships I see, and all brave men they be,
And they were too hard for me, as I sail'd.

Thus being o'ertaken at last, I must die, I must die,
Thus being o'ertaken at last, I must die,
Thus being o'ertaken at last, and into prison cast,
And sentence being cast, I must die.

Farewell to the raging main, for I must die, for I must die,
Farewell to the raging main, for I must die;
Farewell to the raging main, to Turkey, France and Spain[,]
I shall ne'er see you again, for I must die.

To Newgate now I'm cast, and must die, and must die,
To Newgate now I'm cast, and must die;
To Newgate now I'm cast, with a sad heavy heart,
To receive my just desert, I must die.

To Execution-Dock, I must go, I must go,
To Execution-Dock, I must go;
To Execution-Dock, will many thousand flock,
But I must bare the shock, and must die.

Come all you young and old, see me die, see me die,
Come all you young and old, see me die;
Come all you young and old, you're welcome to my gold,
For by't I've lost my soul, and must die.

Take warning now by me, for I must die, for I must die,
Take warning now by me, for I must die;
Take warning now by me, and shun bad company,
Lest you come to hell with me, for I must die,
Lest you come to hell with me, for I must die.

Punks, Pretty Novices, and Persecuted Virgins: Nuns in Broadside Ballads from the Glorious Revolution to the Nunneries Inspection Bill

Catherine Ann Cullen

Nuns have long been the subject of tales that range from the scatological to the sacred. They feature in texts such as Boccaccio's *Decameron*, where an abbess and all nine of the nuns in her convent take advantage of an apparently dumb gardener to satisfy their desires (Third Day, Tale 1), in *The Canterbury Tales*, in the shape of the worldly, social-climbing Prioress, and in folklore about the fourteenth-century St Catherine of Siena who had a vision of Jesus marrying her with a ring made from his holy foreskin, a popular relic at the time.[1] Broadside ballads from these islands reflect a similar range of decidedly post-Reformation nuns. A ballad in support of the Glorious Revolution declares that nuns have gone back to 'their former Profession of Punks' – 'punk' meaning a prostitute.[2] Other English broadsides tell of the 'lusty fryer of Flanders' who got thirty nuns pregnant in the space of three weeks, or of a priest who fasted three days a week, 'But when prayer is done, if he spie a faire Nun, / His stomacke is wonderfull quick'.

The Cashel Ballads collection at Trinity College Dublin has some more serious and sympathetic songs.[3] Examples include an elegy on the persecution of sixty Polish nuns put to death in a purge by Nicholas 1 of Russia in 1845, and a song about the massacre of Christians, nuns among them, in Syria in 1860. Most intriguing are three ballads on the so-called Nunnery Bill, or Nunneries Inspection Bill. These date from between 1851 and 1853, with the last of them celebrating the defeat of the proposed legislation.

---

[1] Andrew S. Jacobs, *Christ Circumcised: A Study in Early Christian History and Difference* (Philadelphia: University of Pennsylvania Press, 2012), pp. ix–x.

[2] *OED*, punk, *n.1* and *adj.2*, 1.

[3] https://www.tcd.ie/library/digitalcollections/home/.

But first, those 'punks' – my tabloid-style title is justified by the discussion of several anti-Catholic 'naughty nuns', but I will go on to interrogate the more serious subject of the 'persecuted virgins' in songs from the Cashel Ballads collection. The treatment of nuns as figures of sexual intrigue pre-dates the Reformation and the printing press, but broadsides provided a gleeful platform both for standard satire and for Protestant pillorying of cloistered congregations, especially at the time of the Glorious Revolution. Nonetheless, long before that nuns were popular figures of fun in Boccaccio's Italy and elsewhere because they were educated, wealthy, and lived lives of luxury. In order to afford the huge price of a dowry for one daughter, noble families frequently sent their other daughters into comfortable convents, on the basis that 'a woman should have a husband or a wall'.[4] As a result, and to give just one example of the intersection of urban wealth and convent life, in the early 1600s in Bologna nuns made up 14 per cent of the population, while in Milan it is estimated that 75 per cent of genteel women were nuns.[5]

It is useful, therefore, to contextualize the portrayal of nuns in broadside ballads by looking at their treatment in notable pre-Reformation texts, the *Decameron* (*c.*1348–53) and the *Canterbury Tales* (*c.*1387–1400). Nuns in the *Decameron* are sexually active, whether they are pretty novices easily persuaded by men to succumb to the pleasures of the flesh, or powerful abbesses who choose to indulge, usually with men of the cloth. Many of Boccaccio's stories bear a certain resemblance to the *Carry On* films of the last century. In one tale, an abbess has heard that one of her young novices is in bed with a young man and in her haste to dress and publicly shame the novice she covers her head not with a wimple (a nun's headdress), as she believes, but with the underpants of the local priest with whom she herself has been sleeping (Ninth Day, Tale 2). In the tale mentioned at the beginning of this paper, Masetto decides that he can satisfy his sexual appetite if he secures the job of gardener at a convent, so he presents himself to the old gardener and the abbess as deaf and dumb, calculating that this will ensure a warmer welcome from the nuns as he would be unable to spread gossip about their scandalous behaviour (Third Day, Tale 1). As he romps with every nun in the convent in turn, he prefigures the 'lusty fryer of Flanders', whom we will meet shortly.

---

[4] Craig A. Monson, *Nuns Behaving Badly: Tales of Music, Magic, Art, and Arson in the Convents of Italy* (Chicago: University of Chicago Press, 2010), p. 8.
[5] Monson, *Nuns Behaving Badly*, p. 9.

That lusty friar might also be a cousin of the one in the *Canterbury Tales*, where Chaucer pillories various pillars of the church. Chaucer's Friar is sexually active: 'He hadde maad ful many a mariage / Of yonge wommen at his owene cost', we are told (General Prologue, ll. 212–13) – that is to say, he had found husbands and dowries for young women whom he himself had seduced. The chief nun of the *Canterbury Tales*, the Prioress, is a worldly social-climber. Her clothes are expensively embroidered and her rosary is made of fine red coral beads. Her massive brooch, which proclaims *Amor vincit omnia* ('Love conquers all') is more a piece of expensive jewellery than a religious item. We do not discover whether the love in question is sacred or profane, but we can guess:

> Of smal coral aboute hire arm she bar
> A peire of bedes, gauded al with grene,
> And theron heng a brooch of gold ful sheene,
> On which ther was first write a crowned A,
> And after *Amor vincit omnia*. (General Prologue, ll. 158–62)

The ballad of *The Lusty Fryer of Flanders* was published in 1688, a vintage year for ballads featuring nuns.[6] This friar is a broadside champion who managed to impregnate thirty nuns in the space of three weeks. There should be a spoiler alert attached to the subtitle, because the main part of the ballad concerns itself with just one nun, 'pretty, young, and fair', and only in the final stanza do we learn that he has behaved in the same way with twenty-nine others:

> This Nun oh she grew big at last,
>   and dayly it increases,
> And e're ten months were fully past,
>   the Nuns fell all a pieces;
> The crafty Fryer away he went,
>   that should 'scape 'twas pity,
> And left behind a Regiment
>   of bastards to the City.
>
> Thus he this Creature did beguile,
>   but tell me wan't he dirty,
> Twenty nine Nuns he'd got with Child,
>   and this made up the thirty:

---

[6] *The Lusty Fryer of Flanders, How in a Nunnery at the City of Gaunt this Fryer Got Thirty Nuns with Child in Three Weeks Time and Afterwards Made his Escape* (printed for I. Blare, 1688) [ESTC R228334].

He had a faculty to Cure,
    each longing expectation.
So this religious Rascal sure,
    is able to stock a nation.

Nuns are also central to an engraved ballad sheet with musical notation, both the title and the presumed date of publication of which are *1688*.[7] This song of the Glorious Revolution is a celebration of the defeat of popery, after which the nuns went back to 'their former Profession of Punks'. Set to the well-known tune 'Lilliburlero', it is worth noting as an aside that the derivation of 'Lilliburlero' puts it on 'the other side'. Irish-language scholar Breandán Ó Buachalla determined that the song and words derived from the Irish, and that the tune was originally used by Catholics as a marching song in the northern part of Ireland. He claims the chorus is a garbled version of an Irish chorus, '*Léir o, Léir o, léir o, léiro, / Lilli bu léir o: bu linn an lá*', which he translates as 'Manifest, manifest, manifest, manifest, / Lilly will be manifest, the day will be ours', referring to a (possible) prophecy of an Irish victory by the English seventeenth-century astrologer William Lilly.[8] Other sources suggest the lily in question is the French fleur de lys. 'Manifest' could be more simply rendered as 'Clear(ly)' and '*bu linn an lá*' means 'we will win the day'.

The term 'manifest' appears with another meaning, as a pageant of many scenes, in a ballad of *c*.1680 written by Elkanah Settle and titled *London's Drollery; or, The Love and Kindness between the Pope and the Devil, Manifested by Some True Protestants Who Utterly Defie the Pope and his Romish Faction, as It Was to be Seen in London, November the 17th. 1680; with Nine Pageants Delightful to Behold*.[9] Here the participants are poking fun at the pope and his acolytes, including nuns, 'who count that Whoring's no Disgrace':

The seventh Pageant that did bear,
The Pope himself in Garments Rare;
Cover'd with Gold and Silver Lace,
A Tripple Crown on him they place:
To fill the Papists full of Hope,
The Loving Devil Kist the Pope.

---

7 *1688* [Edinburgh, National Library of Scotland, Crawford.EB.998].

8 Breandán Ó Buachalla, 'Lillibulero – The New Irish Song', *Familia*, 7 (1991), 47–59.

9 *London's Drollery; or, The Love and Kindness between the Pope and the Devil* (printed for F. Coles, T. Vere, J. Wright, J. Clarke, W. Thackeray, and T. Passenger) [ESTC R228344].

Upon the eighth Olimpia came,
With Former Popes she had great Fame;
She was their Mistris by her Lust,
But long since she is turn'd to Dust:
Four Nuns about her they did place,
Who count that Whoring's no Disgrace.

The author (possibly William Gray) of one of a series of flyting ballads about the execution of Thomas Cromwell in 1540 berates his opponents who have wandered into popish ways:

For here thou upholdest both monkes and fryers
Nunnes and noughty packes / and lewed lowsy lyers
The bysshop of Rome / with all his rotten squyers
To buylde such a church / thou arte moche to blame
Trolle nowe into the way agayne for shame.[10]

The characterization of nuns as 'noughty packes' was not restricted to polemical anti-Catholic ballads and can be paralleled in generically humorous songs such as *A Merry Ballad of a Rich Maid that Had 18. Seuerall Suitors of Seuerall Countries*.[11] The eighteen suitors from different countries provide an opportunity to exploit some racial stereotypes, such as a drunken Irishman, and a suitor from Rome whose habits suggest he is a priest, but who is quick to work up an appetite for a 'faire Nun':

From Rome one came to me, who daily did wo me
He fasted three dayes in the w[ee]ke,
But when prayer is done, if he spie a faire Nun,
His stomacke is wonderfull quick.

These songs are just a few among many examples of ballads in which nuns are portrayed as paying scant attention to their vows of chastity. A contrast is provided by the series of ballads collected by John Davis White of Cashel, Co. Tipperary (1820–93).[12] The background to the Cashel Ballads is worth rehearsing here. In the

---

[10] *A Balade agaynst Malycyous Sclaunderers* (prentyd at London, in Lombard Strete, nere unto the Stockes Market, at the sygne of the Mermayde, by Iohn Gough) [ESTC S2982].

[11] *A Merry Ballad of a Rich Maid that Had 18. Seuerall Suitors of Seuerall Countries; Otherwise Called the Scornefull Maid* (imprinted at London, for Henry Gosson) [ESTC S3252].

[12] Denis G. Marnane, 'John Davis White of Cashel (1820–1893)', *Tipperary Historical Journal* (1994), 97–104.

1850s, 'for my own amusement', Davis White bought the wooden printing press of the defunct *Clonmel Herald*. In 1856 he produced a free single-sheet newspaper called *The Amateur Press* ('with considerable justification', according to one historian). From 1864 he published the popular *Cashel Gazette*. In the meantime, he was not merely producing printed ephemera but collecting it. His treasure trove of approximately a thousand ballads, begun in 1844, was left to Trinity College Dublin, but this fact was not widely known for over a hundred years. Two profiles of White in historical or antiquarian journals (in 1947 and 1994) bemoaned the disappearance of this priceless collection.[13] It was only when Trinity began to digitize its holdings that local historians in Cashel realized that the collection had survived. They were disappointed, however, that the collection contained not local material but ballads from all over Ireland and beyond that had been sold on the streets of Cashel.[14]

From my own research into the collection, it contains a representative sample of songs sold on the streets of a southern Irish town in the nineteenth century. There are nationalist and patriotic songs, love songs and sentimental songs, songs of emigration, local and contemporary ballads about court cases, speeches and parliamentary bills, and imported songs, including from the American minstrel tradition. However, although White himself was a Protestant, the collection reflects the paucity of anti-Catholic ballads in his purview and one thing it does not contain is a single ballad that disparages or mocks nuns in any way. The clergy and religious orders, where they appear in the ballads, are portrayed as virtuous examples to their congregations – heroic martyrs or persecuted virgins.

A Sorrowful Elegy on the Persecution and Martyrdom of Sixty Nuns in Poland, Who Were Put to Death by the Tyrant Nicholas (Cashel Ballads 2.227) relates in harrowing detail the torture and killing of nuns in Poland in 1838–45. The ballad was written in 1845, after the only nun who had survived the persecution of her convent, the mother abbess, arrived in Rome and told her story to the pope:

> In Poland of late, it shall long be remember'd,
> Where tyranny has borne the sway,
> And the vile Russian bear to the convent did enter,
> And the innocent there he did slay.

---

[13] R. Wyse Jackson, 'John Davis White of Cashel', *North Munster Antiquarian Journal*, 5.2–3 (1946), 62–67; Marnane, 'John Davis White of Cashel', p. 102.

[14] Denis G. Marnane, 'The Ballad Collection of John Davis White', *Tipperary Historical Journal* (2005), 61–85 (pp. 61–62).

There were some for the halter and more for the fire,
While some with the fright there alas did expire,
And with some his rude soldiers did please their desire,
Alas! it's heart-rending to hear!

The ballad does not spare the gruesome details and the horror of the defilement of the sisters, 'While for mercy these virgins did call'. The song ends not with a call for vengeance, but by urging the faithful to pray for the conversion of the Russians, a persistent subject of prayers in Irish Catholic churches up to the time of my own childhood (when the Russian bear was atheistic rather than Orthodox):

So let every good Christian with pious supplication,
Their prayers let them send to above
For the conversion of such wicked nations,
Where the true Christian faith is abhorred.

A New Song on the Massacree of the Christians in Syria (Cashel Ballads 2.134), printed by Haly of Cork, records the killing of nuns, priests, and other Christians in 1860 in the course of what was known as the Syrian civil war, or Mount Lebanon War, 'upon the Turkish shore':

Good Christians pay attention to what I now unfold,
The subject I now mention will make your blood run cold,
[']Tis of the Syrian massacre where thousands suffered sore,
By the uncivilized Mahometans upon the Turkish shore.
[...]
It would grieve your heart with pity [to] see how they were used
The men at first were put to death, the women then il[l-]used
[...]
Our chapels and our nunneries those demons did surround,
And set them all on fire till they burned to the ground
Our Priests and Nuns they martyred them and left them in their gore,
The cruel death they underwent it grieves our heart full sore.
[...]
Our Nuns they chased and did not cease till five of them were slained,
Two were Irish ladies and three belonged to Spain
Forty more, thank God escaped, of that community,
And eight Franciscan friars fell in this sad massacre.

There is no praying for the conversion of the perpetrators here, but instead the certainty of God's vengeance on them: 'Now to conclude those feeling lines I will lay down my pen, / The Lord will pour destruction on those savage race of men.'

From the years between these two ballads about the abuse and murder of nuns abroad come the three ballads about the 'Nunnery Bill', or 'Nunneries Inspection Bill', of the early 1850s. In fact, there never was a Nunnery Bill – the name was an inflammatory shorthand for legislation contained in two separate bills, the Religious Houses Bill (1851) and the Recovery of Personal Liberty Bill (1853).[15] The first of these would have permitted Justices of the Peace to make inquiries about any woman suspected of having been forcibly confined in a convent, while the second would have compelled the Home Secretary to send inspectors into any convent suspected of false imprisonment and to apply for *habeas corpus* if necessary. The clear implication was that women were being forcibly confined or falsely imprisoned in convents.

Whatever legitimate suspicions surrounded the circumstances of some nineteenth-century women in convents, serious doubt has been cast on the most celebrated case, that of Maria Monk (1816–49), who in 1836 published a book titled *Awful Disclosures* about her alleged experiences in a convent in Montreal.[16] The book claimed that nuns in the Montreal convent were forced to have sex with priests and any resulting children were strangled. Investigations cast doubt on her credibility, but the story satisfied and fed strong anti-Catholic sentiment during a period when Catholic social and political rights were expanding.

Frank Wallis has posited three focal points for increased anti-Catholic feeling in Britain specifically in the early 1850s: the so-called Papal Aggression affair, centred on the re-establishment of the Catholic hierarchy in Britain by Pope Pius IX in 1850; the issue of state funding for the Catholic seminary in Maynooth, Co. Kildare; and convent inspection and regulation.[17] A significant part of the Catholic response to the proposed regulatory legislation described the intended inspections in terms of violation and defilement. In a letter to *The Times* in 1851, Lady Teresa Arundell wrote:

---

[15] Religious Houses Bill https://api.parliament.uk/historic-hansard/commons/1851/may/14/religious-houses-bill; Recovery of Personal Liberty Bill https://api.parliament.uk/historic-hansard/commons/1853/jul/20/recovery-of-personal-liberty-bill.
[16] *Awful Disclosures of Maria Monk* (New York: Howe & Bates, 1836); *Awful Disclosures*, by Maria Monk, of the Hotel Dieu Nunnery of Montreal, revised with an appendix (New York: published by Maria Monk, and sold by booksellers generally, 1836).
[17] Frank Wallis, 'Anti-Catholicism in Mid-Victorian Britain – Theory and Discipline', *Journal of Religion and Society*, 7 (2005), 1–17 (p. 8).

> To Catholic ladies, who, like myself, have sisters and relatives in convents, it is, indeed, humiliating and most painful, that in England, hitherto considered the land of liberty, we should be forced to exert our influence to save those loved ones from the grossest insults, the most unmanly attempt now being made to deprive them of a security which even the meanest women slaves have insured to them.[18]

The idea that inspecting convents amounted to 'the grossest insults' to the women who lived within them conjures up the imagery of 'persecuted virgins', a refrain that echoed through the ballads written in opposition to the bills.

In Ireland, powerful figures (including many Protestants) rallied to oppose the inspection bills. A public letter to the Lord Mayor of Cork, published in the *Cork Examiner* on 13 June 1853, signed by many Justices of the Peace, aldermen, town councillors, and solicitors, called for a meeting of the citizens of Cork to be convened 'on an early day' to petition Parliament against the proposed bill.[19] The letter was published with a response from the Lord Mayor, John Francis Maguire, calling the meeting for 16 June.

Meanwhile the streets were ringing with songs on the subject. *A New Song on the Nunnery Bill* (Cashel Ballads 2.210), printed by Walter Birmingham of Thomas Street, Dublin, echoes Lady Arundell's letter, describing those who would inspect the convents as 'traitors and bastely fornicators', and the nuns as persecuted virgins in danger of violation.

> You Catholics of Erin come listen now with patience,
> Unto this late dictation that lately I have pen'd
> Concerning of those traitors and bastely fornicators,
> Who want to immolate us and to polute our nuns;
> They are resolutely inclined our convents to defile,
> And to instil the vice of base impurity,
> Unto these lonely creatures who are destined by nature
> For to sing the praises of the blessed trinity.

The other main image in this ballad is of the 'putrid branch' that needs to be removed: 'I hope the time is not far off when that putrid [b]ran[c]h will be lop[p]ed off, / Its sapless vigour enervated, impeded and subdued.' It is not difficult to infer that the balladeer considered

---

18 *The Times*, 6 May 1851, p. 8.
19 *Cork Examiner*, 13 June 1853, p. 2.

this branch to comprise Protestantism in general, not just those Protestants who were promoting the inspection bills.

A New Song on the Nunneries Inspection Bill (Cashel Ballads 2.211) likewise links the proposed legislation with the idea of defilement:

> Come all you Roman Catholics, I hope you will draw near,
> And likewise pay attention the truth you soon shall hear,
> Concerning our blessed nunneries, the pride of Erin's Isle,
> The bigot clan has raised a plan our blessed nuns to defile.
> [. . .]
> It was Chambers first brought in this bill as we do understand,
> Altho he is of Scottish blood he is of a rotten clan,
> To think to rise disturbance all o'er our sainted shore,
> Let shame be stamped upon his name, our nuns are still secure.
> [. . .]
> On the 13th day of June all in the year of fifty-three;
> Sir Thomas Esmonde took the chair, most glorious for to see,
> To join with our blest Clergy throughout the shamrock shore,
> Resolved our blest nuns to protect now and for evermore.

The broadside ballad as 'news of the day' is most clearly evidenced in the third ballad, *Lines on the Defeat of the Nunnery Bill!!* (Cashel Ballads 2.212), which refers to 'last Thursday night':

> You true Roman heroes wherever you be,
> I pray pay attention and listen to me,
> The Nunnery Bill is shoved up the spout,
> Our brave Irish members they soon kicked it out.
> Ladley, fal, de, lal, &c.
> [. . .]
> The moment that Chambers he brough[t] in his bill,
> Whately gave it his sanction he did with good will
> But if they think on Bess and read of her fun,
> It would answer them better than talking of nuns.
> [. . .]
> The old fanatic Chambers he is hurted at last,
> Since the nunnery bill he could not get passed,
> For our brave Irish members on last Thursday night,
> Without any mistake the[y] muzzelled him tight.
> [. . .]
> Not like when our nuns to the scaffold were tore
> By Bessy and Cromwell, sure they suffered sore.
> [. . .]
> Candid I tell, you may rest assured,
> No scorpion shall enter our nunnery doors.

The defeat of the bill is greeted here with a harking back to the persecution of Catholics in the times of Queen Elizabeth I and Oliver Cromwell, and with the triumphant assertion that no 'scorpion' shall enter the Irish convents. 'Whately' was Richard Whately, Church of Ireland archbishop of Dublin, 1831–63. He was lambasted for supporting the bill by the then Catholic archbishop of Dublin, Paul Cullen, who stated that the merits of the nuns 'have been recognised by all that is liberal and generous in this country, and we have often heard with pleasure that in other regions, Protestant cities did not hesitate to decree monuments to the Sisters of Charity who had sacrificed their lives in attending the victims of disease'.[20] The 'Chambers' mentioned as having proposed the bill was Sir Thomas Chambers, a Liberal MP (who does not seem to have been 'of Scottish blood', but of entirely English stock).[21]

Ballads about the Nunnery Bill are scarce today. Aside from the three discussed here, which seem to be unique to the Cashel Ballads collection, I have found only one other song on the theme. This is a ballad by Joseph Sadler titled *Lines Written on the Nunnery Bill*, now in the Helen Hartness Flanders collection.[22] The broadside was printed by P. Brereton in Dublin (the print is of such poor quality that it is difficult to make out many of the words, and the text below has been silently corrected):

> You lovers of honour of truth and fair play
> I'm sure you'll allow that we live in queer days
> The ladies of mercy to knock them about
> In your life did you ever hear such a come out?
>
> *Chorus:*
> But he's desolate of back you'll find it's a fact,
> Our blessed holy convents he can never ransack.

---

[20] William John Fitzpatrick, *Memoirs of Richard Whately, Archbishop of Dublin, with a Glance at his Co[n]temporaries & Times*, 2 vols (London: Richard Bentley, 1864), I, 179.

[21] J. M. Rigg, rev. Patrick Polden, 'Chambers, Sir Thomas (1814–1891)', *ODNB* https://doi.org/10.1093/ref:odnb/5082.

[22] Joseph Saddler [*sic*], *Lines Written on the Nunnery Bill* (P. Brereton, 56 Cooke St, Dublin) [Middlebury, VT, Middlebury College Library, Helen Hartness Flanders Collection https://archive.org/details/hhfbc157-nunnerybill]. Sadler's name also appears as Saddler and Sadlier on ballad sheets, but *A Catalogue of the Bradshaw Collection of Irish Books in the University Library, Cambridge*, 3 vols (Cambridge: printed for the University Library, 1916), III (*Index*), 1632, refers the other variations to the entry for 'Sadler, Joseph'. Little seems to be known about this balladeer, whose works invite further study.

Newdegate is the fomentor of this beautiful tale
But in it I'll tell you he'll certainly fail.
[. . .]
About mother Abbess he's in a great pout
But himself and his bill he may shove by [*sc.* up] the spout.
[. . .]
His vile efforts thank heaven they all are in vain
His sad disappointment now torments his brain
Our nunneries & convents are triumphing still
We'll dance Garryowen on the nunnery bill.

The 'Newdegate' cited here as the 'fomentor' of the bills was Charles Newdigate Newdegate, a Conservative politician well known for his Protestant views and opposition to the parliamentary grant to the Maynooth training college for Catholic priests.[23]

And so the Nunneries Inspection Bill, the bill that never really was, disappeared into obscurity and is barely remembered except for these few Irish ballads from the early 1850s. Nuns in broadside ballads at large are either imaginary figures of fun, romping with lusty friars and priests, or of irreproachable chastity, only occasionally informed by real atrocities and in imminent danger of defilement or slaughter by sectarian forces. In the Cashel collection and beyond, ballads featuring nuns are employed either to portray their own Catholic faith, or else to depict the faith of their enemies, whether Protestant, Russian Orthodox, or Muslim, as hypocritical, corrupt, and monstrous.

---

[23] John Wolffe, 'Newdegate, Charles Newdigate (1816–1887)', *ODNB* https://doi.org /10.1093/ref:odnb/20000.

'Gone to Weave by Steam': The Impact of Steam Power on the Textile Industry of North-West England through Broadside Balladry

Colin Bargery

Before the Industrial Revolution, when poor harvests led to poverty and starvation the government could do relatively little about it. By 1825, however, poverty had become a problem that could be solved.[1] Rather than ameliorating the sufferings of the poor, however, the powerful preferred to blame the victims. Champions of the Protestant work ethic saw the coming of steam power as a gift from God, and it suited the wealthy, and self-made industrialists in particular, to regard their own prosperity as the reward of virtue – and, conversely, poverty as the wages of sin. This poem, published in the *Bolton Chronicle* in March 1827, was written by the clerk to the local magistrate:

> The common people are (excepted few)
> A filthy, drunken, abject, beastly crew.
> So filthy that the very rags they wear
> Are less offensive than the stench they bear!
> So drunken that all the limits they disown
> Save want of cash, long score and landlord's frown!
> So abject that they'll beg with whining din
> For a few pence to purchase beer and gin.[2]

Spinning and weaving were repetitive actions amenable to mechanization and were among the first kinds of work to be moved into urban factories. In the early nineteenth century the textile and clothing industries were often the largest category of urban employment.[3] In 1831 only 10 per cent of British men worked in

---

[1] E. A. Wrigley, *Poverty, Progress, and Population* (Cambridge: Cambridge University Press, 2004), p. 5.

[2] Chris Aspin, *The First Industrial Society, Lancashire, 1750–1850*, rev. edn (Preston: Carnegie Publishing, 1995), p. 100 ('score' = credit).

[3] Wrigley, *Poverty, Progress, and Population*, p. 283.

manufacturing and more than half of that 10 per cent lived in Lancashire and the West Riding of Yorkshire.[4] This textile manufacturing region was the source of a substantial body of street literature addressing the concerns of the workers – spinners and weavers – and their families. This paper describes some of the ways in which those concerns were expressed in the street literature of Lancashire.

'Those terrible machines'

Before the French Revolutionary and Napoleonic Wars of 1793–1815 the labouring poor had exerted economic influence by exercising what Eric Hobsbawm called 'collective bargaining by riot'.[5] In 1790, Robert Grimshaw built a weaving factory incorporating thirty steam-powered looms at Knott Mill, Manchester, but just two years later it 'took fire in the night'. Most believed the fire had been set by weavers fearing for their livelihoods. John Harland recorded that a ballad of *Grimshaw's Factory Fire* was 'regularly set to music, printed, and sold by the ballad-dealers of Manchester':

> The floor was over shavings,
> Took fire in the night, sir;
> But now he [Grimshaw]'s sick in bed
> Some say it's with affright, sir.[6]

Spinners were among the first to feel the effects of steam power, notably at Murray's Spinning Mill, also in Manchester. The mill was established in 1797 and by 1805 it was powered by steam and had become the largest factory in the world. The impact of steam power was immediate. Looking back in 1818 a journeyman cotton spinner wrote in the satirical radical journal the *Black Dwarf*:

> When the spinning of cotton was in its infancy, and before those terrible machines for superseding the necessity of human labour, called steam engines came into use, there were a great number of

---

[4] Wrigley, *Poverty, Progress, and Population*, p. 89.

[5] Eric Hobsbawm, *Labouring Men: Studies in the History of Labour* (London: Weidenfeld and Nicolson, 1964), p. 7. Hobsbawm cites the example of clothiers in the west of England complaining that weavers had threatened to pull down their houses and burn their work unless they acceded to the weavers' demands.

[6] John Harland (ed.), *Ballads & Songs of Lancashire, Ancient and Modern*, 2nd edn, rev. T. T. Wilkinson (London: George Routledge and Sons, and L. C. Gent, 1875), pp. 202–04.

what were then called *little masters*; men who with a small capital, could
procure a few machines, and employ a few hands [. . .] But none are
thus employed now; for all the cotton is broke up by a machine,
turned by the steam engine, called a devil: so that the spinners['] wives
have no employment, except that they go work in the factory all day
at what can be done by children for a few shillings, four or five per
week.[7]

Many textile workers took the well-worn path of the destitute and
joined the army, like the impoverished Oldham worker of *The Original
Jone o' Grinfield!*:

Fare thee weel Grinfield to order am made,
Aw[']ve getten new shoon an a rare Cockade,
Aw'll fight for owd England as hard as a con,
Either French, Dutch, or Spanish to me it[']s all [one],
Aw'll mak um to stare like a new started hare,
And aw'll tell um fro Owdham aw'm come.[8]

The military historian Richard Holmes states that handloom weavers
were an important component of Wellington's army and estimates
that they constituted more than 25 per cent of the Royal Artillery.[9]
After the war, unemployment was worsened by population growth,
estimated to have produced an increase in the supply of labour of 143
per cent between 1780 and 1850,[10] by discharged soldiers and sailors
seeking work, and by the calamitous failure of the harvest in 1816, the
infamous year without a summer.

More than a third of the non-commissioned officers and men in
many regiments were Irish.[11] Irish weavers, like their English
counterparts, found themselves in search of work. Unsurprisingly,
they were met with hostility by starving English textile workers. In
1824 the government, alarmed by the numbers of poor people on the
tramp, passed the Vagrancy Act which enabled parish authorities to

---

[7] A Journeyman Cotton Spinner, 'The Manchester Cotton Spinners to their
Employers, and the Public', *Black Dwarf*, 30 September 1818, cols 622–24; cited in E.
P. Thompson, *The Making of the English Working Class* (London: Penguin, 1968 [1963]),
p. 220.
[8] *The Original Jone o' Grinfield!* (Manchester: T. Pearson, printer, 4 & 6, Chadderton
Street) [Oxford, Bodleian Library, Firth c.14(104)].
[9] Richard Holmes, *Redcoat: The British Soldier in the Age of Horse and Musket* (London:
HarperCollins, 2001), p. 57.
[10] John Rule, *The Labouring Classes in Early Industrial England, 1750–1850* (Harlow:
Longman, 1986), p. 1.
[11] Holmes, *Redcoat*, p. 56.

transport destitute Irish families to Liverpool and send them home by sea, a crossing that could take a week or more in a sail-driven vessel, without any food.[12] Their experience was voiced by the eponymous *Larry O'Broom*:

I am a poor weaver that's out of employ,
And my name it is Larry O'Broom, sir;
I have got no parish my wants to supply,
Nor a web to [p]ut in the loom, sir;
To old England I came in the sweet prime of life,
I deserted my country, my friends and my wife,
But now, sir, grown old, and without any strife,
They will send home poor Larry O'Broom, sir.

Just the other day to the parish I went,
And I told them of my situation,
They mock'd me and said that no one for me sent,
And they order'd me to my own nation.
They said, since the peace it is very well known,
We're oppressed by the Irish as much as our own,
But a bill is now pass'd & we'll send them all home,
As well as poor Larry O'Broom, sir.[13]

A broadside headed *Cotton Spinners from Manchester*, distributed in order to support the sale of reels of cotton by two unemployed cotton spinners, states: 'Machinery has so overstocked the market, that it is impossible to obtain employment; and the parish is so overburthened that we could get but little relief.'[14] There follows a set of verses beginning:

We are cotton spinners by our trade;
Employ we cannot find:
Hundreds are by want compell'd
To leave their friends behind.

Following the verses is the statement: 'There are more than Four Hundred out of Employment at this time.' The *Cotton Spinners from Manchester* broadside was printed in London. It seems that destitute

---

[12] Ben Wilson, *Decency and Disorder: The Age of Cant, 1789–1837* (London: Faber and Faber, 2007), p. 243.

[13] *Larry O'Broom* (printed for W. Armstrong, Banastre St, Liverpool) [Oxford, Bodleian Library, Harding B 28(45)].

[14] *Cotton Spinners from Manchester* (James Paul & Co., printers, 2 & 3, Monmouth Court, Seven Dials) [Oxford, Bodleian Library, Johnson Ballads 646].

weavers travelled considerable distances. William Cobbett encountered them in Wiltshire in 1826: 'throughout this country, weavers from the North, singing about the towns, ballads of Distress!'[15] The landlord told him that people that could afford it generally gave them something. William Dodd wrote in *The Factory System Illustrated*, published in 1842, that unemployed Manchester spinners were resorting to 'going errands, waiting upon the market-people, selling pins and needles, ballads, tapes and laces, oranges, gingerbread, &c. &c.'[16]

The application of steam power to weaving had followed quickly upon its application to spinning, and *The Weaver's Lamentation* has much in common with *Cotton Spinners from Manchester*. Both songs find unemployed textile workers forced to travel far from home and both lament that their children are starving:

Good people all attend a while,
And lend an ear I pray,
While we unfold the reason why,
We're travelling here to-day.

It is because we are out of work,
And bread cannot procure,
To see our children starve for food,
What parent can endure.[17]

Both songs end, too, by paraphrasing the biblical text 'He that hath pity upon the poor lendeth unto the Lord; and that which He hath given will He pay him again' (Proverbs 19:17):

Cotton Spinners from Manchester	*The Weaver's Lamentation*
For he that giveth to the poor,	All that giveth to the poor,
But lendeth to the Lord;	Lendeth to the Lord,
So now, kind friends, on us bestow	Now, kind friends, on us bestow,
Whate'er you can afford.	Whatever you can afford.

---

[15] William Cobbett, *Rural Rides*, new edn, 2 vols (London: Reeves and Turner, 1908), II, 105.

[16] William Dodd, *The Factory System Illustrated, in a Series of Letters to the Right Hon. Lord Ashley* (London: John Murray, 1842), p. 113; cited in Thompson, *Making of the English Working Class*, p. 364.

[17] *The Weaver's Lamentation* ([Harkness, printer, Preston]) [Oxford, Bodleian Library, Harding B 11(4073), Harding B 20(211)].

Many families maintained themselves by a mixture of weaving and farming. Around Burnley in the mid-1820s it was reported that 'the principal part of the farmers depend on weaving for the support of their families'.[18] Not only were factory rules irksome, but the long working hours prevented weavers from working the land, as described in the song *Hand-Loom v. Power-Loom*:

> So, come all you cotton-weavers, you must rise up very soon,
> For you must work in factories from morning until noon:
> You mustn't walk in your garden for two or three hours a-day,
> For you must stand at their command, and keep your shuttles in play.[19]

Probably the best known broadside concerning the coming of steam power in the textile industry is *Joan O'Grinfield!*:

> I sed to our Margit as we lay on the floor,
> We ne'er shall be lower in this world I'm sure,
> But if we alter I'm sure we mun mend,
> For I think in my heart we are both at far end.
> For meat we have none nor looms to weave on,
> Egad they're as good lost as found.[20]

The assertion 'meat we have none' is no exaggeration. A. N. Wilson writes that between 1837 and 1844 more than a million people died of starvation resulting from unemployment.[21] Towards the end of the ballad, John's redoubtable wife Margaret determines to take violent action:

> Our Margit declared if hoo'd cloose to put on,
> Hoo'd go up to London to see th' great mon,
> And if things wur not altered when she had been,
> Hoo swears hoo would fight blood up to the een.
> Hoos nowt agen th' King but hoo likes a fair thing,
> And hoo ses hoo can tell when hoos hurt.

In 1826 handloom weavers rioted in Darwen and power looms were destroyed. Machine-breaking was a capital offence but sentences were

---

18 Aspin, *First Industrial Society*, p. 66.
19 Harland (ed.), *Ballads & Songs of Lancashire*, pp. 188–89.
20 *Joan O'Grinfield!* ([Harkness, printer, Preston]) [Oxford, Bodleian Library, Firth b.27(270), Harding B 20(80)].
21 A. N. Wilson, *The Victorians* (London: Hutchinson, 2002), p. 28.

often commuted to transportation, as was the case with forty-two machine-breakers convicted at Lancaster in August 1826.[22]

In the politically repressive atmosphere of the time the printing of protest songs might well result in unwanted attention from the magistrates. Among the brave souls prepared to commit themselves to print was the handloom weaver and poet Joseph Hodgson of Blackburn (c.1783–1856):

> Ye weavers of Blackburn, come hear to my song
>> When I sing of tyrants I seldom do wrong;
> For if they transport me to Canada's wild shore,
>> I then shall have freedom when I have sailed o'er;
>> Free from slavery,
>> Fetters and knavery,
> Never tormented with tyrants again![23]

The Sovereign Mills in Wigan were particularly notorious. Children employed there were beaten if they fell asleep at their work. The author of a broadside about the mills employed heavy sarcasm, perhaps in the hope of avoiding retribution:

> Those Sovran Mills, those Sovran Mills,
> If you go there, you'll get no ills:
> For daily working fourteen hours
> Will only renovate your powers.[24]

Before the French Wars 'collective bargaining by riot' had been reasonably effective, but after Waterloo the mill owners were firmly in control. The cottage industry hung on for a couple more decades. The census of 1841 records 49,280 'weavers', plus 63,734 people employed in 'cotton manufacture'; the 1851 census records 106,082 people employed in 'cotton manufacture', but 'weaver' was no longer recognized as a category.[25]

---

[22] *An Account of the Proceedings at the Lancaster Assizes against the Rioters in Lancashire; When No Less than 35 Men and 7 Women Received the Awful Sentence of Death on Monday Last, for Destroying the Steam-Power Looms* (John Muir, printer, Glasgow, 21 August 1826) [Edinburgh, National Library of Scotland, L.C.Fol.73(088)].

[23] Aspin, *First Industrial Society*, p. 79. Hodgson was a bit out of touch – transportation to Canada ceased with American independence in 1783.

[24] Aspin, *First Industrial Society*, p. 119.

[25] Wrigley, *Poverty, Progress, and Population*, Table 5.A1.2.

'Where are the girls?'

The factory workforce was overwhelmingly female. Census figures for the period reveal that in the period after the wars there were far more women than men. The mortality rate for boys was higher than for girls, the wars had taken their toll, and men were more likely to emigrate than women. As the income of handloom weaving families fell, young women were expected to go in search of work:

> Now where are the girls? I'll tell you plain,
> The girls have gone to weave by steam.
> And if you'd find 'em you must rise at dawn
> And trudge to the factory in the early morn.[26]

Rural society had governed sexual relationships by means of widely respected conventions. Françoise Barret-Ducrocq summarizes the stages of rural courtship:

- Speaking
- Walking out together
- Keeping company
- Bundling (bed sharing short of sexual intercourse)
- Public exchange of gifts (not in all cases)
- Marriage.[27]

However, these conventions were disrupted by urbanization, and in particular by the movement of young people into factory towns. During the 1840s the illegitimacy rate among Lancashire weavers was more than 25 per cent, although while 90 per cent of first births were conceived outside marriage it was still expected that pregnancy would lead to marriage.[28] Convention was further undermined when the Poor Law reform of 1834 removed the right of women to prosecute the father and exact support from him. Paternity suits and actions for breach of promise were reduced to symbolic status, although some women did still try to ensure their rights were respected.[29] In the absence of support from the father, a mother might use some of her

---

[26] Roy Palmer, 'The Weaver in Love', *Folk Music Journal*, 3.3 (1977), 261–74 (pp. 273–74).

[27] Françoise Barret-Ducrocq, *Love in the Time of Victoria: Sexuality, Class and Gender in Nineteenth-Century London*, trans. John Howe (London: Penguin, 1992 [1989]), p. 86.

[28] Rule, *Labouring Classes*, p. 196.

[29] Barret-Ducrocq, *Love in the Time of Victoria*, pp. 154–56.

meagre wages to employ a wet nurse.[30] High infant mortality rates ensured a steady supply of potential wet nurses.

In this light, *The Flashie Steam-Loom Weaver* tells an old story against this new background of industrialization, in which a woman is deserted by the father of her unborn child in favour of a steam-loom weaver, whom she regards as her inferior:

> I was courted by a chap, a fickle false deceiver,
> Who has given to me the slip, for a flashie steam loom weaver.
> [...]
> She is not to[o] short nor tall, but she is a little fattish,
> And she's what the people call, rather proud and pe[e]vish.
> Gold earerings [*sic*] to[o] she wears, with a necklace that he gave her,
> And she's full of ladies airs, is this flashie steam loom weaver.
>
> Now they say I'm getting fat, for my stays I scarce can [tie] them,
> But there is a case for that, and my friends I dare not face them.
> If I'd send my brothers word, where to find that base deceiver,
> They would send him home a bairn, to his flashie steam loom weaver.
>
> Time and tide on none will wait, and the frost will try the pratties,
> I'll be even with him yet, he'll be brought before his betters.
> Half a crown a week he'll pay, unto me for his behaviour,
> Or long he will not stay, with his flashie steam-loom weaver.
>
> To a nurse I'll send him out, if my child should be a laddy,
> Untill he grows big and stout, and a sparter like his dad[d]y.
> Then won[']t I make him whack, his father the deceiver,
> Who on us turned his back, for his flashie steam loom weaver.[31]

The widening geographical separation between the families of factory owners and their employees saw the withdrawal of middle-class women from urban life. The streets through which young women walked to and from the mill became the domain of the poor. The dishevelment produced by sixteen hours working in a mill was seen as a sign of moral laxity. The *Flare Up Factory Girl* typifies the way in which such women were depicted:

> Mother sells apples, nuts and cakes,
> Of which my whack I always takes,
> Each morning I my pockets cram,
> To give to Harry Dick or Sam,
> As I am a handsome gal, you see,

---

[30] Barret-Ducrocq, *Love in the Time of Victoria*, p. 135.
[31] *The Flashie Steam-Loom Weaver* [Oxford, Bodleian Library, Firth c.18(225)].

One chap is not enough for me,
I've three or four cause I can,
Always pick a nice young man.[32]

Conversely, an observer of Lancashire's mill girls in 1849 remarked on the contrast between their talk and their actual standards of behaviour, noting that they displayed a 'saucy prudery' and kept a strict watch upon one another's morals.[33]

Nevertheless, recent genetic research has shown that as a result of industrialization in Western Europe the number of children resulting from extra-pair paternity (female extramarital sex) increased from about 0.5 per cent to more like 5 per cent (1 in 200 to 1 in 20).[34] Other historical evidence suggests that the number of informal marriage arrangements increased with urbanization to about 25 per cent of all couples.[35] In rural areas the church could put pressure on cohabitees to marry, but in the crowded cities its influence was much diminished. These were social changes that took place following industrialization right across Europe and the experiences of the labouring poor of Lancashire were no exception.

'Manchester's improving daily'

As handloom weaving collapsed some young people saw the move to a factory town as an opportunity to cut the apron strings, as described in a broadside titled *Oldham Workshops*:

When I'd finished off my work last Saturday at neet,
Wi' new hat and Sunday cloas I dress'd myself complete;
I took leof o' my mother wi' a very woeful face,
And started off for Owdhum soon, that famous thriving place.[36]

---

[32] *The Flare Up Factory Girl* (Harkness, printer, 8, Water Street, Preston) [Oxford, Bodleian Library, Harding B 20(209)] (flare up = spirited, lively, fun-loving, extrovert).

[33] Rule, *Labouring Classes*, p. 160.

[34] Maarten H. D. Larmuseau, Pieter van den Berg, Sofie Claerhout, Francesc Calafell, Alessio Boattini, Leen Gruyters, Michiel Vandenbosch, Kelly Nivelle, Ronny Decorte, and Tom Wenseleers, 'A Historical-Genetic Reconstruction of Human Extra-Pair Paternity', *Current Biology*, 29 (2019), 4102–07.

[35] Ginger S. Frost, *Living in Sin: Cohabiting as Husband and Wife in Nineteenth-Century England* (Manchester: Manchester University Press, 2008).

[36] *Oldham Workshops* (Cadman, printer, 152, Great Ancoats Street, [Manchester]) [Frank Kidson Broadside Collection, vol. 9, p. 163; VWML Digital Archive, FK/17/163/1].

Likewise, in *The Dashing Steam-Loom Weaver* the young protagonist sets out to seek his fortune in the textile industry:

One day I got out on the spree
I fell out with my mother,
She says we can't agree,
[Y]ou'd better find another;
I said yo need not fret,
For I'se i'th' humour i' starting
So straightway I did set,
On purpose to seek my fortune.[37]

Factories created new sorts of job opportunities for aspiring young men. Overseers and mechanics were early members of the emerging aristocracy of labour:

I come to . . . . . . Town,
I met all things satisfactory;
I tried at mony a Loom,
Tin I geet to weave at Factory.
I had not long been i'th' shade, [= weaving shed]
Before my merit took, sir,
I geet so weel on with trade,
They made me Overlooker.

The sorts of men who took up these new jobs also attended the new Mechanics' Institutions that were established as part of a general movement to spread scientific and technical knowledge, described in *The Scenes of Manchester*:

We've buildings large and grand to view,
Likewise Mechanics' Institutions, too,
Where gentlemen go to learn gastronomy,
Gymnastics, optics and physio[g]nomy.
Where Doctor Lardner's LLD, sir,
A-lecturing on steam power you'll see, sir.
'Twould look better on to turn his head,
And teach poor folk to get cheap bread.[38]

---

[37] *The Dashing Steam-Loom Weaver* ([Harkness, printer, Preston]) [Oxford, Bodleian Library, 2806 c.13(148)].
[38] Roy Palmer, *A Touch on the Times: Songs of Social Change, 1770–1914* (Harmondsworth: Penguin, 1974), pp. 62–64. The first Mechanics' Institution opened in Manchester in 1825. Dionysius Lardner, scientific writer and lecturer, was an outspoken advocate of steam power, although also a controversial figure. See J. N.

Men like these rapidly established themselves as a class superior to their factory colleagues, to some extent reinstating the sort of distinctions that had previously discriminated between various classes of weavers. A contemporary observer, W. A. Abram, wrote that the first qualification required of an overlooker was 'not superior education or exceptional intelligence, but a rough force of character and activity of habit, which enable the man to keep in check the heterogeneous and at times mutinous mass of a mill population'.[39]

Women were excluded from supervisory roles, but the factory could still offer them a chance to cut the apron strings. Roy Palmer quotes a song called *The Factory Girl*, which seems to have found its way to America, about a young Irish woman in Manchester who, while acknowledging the hardships of the factory, values her new friends and welcomes the chance of a new life:

> When I set out for Manchester, some factory to find,
> I left my native country, and all my friends behind.
> [. . .]
> But now I am in Manchester, and summoned by the bell,
> I think more of the factory girls than of my native dell.[40]

Textile workers were among the first to live in an industrial society where the geography of the workplace echoed the geographic separation of social classes. Mill owners lived far away from the smoke and noise of their factories; some of them organized private trains to bring them in to the city from their homes on the coast of North Wales.[41] A rising population and the drift from countryside to town crowded young people together in houses built close to the mills and brought about the creation of a new community. Pubs with concert rooms provided places both to make new friends and to enjoy entertainment, as described in *Oldham Workshops*:

Hays, 'Lardner, Dionysius (1793–1859)', *ODNB* https://doi.org/10.1093/ref:odnb/16068.

[39] David Vincent *Literacy and Popular Culture: England, 1750–1914* (Cambridge: Cambridge University Press, 1989), p. 128.

[40] Roy Palmer, *Working Songs: Industrial Ballads and Poems from Britain and Ireland, 1780s–1980s* (Todmorden: Herron Publishing, 2010), pp. 81–82.

[41] Michael Harris, 'Rolling Stock: The Railway User and Competition', in *The Impact of Railways on Society in Britain: Essays in Honour of Jack Simmons*, ed. A. K. B. Evans and J. V. Gough (Aldershot and Burlington, VT: Ashgate, 2003), pp. 47–60.

I come again up th' town, reet opposite Swan door,[42]
Un there I heard an organ, like a lion it did roar,
Un folk were all a crowdin up stairs there like station,
I sure there's a church here they'n a famous congregation.

I wanted to see all so I clammer'd up aloft,
Un to show at I'd good manners my hat I quickly doft:
But when the singin started I stood just like a gobbin,
For instead of hallelujah, they blowed out gee wo dobbin.

When I fun it wur a alehouse I sit me down i'th throng,
When a chap ut they cawed Bardsley he sang a reet good song;
Un when he coom to th' end on't they gave him some fine claps
There were chaps for lasses lookin out, and lasses for their chaps.

After 1840 the concert room at the rear of the Star Inn, Churchgate, Bolton, was attracting crowds.[43] The Star is generally considered to have been the first music hall in the north of England.[44] Newly built railways enabled ordinary folk to travel in search of entertainments like these. *A New Song; or, A Visit to Knott Mill Fair* tells of an outing from Ashton-under-Lyne to the fair that was held near to what is now Manchester's Deansgate Station:

L[ast] Easter Monday off I went,
Like other folks on pleasure bent,
The Railway Station soon I gain,
Where crowds were waiting for the Train.

I got my ticket, paid my fare,
Fine weather banish'd every care,
And as along the rails we flew
Fair Ashton faded from our view.
[. . .]
In Manchester we did arrive,
After a quick and pleasant drive,
And presently the townsfolk found
Us country Johnnies gazing round.[45]

---

[42] The Swan was probably the building of that name that stands (or stood) at 89, High Street, Oldham.
[43] Lost Pubs of Bolton http://lostpubsofbolton.blogspot.co.uk/2014/10/bush-hotel-star-inn-star-concert-room.html.
[44] Richard Anthony Baker, *British Music Hall: An Illustrated History* (Barnsley: Pen & Sword History, 2014), p. 49.
[45] *A New Song; or, A Visit to Knott Mill Fair* (George Booth, printer, Hyde) [Oxford, Bodleian Library, Harding B 11(2014)].

When the broadside was printed Easter Monday was not yet a bank holiday but 'Saint Monday' was almost universally observed among weavers and other workers.[46]

Inside the mills, older workers were deafened by the unceasing noise, and fibre fragments caused lung disease. Outside the mills, smoke filled the air, as described in *The Scenes of Manchester*:

> The scenes of Manchester I sing,
> Where the arts and sciences are flourishing;
> Where smoke from factory chimneys bring
> The air so black, so thick and nourishing.
> Where factories that by steam are gated, [= driven]
> And children work half suffocated,
> It makes me mad to hear folk, really,
> Cry 'Manchester's improving daily.'

The River Irwell in Manchester was one of the most polluted rivers in the world well into the twentieth century:

> Once on a time were you inclin'd, your weary limbs to lave, sir,
> In summer's scorching heat in the Irwell's cooling wave, sir;
> You had only got to go to the Old Church for the shore, sir,
> But since those days the fish have died, and now they are no more[,] sir.[47]

Mechanics Institutions ran excursions that provided a brief escape from smoke and noise, and organizers complained that the number of excursionists taking advantage of the cheap fares often exceeded the total membership of the institution.[48] The *Burnley Express* in 1849 printed a song celebrating the first railway trip from the village of Trawden:

> On the sixth day of August, as I have heard folks say,
> All th' people left Trawden, on that varry day;
> Wi' big packs on ther backs, coome marching thro Colne,
> For ther wer a chep trip on, for Liverpool teawn.[49]

---

[46] Rule, *Labouring Classes*, p. 131.

[47] *Manchester's an Altered Town* ([Harkness, printer, Preston]) [Oxford, Bodleian Library, Harding B 20(105)].

[48] Susan Barton, *Working-Class Organisations and Popular Tourism, 1840–1970* (Manchester: Manchester University Press, 2005), p. 31.

[49] 'Trawden Bloeberry Cake', *Burnley Express*, 1 September 1894, p. 3. The introduction to the verses reads: 'The following is a sample of one of the folk-songs of Lancashire worth preserving. It was written to commemorate the first railway trip

The sixth of August that year, which was the year after the railway reached Colne, was a Monday. The trip from Trawden to Liverpool was a considerable undertaking, but some of the excursionists still found time to include a steamboat trip to New Brighton:

> Then deawn to i' scores they did run,
> An' ower New Brighton to see that big gun, [= Perch Rock Battery]
> Says Tommy o' Mary my belly it aches,
> I'm sea-sick wi' eytin' these bloeberry cakes.

'Ten Per Cent and No Surrender'

Workers who had been forced to accept a reduction in their wages during the hungry forties read in the press about a 10 per cent growth in national prosperity during the following decade.[50] They took strike action and adopted the slogan 'Ten Per Cent and No Surrender'.[51] They wrote and sang songs like *The Cotton Lords of Preston* to raise support:

> So with our ballads we've come out,
> To tramp the country round about,
> And try if we cannot live without
> The Cotton Lords of Preston.[52]

The Preston strikers received widespread support, including donations from Manchester, Liverpool, Sheffield, Bristol, and the Midlands, and from a wide variety of workers including carpenters, boilermakers, printers, stonemasons, and tailors,[53] and raised £105,000 in subscriptions.[54] In a remarkable gesture of generosity, even the surviving handloom weavers provided assistance.[55] Conversely, a series of pictures made about the strike gave Irish accents to the

---

taken from the village of Trawden.' The moorland to the east of Trawden was a likely source of blueberries (whortleberries).

[50] Palmer, *Working Songs*, pp. 183–97.

[51] H. I. Dutton and J. E. King, *'Ten Per Cent and No Surrender': The Preston Strike, 1853–1854* (Cambridge: Cambridge University Press, 1981), p. 1.

[52] *The Cotton Lords of Preston* [Madden Ballads 18.1312]; Palmer, *Working Songs*, pp. 194–95; Preston Digital Archive https://www.flickr.com/photos/rpsmithbarney/428 0308352/.

[53] Dutton and King, *'Ten Per Cent and No Surrender'*, p. 71.

[54] Dutton and King, *'Ten Per Cent and No Surrender'*, p. 191.

[55] Dutton and King, *'Ten Per Cent and No Surrender'*, p. 97.

blackleg workers recruited by the mill owners.[56] Roy Palmer suggests that the tune for *Betty Martin; or, the Steam Loom Lass* was the Irish melody 'The Shan Van Vocht':

> We will stand the grand attack,
>   Says the steam loom lass,
> We've the public at our back,
>   Says the steam loom lass,
>   Until we get the Ten per Cent.
>   We will never be content,
> For no less will pay the rent,
>   Says the steam loom lass.[57]

Prominent among the new music popular with audiences at halls like the Star in Bradford was blackface minstrelsy. A meeting of strikers held in the meadow of the Railway Hotel at Houghton, midway between Preston and Blackburn, began with a song set to the tune of 'Uncle Ned', a minstrel song by Stephen Foster:

> You may see of a truth that the people are not dead,
> Though 'tis said that they died long ago;
> But we've risen from our sleep, a holiday to keep,
> Determined to work under price no more.
>
> [*Chorus.*]
> So we've put by the reed-hook and the comb,
> And hung up the shuttle on the loom;
> And we'll never be content
> 'Till we get the ten per cent,
> In spite of their let well alone.[58]

Preston was the crucial battlefield, but nearby towns were also affected. Strikers at Haslingden sang these words to 'Oh! Susanna', another blackface minstrel song by Stephen Foster:

> When trade was bad in 47, the food was very high,
> And mothers had to learn again, the art of cookery,
> For instead of flour we'd yellow meal, not so pleasant to the eye,

[56] Preston Digital Archive https://www.flickr.com/photos/rpsmithbarney/8156299985/.
[57] *Betty Martin; or, The Steam Loom Lass* [Oxford, Bodleian Library, Firth c.16(255), Firth c.16(273)]; Palmer, *Working Songs*, pp. 196–97.
[58] *Uncle Ned; or, The Preston Strike* [Madden Ballads 18.1302]; Dutton and King, 'Ten Per Cent and No Surrender', p. 1; Palmer, *Working Songs*, pp. 192–94.

Steam Engines superceded [*sic*] were by American bean pie.

[*Chorus.*]
So now we'll try to make their hearts relent,
And never rest until we've gained the advance of Ten Per Cent.[59]

Dave Russell writes that just as the working population came to appreciate the need for sustained industrial and political organization as opposed to traditional, sporadic forms of protest, so, too, rehearsals at a set place and time were a necessary replacement for informal gatherings, which had been rendered less common by the new work discipline, and that such rehearsals were often firmly rooted in evangelical culture.[60] Charles Dickens attended a strike meeting and reported:

> The proceedings commenced with the following sufficiently general and discursive hymn, given out by a workman from Burnley, and sung in long meter by the whole audience:
>
> Assembled beneath thy broad blue sky,
> To thee, O God, thy children cry.
> Thy needy creatures on Thee call,
> For thou art great and good to all.
>
> Thy bounty smiles on every side,
> And no good thing hast thou denied;
> But men of wealth and men of power,
> Like locusts, all our gifts devour.
>
> Awake, ye sons of toil! nor sleep
> While millions starve, while millions weep;
> Demand your rights; let tyrants see
> You are resolved that you'll be free. [61]

Conclusions

Weavers returning from the Battle of Waterloo came back to families living by a mixture of farming and weaving – one might say that they were among the last English peasants. In less than two generations they became some of the first members of the working class. Songs from immediately after Waterloo express the grief and anger of

---

[59] Aspin, *First Industrial Society*, p. 74 ('yellow meal' is corn meal, very different from the wheat meal with which cooks were familiar).
[60] Dave Russell, *Popular Music in England, 1840–1914: A Social History*, 2nd edn (Manchester: Manchester University Press, 1997), pp. 197–98.
[61] 'On Strike', *Household Words*, 8 (11 February 1854), 553–59 (p. 558).

starving spinners and weavers as their world collapsed about them. Next come a group of songs about the technology and its impact on the community and individuals within it, some resenting the constraints of industrialization, others anticipating the opportunities of city and factory life. Lastly come songs in which steam power is accepted as the daily norm. These tell of the establishment of a new community, defining who was out as well as who was in.

While *Cotton Spinners from Manchester*, which includes stanzas current in 1826,[62] and *The Cotton Lords of Preston*, from the strike of 1853–54, were both used to raise funds, their tone could not have been more different. The cotton spinners made a humble plea for alms, whereas the Preston strikers made demands in the confidence that the justice of their cause would be recognized. Community arises from shared experience, especially shared adversity. Harland remarks on the lasting popularity of the Joan O'Grinfield songs in Lancashire, thus carrying the folk memory across the generations.[63] It is likely, too, that the balladeer who put the words 'We will stand the grand attack' into the mouth of Betty Martin was also thinking of the Lune Street shootings in Preston when soldiers shot protesting weavers during the Plug Plot Riots of 1842.[64]

Railway excursions to Knott Mill Fair, or all the way from Trawden to Liverpool, were a new kind of communal experience which could also elicit vivid shared memories. We have seen people singing together in the concert rooms of the Swan in Oldham, at the Star music hall in Bolton, and at the Preston strike meeting. Singing together serves to strengthen bonds of friendship, and street literature provided a repertoire of songs that could be shared. Broadside literature was simultaneously a record of the changes brought about by the rise of steam power, and an agent of change that contributed to the evolution of the communal identity of the people of north-west England.

---

[62] *Framework Knitters Petition* [Oxford, Bodleian Library, Johnson Ballads 2509], which bears the manuscript inscription, 'singing in Sunderland streets by two frame knitters June 24th 1826', has eight lines in common with *Cotton Spinners from Manchester*.
[63] Harland (ed.), *Ballads & Songs of Lancashire*, pp. 162–75.
[64] *Preston Chronicle and Lancashire Advertiser*, 20 August 1842, pp. 2–3.

Newcastle Chapbooks, Broadsides, and Garlands: A Study of the Collection of Woodblocks in McGill University Library, Rare Books and Special Collections

Leo John De Freitas

Some thirty years ago, Professor Pat Rogers questioned whether a study of the literary texts of street literature can 'ever tell us anything directly about the audience who read them', and advised a concentration on the producers as well as the consumers in any future research.[1] Partly in response to Rogers's clarion call, I made a 6,500-mile round trip from Oxfordshire to Montreal to examine a collection of some eight hundred woodblocks. My interest in these blocks was driven by a desire to know more about the *manufacture* of street literature – the *realia* of its making – with the intention of contributing to the better understanding of the genre. It was conjectured whether surviving printing blocks – the surfaces from which the illustrations to broadsides and chapbooks were actually printed – might reveal something.

But what? This was unknown, but the fact that they are some of the few printing artefacts surviving from the era, and that they might harbour information, encouraged the research. This near-unique collection of printing blocks was initially in the hands of trade printers in eighteenth-century Newcastle, engaged in the miscellaneous work of provincial printers but with a particular reputation for street literature.[2] These blocks are now held in McGill University Library.[3]

---

[1] Pat Rogers, *Literature and Popular Culture in Eighteenth Century England* (Brighton: Harvester Press; Totowa, NJ: Barnes & Noble, 1985), p. 183
[2] Here I acknowledge the work that has already been done on printing activities in Newcastle and the North-East, especially by contributors to the History of the Book Trade in the North publications.
[3] All the woodblock images shown here are from Montreal, McGill University Library, Rare Books and Special Collections, Woodblock Collection. (A similar collection of woodblocks is to be found in the Huntington Library, Armstrong Collection.)

The use of woodblocks in chapbooks and ballads

Both chapbooks and ballads were illustrated by these blocks, together with the songbook version of the chapbook, known as the garland. Many chapbooks and ballad sheets are without imprint details and there is a sliding scale from absolute zero information to full bibliographical description. The Newcastle publications are no exception to this and the commercially shrewd phrases 'licensed and entered according to order', 'entered according to order', and, the most misleading, 'printed in this present year' are frequently to be found. In the absence of a date and publisher the purchaser had no idea of whether they were current publications or not – a canny marketing ploy at the very least. Clearly, in such instances the ability to marry the block to the image to the publication is a valuable aid to the bibliographer and historian (*Figure 1*).

Figure 1.
(*left*) Block box 14, item 706.
(*right*) Woodcut image from *The Lovers Quarrel; or, Cupid's Triumph* (Newcastle: printed in this year) [Oxford, Bodleian Library, Harding A 146 (9)].

Many examples of Newcastle street literature do, however, carry identifying imprint information. Both chapbooks and broadsides can be associated with specific blocks, and the same blocks can be found illustrating both chapbooks and ballad sheets (*Figure 2*). It will take time to associate all the known Newcastle blocks with known publications, but the fact that we are able to do so encourages the ambition of constructing a particular printing/publishing profile that will be unique in the popular print culture of the eighteenth century. What this might result in, and how we might use this knowledge better to figure out the relationship between producers and consumers, is a challenge for the future, but if successful we will have enriched our knowledge and understanding of the past by such an exercise.

Figure 2.
(*above left*) Block box 14, item 705 (75 × 87 × 22 mm), annotated 'Very early valentine block(?) WHITE collection'.
(*above right*) Woodcut image from *The Delightful New Academy of Compliments* (Newcastle: printed in this present year) [Oxford, Bodleian Library, Harding A 147 (8)].
(*below*) Woodcut image from *The Kind Virgin's Complaint* [Oxford, Bodleian Library, Douce Ballads 3(51b)].

Description of the blocks

The materials in the McGill collection are of all sizes but, with few exceptions, of a uniform height, or 'type-height', that being the standard measurement (23.32 mm or 0.918 inch) for them to print correctly in a traditional handpress. Some blocks fall below this necessary height and are made up with 'spacers'. A small number of printing surfaces are unexpectedly very thin, around 6–8 mm, and are mounted on inferior wood to bring them up to the correct height. These last are intriguing to the print historian, but suffice it to say that they pose questions about working practices that may yet prove insightful: for example, who manufactured the blocks, and how, and questions around the role of the amateur in the production of ballad sheet and chapbook imagery.[4]

The earlier blocks are distinguished, among other criteria, by the marks of the carpenter's sawing and shaping implements, whereas the later, nineteenth-century, blocks are characterized by the smoothness of the machine-manufactured sides. It will be appreciated that this difference is one feature that can help in the rough dating of printing blocks and hence publications. The surfaces of all but a few of the blocks are stained with the ink with which they were covered for printing, thus betokening heavy use.

The very survival of the blocks, and the generally good condition of many of them, are quite remarkable for objects of practical trade. For at least the first hundred years of their life they were housed, and used, in the workaday environment of printers' workshops. Thereafter they were kept by collectors, antiquarians, and librarians in various 'safer' milieux (*Figure 3*). A few of the blocks are fundamentally or seriously damaged and unlikely ever to be printed from again. Others need a little attention before attempting anything with them, but the majority appear ready for printing.

The generally good condition of the blocks is significant, especially in the context of their early working life. Their long life in the workshops of the printers/publishers shows that they were safeguarded and maintained in good repair. These were valued artefacts that their end use, the illustration of chapbooks and broadsides, seemingly belies. We might be charmed or entertained by, or feel indifferent towards, the ephemeral nature of popular print, but we are not free to disparage the means of its production.[5] These blocks were serious commercial undertakings and they invite careful consideration, with undoubted implications for our understanding of the printed texts they accompanied.

---

[4] Remarkably, even the few contemporary sources that engage with the printing of woodblocks seem to have seen these questions of manufacture as of no interest.

[5] It is important to bear this in mind when, not infrequently, one comes across a reference to the making of chapbook illustrations by means of 'penknives'.

Figure 3.
(*above*) A contemporary collection of well-preserved woodblocks.
(*below*) Interior of an eighteenth-century print shop, from *The Most Delectable, Scriptural and Pious History of the Famous and Magnificent Great Eastern Window (According to Beautiful Portraitures) in St. Peter's Cathedral, York* (impressed for the author, in St Peter's Gate, [1762]).

What do the blocks reveal?

Previous research on old blocks had prepared me against any disappointment at not finding much documentary evidence on the blocks in the McGill collection. But what there was suggests how students might approach and use such information. By 'documentary evidence' is meant manuscript or printed annotations appended to a block. It is prudent to assess these snippets of information circumspectly; they are most likely to have been added to the blocks sometime after their creation, by collectors and dealers, and librarians, archivists, and curators. Nevertheless, they should not be ignored, because they may point us in a useful direction. One example, however, acts as a warning. It reads, 'Thomas Bewick. Early Robinson Crusoe 1st York edition', which seems specific and reasonable enough. But is it? The block in question is shown in *Figure 4*.

Now anyone who has even the most limited acquaintance with Bewick's style of wood *engraving* – and the 'Robinson Crusoe' is most clearly a wood or metal *cut* – will recognize that this cannot be the work of the acknowledged master of the process. The original upon which the 'Robinson Crusoe' illustration was based was published in 1722, some thirty or so years before Bewick's birth, and while that in itself is not sufficient proof that Bewick did not engrave a later copy, we have his own words to the effect that it was precisely poor work such as this that he was committed to challenging, right from his earliest endeavours in wood engraving.[6]

The clincher, however, lies in the clumsy initialling of the block and the subsequent print taken from it by one 'R.M.' (*Figure 5*). 'R.M.' did cut some other blocks associated with northern chapbook printers/publishers and much has been done to try to identify this elusive character and the work he did for the Cumbrian chapbook trade.[7] In order to make a sale (and hardly as a result of honest error) unscrupulous booksellers have constantly and confidently identified *any* late eighteenth- or early nineteenth-century wood-engraved image as being by 'Thomas Bewick' or his 'workshop' – a practice that persists to the present day, so that the researcher needs to be alert when examining such 'documentary evidence' pertaining to a block.

A rare source of optimism provided by the McGill collection comes from some seemingly authentic ink inscriptions found with one

---

[6] *A Memoir of Thomas Bewick, Written by Himself* (Newcastle-on-Tyne: Robert Ward, for Jane Bewick; London: Longman, Green, Longman, and Roberts, 1862), p. 144.

[7] Barry McKay, 'Cumbrian Chapbooks Cuts: Some Sources and Other Versions', in *The Reach of Print: Making, Selling and Using Books*, ed. Peter Isaac and Barry McKay (Winchester: St Paul's Bibliographies; New Castle, DE: Oak Knoll Press, 1988), pp. 65–84; Barry McKay, 'R.M. Who He?', unpublished notes from Bodleian Library seminar, June 2017.

Figure 4. Block box 2, item 113 (61 × 75 × 21 mm), annotated 'Thomas Bewick. Early Robinson Crusoe 1st York edition', with the initials 'RM' (top right).

Figure 5. Print taken from the block shown in *Figure 4,* with the clumsy initials 'RM' (top left).

of the blocks (the aged and stained appearance of the inscriptions places them back in time, but without a corroborating date it is still a guess as to their origin).[8] Along with a more or less indecipherable label, the block in question has inscriptions on all sides which provide a title, 'Shooting the witch from the river', some as yet indecipherable information, and a name, 'W. Kidd'. The publication in which the block was used has not yet been identified. The British Book Trade Index does not list a 'W. Kidd', but it does list a John Andrew Kidd, a Newcastle engraver/etcher working at the end of the eighteenth century.[9] With the discovery of this block and its inscriptions biographical research into this 'W. Kidd', an otherwise unknown player in the field, has now acquired a certain urgency. Such leads are rarely come by, but they are there, and the hunt goes on. References to the 'White collection' or 'Bewick' can provide a starting point for associating a block with a printer or supposed wood-cutter, and cross-referencing blocks with actual publications can confirm trade connections.

Finally, several blocks have been numbered by means of punches. Without corresponding ledgers they are merely isolated markings and remain enigmatic, unless and until relevant workbooks – accounts, tally sheets, catalogues – can be unearthed. They must, however, be recorded for possible future use. So far this practice has been found only with nineteenth-century blocks.

Repair and recycling of blocks

Some blocks have been carefully repaired and one in particular is rather exceptional for the level of carpentry skills that went into its maintenance and renovation (*Figure 6*). It is neither a large nor a complicated block, approximately the size of a small matchbox, but it was evidently considered by the printer/publisher important enough to be kept in working condition, and time and energy, and presumably money, were expended to ensure its survival. Use of this block has yet to be identified in printed sources, but here is evidence of practical printing practice that could not have been deduced from the image alone.

---

[8] McGill University Library, block box 1, item 6 (34 × 59 mm), annotated 'Shooting the witch from the river'.
[9] BBTI. There is also a William Kidd, of South Shields, bookseller, stationer, and map and chart seller, active in the 1840s–50s.

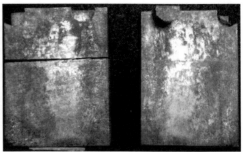

Figure 6. Block box 8, item 426 (61 × 45 × 23 mm). (*left*) Surface image. (*right*) Reverse of the block showing repairs designed to keep it in service.

There is evidence, too, of later printers having extended the life of damaged blocks by means of electrotyping. An example is shown in *Figure 7.* The publication the original woodblock illustrated was *The Second Part of Jack and the Giants*, printed by John White, *c.*1711–30. However, the process of electrotyping was not introduced until the 1830s, so here is evidence of the length of time over which the block was 'kept alive'.[10] The electrotyped block again represents tangible evidence of a workaday practice that would have remained unknown had not both the original printed woodcut and the metal replacement block survived. Discoveries like these extend beyond the mere curiosity of collectors – they are, to repeat the point, indicators of printing practices in the real world of street literature which underlie business practices that we ought to be investigating more closely.

---

[10] The process was first announced in 1838 by M. H. von Jacobi, a German working in St Petersburg. In England the first use of electrotyping for printing appeared in the *London Journal* of April 1840, and other English examples are known from later in that year. It is worth noting in addition that stereotyping, an early method of copying original material, was invented by William Ged in 1725 and was used by John White in an edition of Sallust printed in 1738. See Richard Welford, 'Early Newcastle Typography, 1639–1800', *Archaeologia Aeliana*, 3rd ser., 3 (1907), 1–134 (p. 21).

(*Figure 7*.
(*a*) Woodcut image from *The Second Part of Jack and the Giants* [Oxford, Bodleian Library, Opie C 946] (approx. 85 × 79 mm).

(*b*) Block box 2, item 80 (88 × 79 × 23 mm). The beginning of the problem can be seen in the print (above) as a white patch to the left of the dragon's chest, indicating missing wood and the fracture at the bottom of the block. This is seen reversed in the lower right of the block.

(*c*) Block box 3, item 161, electrotyped metal block (88 × 80 mm), where the break in the original woodblock (above) has been repaired in the metal copy – an easy enough job compared with repairing the woodblock.

A small number of blocks were cut on both sides. This is not so uncommon among the nineteenth-century blocks examined, but very few examples have so far been found from earlier periods. For one reason or another, this expedient was resorted to because a block was needed when virgin wood was not available. In the nineteenth century this was not infrequently a consequence of the increasing demands of industry for boxwood, which was also the preferred type of wood for engraving pictorial blocks. Machine-driven mills, for example, were major users of boxwood for making shuttles. Old woodblocks that had passed down through the trade into the nineteenth century, or rejected blocks, were considered recyclable and were reused.

Another teasing indicator of trade practice is suggested by an example of a double-sided block where it can be argued that we are witnessing an apprentice hand at work. Offcuts of boxwood, or blocks considered useless, would have been made available to apprentices to enable them to try out their skills with a graver. The fact that the incomplete word 'Tria[ll]' on the block in question would have printed white suggests a novice getting used to handling the tool in the simplest of exercises.

The printers

The earliest of the blocks in the McGill collection are likely to date from the end of the seventeenth century, and most certainly from the early years of the eighteenth century, when they were in the possession of the first important Newcastle printer, John White II. There had been earlier printers in Newcastle but they are not believed to have been engaged with the street literature in which we are interested.[11] John White II was the son of John White I, the king's royal printer for York and the five northern counties.[12] It is important to emphasize that these early northern printers were not isolated from the centre of printing and publishing in London. John White I had been a printer in London before moving to York after 1688. When his son moved to Newcastle and began publishing his *Newcastle Courant* newspaper in 1711 he would have carried with him not only printing artefacts but also, it can be assumed, metropolitan contacts.[13]

Several printer's devices and decorations attributable to John White II, and later used by his successors, are traceable through

---

[11] Welford, 'Early Newcastle Typography', pp. 3–18.
[12] Welford, 'Early Newcastle Typography', p. 18.
[13] Welford, 'Early Newcastle Typography', p. 19.

printed sources.[14] Unhappily, none of the actual blocks for these images were found in Montreal.[15] Nevertheless, a number of woodcuts designed and cut in a familiar manner can, unless proved otherwise, be considered as belonging to the same hand. And whose hand might that have been? Some of the ornaments printed by White show, hidden away in intricate rococo designs, the letters 'W' and 'P' (*Figure 8*). The 'W' and 'P' refer to William Pennock (*c*.1709–*c*.1752), a multifarious worker in the London world of printing and publishing where he was, in addition to his work as a wood-cutter, a copper-plate engraver/etcher, printer, print seller, bookseller, and publisher.[16] Although a metropolitan engraver, Pennock corresponded with and worked for clients outside of the capital.[17] It is probable that John White sourced several woodcuts from him, either directly or through an agent.[18]

Figure 8. Headpiece ornament from *The History of the Wicked Life and Miserable End of Doctor John Faustus* (Newcastle upon Tyne: printed and sold by John White) [Oxford, Bodleian Library, Douce BB 394].

The initials 'R.M.' have already been mentioned, and other blocks in the collection are signed with anonymous initials and positive identification of the cutters is still in abeyance. What these initials do not tell us, of course, is whether the wood-cutters were also the

---

[14] Leo John De Freitas, 'Squabbling Eagles: A Huntington Wood Block's Passage through Time', forthcoming.

[15] I now think a number may have ended up in the Huntington Library (see n. 14 above).

[16] BBTI.

[17] David Stoker (ed.), *The Correspondence of the Reverend Francis Blomefield* (1705–52) (Norwich: Norfolk Record Society, 1992). Pennock also contributed to Thomas Gent's *The Antient and Modern History of the Loyal Town of Rippon* (1733).

[18] Pennock had been recommended to the Rev. Francis Blomefield by an agent called Dr Gaylard (n. 17 above).

designers of the images. Such information would be invaluable for the reconstruction of the sources and aesthetics of popular imagery and for answering the question to what degree did they represent an innate or an imposed visual vocabulary for the *hoi polloi*?

The blocks were commissioned, or passed through the trade, by the important printers associated with the Newcastle street literature trade. John White II was followed by Thomas Saint, White's partner and successor, and then by various members of the Angus family until the bankruptcy of George Angus in 1825, after which the blocks came into the hands of collectors. By that date the chapbook's days were effectively numbered, and with the coming of the penny illustrated press in the 1830s, printed on the new machine presses, the chapbooks and ballad sheets themselves became collectors' items.

* * *

There is an unhelpful and unqualified belief in some quarters that the manufacture of chapbooks and broadsides was 'an art of the people by the people', akin to a domestic industry.[19] Only under special pleading can this be argued. Except for the small scale of provincial printers' workshops, there is no evidence of the production of street literature at all within a domestic setting. The blocks examined here are witnesses to the efforts of the tradesmen and businessmen in their workshops who made the chapbooks and song sheets, and who sold them from their workshops to local callers, booksellers, and itinerant chapmen (*Figure 9*).

The condition and level of care of the blocks in Montreal supports this inference of a commercial origin. As far as researchers are aware, this collection is (along with the Armstrong Collection of woodblocks in the Huntington Library) unique in being so firmly associated with known printers/publishers working during a specific period in a specific locale, Newcastle, which after London was the most important centre for the production of eighteenth-century street

---

[19] For example, https://www.bl.uk/romantics-and-victorians/articles/chapbooks (italics added): '*Most chapbooks were the products of domestic-scale industry.* They were hand-printed on manual presses, and the folding, sewing and trimming would all also be done by hand; so too would the colouring of illustrations, the folding and tipping-in of frontispieces and the pasting on of wrappers. Much of this labour would have been carried out by women and/or children, who were cheap to employ because they were poorly paid. *Perhaps* in some cases output would be a family affair, with the whole of the printer's family contributing to the manufacturing effort; *but doubtless* busy printers also employed poorer folk to undertake the work in their own homes.'

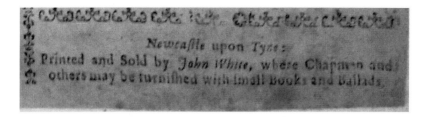

Figure 9. Imprint from *Hind's Progress and Ramble* (Newcastle upon Tyne: printed and sold by John White; where chapmen and others may be furnished with small books and ballads) [Oxford, Bodleian Library, Douce Ballads 3(122a)].

literature. Examination of the blocks argues for a more nuanced assessment of the making of woodcuts for street literature, with implications for a richer appreciation of the genre's place in popular culture. There is a need to wean ourselves away from generations of uncritical acceptance of the idea that the images were 'hacked out with a knife'.[20] To confuse the printed image with the manufactured block is to set discovery on to a wrong track, leading to false premises and preconceptions and the stifling of insightful research.

How far the information and arguments derived from the McGill woodblocks can be extended to other printers and other areas will only become clear when, and if, other blocks are discovered and made available for research. It is a great shame that this particular collection of identifiable blocks has become widely dispersed, far from the shores of their origin. But it must be conceded that where our own national libraries and museums apparently took little interest in such lowly artefacts from our past, others, more forward-looking perhaps and less prejudiced, did value them and are now caring for them. Likewise, it is to be hoped that examples of such blocks in private hands are being carefully maintained and will eventually become available to serious researchers so that the work of detailed reconstruction of their making and their use can contribute to a better understanding of the commercial milieux of street literature.

---

[20] *Newcastle Daily Journal,* 9 July 1896, quoted in Charles S. Felver. *Joseph Crawhall: The Newcastle Wood Engraver, 1821–1896* (Newcastle upon Tyne: Frank Graham, 1972), p. 91. Such characterization of chapbook and ballad-sheet woodblocks is common throughout the literature, if perhaps not so baldly stated.

The author in McGill University Library, Rare Books and Special Collections.

Fairburn's Editions: Songs, Songsters, and Handbooks for Plebeian Modernity

Gary Kelly

This essay suggests some commercial, social, cultural, and political meanings and values that could be assigned to songs, songsters, and related material produced by the London firm of John Fairburn, father and son. They were printers and book, map, and print sellers, active from the 1790s to the 1840s, but principally during the first three decades of the nineteenth century. The firm's products were often branded as Fairburn's Editions. I examine in particular two of these volumes, related to popular song as broadly understood.

'Popular' may have several senses: much frequented or practised; using certain formal and thematic resources constituting a particular idiom or cluster of idioms; responded to (though in many different ways) by large numbers; widely circulated; expressing or deriving from the social and cultural life of the common people; using forms and themes of popular arts even when by and for a social minority; cheap in price and/or quality. 'Popular' may have a positive, pejorative, and/or descriptive connotation, depending on the speaker/writer, maker/user, seller/buyer, observer/practitioner in a particular social context.

As performed and/or printed artefacts, popular song in Fairburn's day could range from what was later termed 'folk song' through printed 'street' ballads, garlands, and songsters, to theatrical performances of several kinds, including entr'acte exhibitions in a playhouse or turns in a commercial pleasure garden, professional or amateur musical drama, and domestic social performance. Further, in Fairburn's day 'song' could signify words in verse musically performed, solo or ensemble, with or without musical accompaniment, or poetry in general, including performed recitation without musical form or accompaniment. Like 'popular', 'song' could be pejorative, signifying something of little commercial or aesthetic value. In short, songs could signify as objects and practices in various ways for various users in various situations.

Songs, with other cultural and communicative objects and practices, are instruments in and objects of social and cultural difference and contest. As one musicologist of popular song puts it:

> music gives us a way of being in the world, a way of making sense of it: musical response is, by its nature, a process of musical identification; aesthetic response is, by its nature, an ethical agreement. The critical issue, in other words, is not meaning and its interpretation – musical appreciation as a kind of decoding – but experience and collusion: the 'aesthetic' describes a kind of self-consciousness, a coming together of the sensual, the emotional, and the social performance. In short, music doesn't represent values but lives them.[1]

Or, as proponents of integrational linguistics and effective semiotics would argue, meaning is always meaning in use. Meaning does not inhere in the object or practice but is created by users and practitioners in particular moments of meaning-making. In such moments, everything that the user/practitioner is, right there and then, and everything about the moment and place, right then and there, may be made part of the meaning in that instance, depending on the perceived and felt needs and interests, personal and social, of those present in that moment. Archival, historiographical, classroom, or similar meanings given to songs and songsters cannot trump the meanings they may be given in everyday life, but are just other meanings in use. So a song is always more than a song, a songster always more than that, as suggested by considering the social and cultural lives of two of Fairburn's Editions, the three-volume, serially published *Universal Songster* of the mid-1820s, and the pamphlet *The Laughable Tale of the Farmer's Blunder*, probably published in the 1830s or 1840s.

The Universal Songster; or, Museum of Mirth, forming the Most Complete, Extensive, and Valuable Collection of Ancient and Modern Songs in the English Language was one of many such songsters to be found in the archival record from at least the mid-eighteenth century through to the nineteenth century and beyond, although it is one of the largest of them (*Figure 1*). It was offered by Fairburn and apparently obtainable throughout Britain from December 1824 in weekly numbers at 3*d.* or in monthly parts at 1*s.*[2] The title page states that it was 'printed for'

---

[1] Simon Frith, *Performing Rites: On the Value of Popular Music* (Cambridge, MA: Harvard University Press, 1998), p. 272.
[2] *Newcastle Courant*, 25 December 1824, p. 1.

Fairburn as part of a consortium that included Simpkin and Marshall, and Sherwood, Gilbert, and Piper.[3]

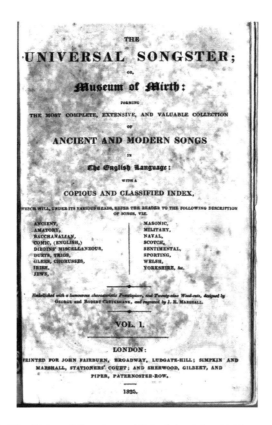

THE

·UNIVERSAL SONGSTER;

OR,

Museum of Mirth:

FORMING

THE MOST COMPLETE, EXTENSIVE, AND VALUABLE COLLECTION

OF

ANCIENT AND MODERN SONGS

IN

The English Language:

WITH A

COPIOUS AND CLASSIFIED INDEX,

WHICH WILL, UNDER ITS VARIOUS HEADS, REFER THE READER TO THE FOLLOWING DESCRIPTION
OF SONGS, VIZ.

ANCIENT,	MASONIC,
AMATORY,	MILITARY,
BACCHANALIAN,	NAVAL,
COMIC, (ENGLISH,)	SCOTCH,
DIBDINS' MISCELLANEOUS,	SENTIMENTAL,
DUETS, TRIOS,	SPORTING,
GLEES, CHORUSSES,	WELSH,
IRISH,	YORKSHIRE, &c.
JEWS,	

Embellished with a humorous characteristic Frontispiece, and Twenty-nine Wood-cuts, designed by
GEORGE and ROBERT CRUIKSHANK, and engraved by J. R. MARSHALL.

VOL. 1.

LONDON:

PRINTED FOR JOHN FAIRBURN, BROADWAY, LUDGATE-HILL; SIMPKIN AND
MARSHALL, STATIONERS' COURT; AND SHERWOOD, GILBERT, AND
PIPER, PATERNOSTER-ROW.

1825.

Figure 1. The Universal Songster, published by John Fairburn; Simpkin and Marshall; Sherwood, Gilbert, and Piper.

A temporary investment consortium, or 'conger', was a common practice for ambitious projects, spreading risk. Sale in numbers and/or parts was also a practice that eased capitalization of such projects by ensuring the receipt of payments while publication went on, rather than requiring full capitalization before a copy could be sold. Each number of the *Universal Songster* comprised sixteen double-column pages and was headed by a woodcut vignette, comic and satirical in

---

[3] *The Universal Songster; or, Museum of Mirth, forming the Most Complete, Extensive, and Valuable Collection of Ancient and Modern Songs in the English Language*, 3 vols (London: printed for John Fairburn, Broadway, Ludgate Hill; Simpkin and Marshall, Stationer's Court; and Sherwood, Gilbert, and Piper, Paternoster Row, 1825–26).

style, designed by Robert or George Cruikshank and executed by J. R. Marshall. Numbers and parts were meant to be bound into volumes. I have not come across an individual number or part, but if a familiar pattern of production was followed each would have been issued with coloured-paper covers, likely bearing advertisements for Fairburn's other products. If a familiar distribution pattern was followed, numbers and parts could be subscribed to, and delivered and paid for, through peripatetic newsmen, or at newspaper and stationery shops and booksellers.

Each volume of the completed three-volume set contained about 1,500 songs.[4] Each number mixed types of songs indiscriminately. The categories of songs were listed on the title pages and in the indexes supplied with each volume and include, variously: Ancient; Amatory; Bacchanalian; Comic; Dibdin's Songs; Duets, Trios, Catches, Glees, and Choruses; Irish; Jews' Songs; Masonic Songs; Military Songs; Naval Songs; Scotch; Sentimental; Sporting; Yorkshire and Provincial; Welsh; and Miscellaneous. The most numerous categories, at about a fifth each, were Comic and Amatory.

The majority of songs were ascribed to a creator and/or associated with a celebrity singer, such as Charles Dibdin, master of cabaret and synonymous with commercial popular song through the century, John Braham, Jewish international opera tenor and theatre manager, and Charles Incledon, pre-eminent ballad singer of his day. Many of the songs came from or were associated with the theatres, where songs were integral to many popular plays and were also performed between plays in the characteristic multi-play programme of the time. As with most songsters, musical notation was not included in the *Universal Songster*, as this had to be printed by costly engraving, although tunes were sometimes indicated in songs' subtitles. There were eighty-four numbers, twenty-eight per volume.

Almost simultaneously, an edition of the *Universal Songster* appeared with the imprint of Jones and Co., who succeeded the famous suppliers of cheap books Lackington and Allen at the Temple of the Muses in Finsbury Square (*Figure 2*).[5] Whereas Fairburn specialized in pamphlets and numbers, Jones specialized in cheap volumes. In time, a collection with the same title was published by another firm

---

[4] See further Anthony Bennett, 'Sources of Popular Song in Early Nineteenth-Century Britain: Problems and Methods of Research', *Popular Music*, 2 (1982), 69–89 (pp. 81–82) (although further research suggests some refinements to Bennett's description).

[5] *The Universal Songster; or, Museum of Mirth, forming the Most Complete, Extensive, and Valuable Collection of Ancient and Modern Songs in the English Language*, 3 vols (London: published by Jones and Co., Temple of the Muses, Finsbury Square).

specializing in cheap volumes, George Routledge, initiator of the celebrated Railway Library and with empire-wide reach. By 1864, Routledge was operating from Ludgate Broadway, former locale of one of Fairburn's shops. The Fairburns and their songsters were, then, deeply involved in and associated with cheap print, for better and worse. This was true even before the appearance of the *Universal Songster*.

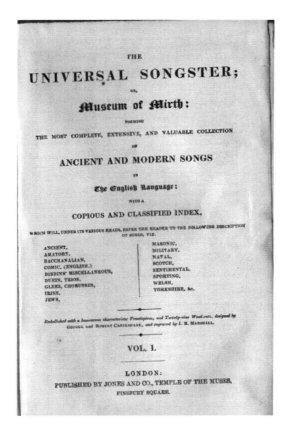

Figure 2. The Universal Songster, published by Jones and Co.

For example, a year before the first number of the songster was advertised, a review in the conservative *British Critic* of cantos XII to XIV of Byron's *Don Juan* smeared the well-known liberal poet and his scandalous poem by associating them with Fairburn and his songsters, and with cheap print generally.[6] The review declared that Byron 'can

---

[6] *British Critic*, 20 (December 1823), 662–68 (p. 662).

hardly be ignorant that his hero is sunk from the Don Juan of Moliere, into the "Giovanni in London" of the minor theatres', regarded by many as promoters of moral, religious, artistic, and even political subversion. It went on to assert that Don Juan had degenerated into a 'humble second' to the protagonists of Pierce Egan's comic, impudent, louche, and hugely successful novel *Life in London* (which Fairburn quickly ripped off with *Life in Paris*) and to make the point that Byron's works were no longer published by the upmarket firm of John Murray, located in London's fashionable West End, but were now 'gibbetted in effigy in every twopenny book-stall, side by side with grim wood-cuts of Hunt and Thurtell [notorious murderers featured in trials published by Fairburn and others] and the features of our poor old friend Grimaldi [. . .] grinning at the head of Fairburn's Songster'.

The last reference is probably to Fairburn's six-volume *Songster's Multum in Parvo; or, New Pocket Companion for the Lovers of Harmony, embracing All the Popular New Songs Singing at the Theatres Royal, Minor Places of Amusement, &c.* (1808–10). This was published in weekly 2*d.* numbers, with a grinning head, presumably that of Grimaldi, on each volume's title page. Other songsters from Fairburn also featured Grimaldi, the most famous theatrical acrobat-clown of the era, including *Fairburn's Gallimaufry Songster and Comical Budget for 1812, Songs Now Singing at the Theatre Royal, Sadler's Wells, etc.* (1812). At the time, Sadler's Wells Theatre was regarded as a purveyor of low drama and entertainment, and a scene of plebeian revelry and riot. As was common with critical commentary of this period, differences of politics, class, aesthetics, and price were aligned in a hierarchical binary.

Fairburn's Editions included numerous songsters. For example, Sir John Stainer's 1891 annotated *Catalogue of English Songbooks* listed *The Brilliant Songster, British Songster, Annual Songster for 1837, Catamaran Songster, Comic Constellation, Comic Highflyer, Dashing Songster, Everlasting Songster, Incledonian and Vauxhall Songster, Larking Songster for 1823, Laughable Songster and Fashionable Quizzer, Laughable Songster or High Cockalorum Jig, Naval Songster, Odd Fellows Song Book and Comic Peg-ass-us of Wit, Wonderful Songster for 1829, Harmonist's Preceptor,* and the *Songster's Multum in Parvo,* and there were others besides (Stainer lists the *Universal Songster* as published by Jones and Co.).[7] Stainer, son of a London cabinet-maker, was eventually knighted for his work as

---

[7] *Catalogue of English Song Books, forming a Portion of the Library of Sir John Stainer* (London: printed for private circulation, 1891).

cathedral organist, composer of Anglican liturgical music, music educator, and Oxford Professor of Music, and for promoting music in schools and professionalizing English musical life, especially choirs, at a local level. Stainer, with friends such as Sir Arthur Sullivan and W. A. Barrett, resisted the contemporary denigration of popular, especially commercial, song in favour of 'art song' on one hand and a supposedly authentic tradition of 'folk song' on the other. Sullivan, co-creator with W. S. Gilbert of the Savoy operas, and initially regarded as the future genius of English classical music, was commonly perceived to have sold out to the popular. Stainer devoted his career to bringing 'high' and 'popular' song and music together as the foundation of a modern national identity and clearly had more than a professional interest in songsters such as Fairburn's.

The *British Critic*'s alignment of differences of class, culture, and politics for Fairburn's songsters seems borne out, though reversed, by an advertisement placed by the printer, publisher, bookseller, and commercial circulating-library proprietor Joseph Russell of Moor Street, Birmingham, in 1826.[8] In 1819, shortly after the Peterloo Massacre, Russell been convicted for libel for publishing William Hone's anti-establishment reformist parody the *Political Litany*. He would go on to be a member of the Birmingham Political Union, founded to campaign for parliamentary reform. His commercial circulating library of two thousand volumes offered best-selling novels by the likes of Scott and Lister, and other books of the day such as Moore's life of Sheridan. He also sold cheap books, many of which were published in numbers and were associated with plebeian and reformist politics. They included Volney's rationalist *Ruins of Empire* and deistic *Law of Nature*, popular humanitarian titles such as Pope's *Essay on Man*, Goldsmith's *Deserted Village*, and Gray's *Elegy*, and works of everyday utility, such as Walker's pronouncing dictionary (for plebeians anxious about their 'vulgar' and 'provincial' language), Buchan's *Domestic Medicine* (a pseudo-scientific presentation of historic folk medicine), and John Wesley's *Primitive Physic*. Russell's advertisement also boasted of his having for sale '[s]everal thousand volumes of Books, new and second-hand, in the various branches of Literature and Science', two terms that would have had broader signification than they do now and which together indicated a certain kind of modernity.

What constituted that modernity – and indicative of Russell's market – was his offering of 'Cheap and Popular LONDON

---

8 *Aris's Birmingham Gazette*, 5 June 1826, p. 1.

PUBLICATIONS [. . .] weekly as published'. These were works in numbers, listed according to price per issue. A number were entertaining and sensationalist literature priced at 2*d*., such as the *Arabian Nights*, the *British Novelist*, *Legends of Terror*, the *Terrific Register*, and the *Seaman's Recorder, containing Shipwrecks, Battles, and Miraculous Escapes*. At 3*d*. there were Oxberry's *Dramatic Biography*, the *London Stage*, 120 numbers of Editions of the Drama, the *Universal Songster*, Shakespeare's works, and Cook's voyages (exotic adventures of the popular common-man hero). At 6*d*., the historic price point for cheap print and entertainments, were numbers of Dolby's *British Theatre*. A wide range of works contained burgeoning kinds of 'modern' knowledge, especially those involved in transforming customary artisanal manufacture into industrial, machine-driven manufacture, as well as other kinds of self-education, reference, and self-improvement.

Plutarch's Lives were available at 2*d*. per number. At 3*d*. were the *Mechanics' Magazine*, the *Mechanics' Register*, the *Popular Encyclopedia*, Bayle's *Historical and Critical Dictionary*, and Rollin's *Ancient History* (a favourite of republicans and reformists). The *Register of Arts and Sciences* was priced at 4*d*. The *Medical Adviser*, the *Female Friend, or; Domestic Advisor*, and an *Architectural Dictionary* were all at 6*d*. Offered at 1*s*. were a *Biographical Dictionary*, the memoirs of the organic intellectual Benjamin Franklin, and the Enlightenment rationalist and sceptic Pierre Bayle's *Historical and Critical Dictionary*. At 1*s*. 6*d*. per part were Hume and Smollett's history of England and Nathaniel Hooke's Roman history (perhaps read as a proponent of classical republicanism). Most clearly indicative of the company that Fairburn's *Universal Songster* was keeping in Russell's shop was the political literature: Cobbett's *Political Register* at 6*d*. per number, and Voltaire's *Philosophical Dictionary*, Mignet's liberal history of the French Revolution, and Ségur's account of Napoleon's Russian campaign, all at 1*s*. per part.

Thereafter, the *Universal Songster* can be found in the company of a certain strain of print often denominated at the time as 'popular', 'standard', or 'classic', but also affordable or cut-price. Many of these print objects would be reprints of 'serious' and 'respectable' literature of the previous century, and more recent 'books of the day', typically illustrated, and advertised as both 'elegant' and 'cheap', with newly designed type and high-quality paper. Their materiality, then, could connote both enduring and modern value, even when they had originally been published generations earlier. Some were standard sacred and religious works, usually neo-puritan in character and leaning towards ecclesiastical and theological nonconformity.

Nonconformity with or dissent from the established church provided a spiritual and social home for many of the new commercial and manufacturing classes, until increasing wealth and status would nudge some of them into the Church of England. Some of these works, too, could be classed as 'furniture books', not necessarily intended to be read but rather to be displayed in the home and/or commercial or professional workplace, as an indication of prosperity, respectability, and culture – that is to say, not plebeian culture.

The *Universal Songster* found itself in such company in an advertisement placed by the bookseller, occasional publisher, and half-price specialist F. Loraine, located in the recently completed neoclassical Grey Street in the heart of manifestly modern Newcastle upon Tyne, in 1838.[9] Loraine's book list indicates the scope, content, and character of this widely diffused repertoire, reproduced by publishers across nation and empire, and suggesting a market that was interested in recognized forms of modern knowledge, classic British non-fiction, neo-puritan religious classics associated with Protestant nonconformity, respectable novelists and novel collections, romanticized travels and histories, sets of Shakespeare, the *Penny Magazine* of the utilitarian Society for the Diffusion of Useful Knowledge, aimed at artisans and petty shopkeepers, and Hone's *Every-Day Book,* a secularization and folklorization of the ecclesiastical and agricultural year and a major contribution to the incorporation of 'customs in common' into a distinctive plebeian modernity. Loraine advertised the three-volume *Universal Songster* at half-price for 15*s*.

The newspaper record suggests, however, that with time the value (in several senses) of the *Universal Songster* shifted again, as it came to be prized by bibliophiles, probably boosted by its association with the humorous art of the Cruikshank brothers and Victorian nostalgia for an imagined Georgian culture of genteel, if naughty, fun. In 1884, for example, the Local Board of Oswaldtwistle in Lancashire, a cotton town developed by the family of Robert Peel, ordered the sale of books found in the office of William Gourlay, a Scot, former editor of the *Blackburn Standard* newspaper, and recently clerk to the Oswaldtwistle Local Board. Gourlay was considered to have lived unusually well on his clerk's salary, with a fine house, sumptuous living, numerous investments, and 'had a great interest in books and was an avid collector', who 'had acquired a very substantial and

---

[9] *Newcastle Courant*, 15 June 1838, p. 1.

valuable library'.[10] In 1879, however, he had been convicted and sentenced to ten years in jail for forgery and embezzlement of about £40,000 from the municipal board. In an article headed 'Gourlay's Collection of Literature and Art', the *Blackburn Standard* reported:

> The somewhat curious medley of the sacred and profane in his office collection of books would lead one to suppose that Gourlay had a great taste for variety in his literature.
>
> The books, some of which are richly bound, include a splendid copy of Hogarth's works [an often republished furniture book], Bible Commentaries, two copies of Burns's works, nine volumes of Thackeray's works, 37 parts of the Imperial Family Bible, Vanity Fair Album [published by the British *Vanity Fair* magazine of 1868–1914, known for its full-page caricatures of personalities of the day], two beautiful copies of the Gospels of St. Luke and St. Mark, seven volumes of the National Gallery, a Martyrology of the Church of Christ, a Dictionary of Slang, 'The Bloudy Tenent of Persecution' [by seventeenth-century Puritan minister and founder of Rhode Island colony Roger Williams], Notes on Dancing [about ballet], The Christian Year (Keble), Moore's Irish Melodies [thought by some to be a bit risqué], Bunyan's Pilgrim's Progress, a book on the necessity of separation from the Church of England [Gourlay was a chapel-going Presbyterian], 'Records of the Church of Christ', 'Confessions of Faith', 'Felltham's Resolves', Manchester Corporation Engineering Records, two volumes of landscape illustrations of the Bible, tracts on liberty of conscience, Clarke's Marrow of Ecclesiastical History, and three volumes of the Universal Songster. There are some nice engravings.[11]

The board expected Gourlay's collection to fetch £40, presumably to be set against the £40,000 he had embezzled. Several possibilities are suggested by the company kept by the *Universal Songster* here: it could have been seen as a fine book and a bibliophile's prize, as 'safe' reading, as non-canonical literature, as representing a racier earlier time – or as all of these things. Perhaps Gourlay, as a Scot, regarded the Cruikshanks as fellow countrymen. Since he kept the books in his professional office, they may have been at least in part furniture books, assembled in order to display to co-workers, clients, and visitors his piety, modern culture, and self-conscious Britishness.

---

[10] Stephen Smith, 'The William Gourlay Embezzlement' http://www.cottontown. org/Health%20and%20Welfare/Pages/Law-and-Order.aspx.

[11] *Blackburn Standard*, 16 February 1884, p. 3.

In that regard, a further suggestion may be made, prompted by a newspaper article of 1890. The *Universal Songster* had come to be a quarry for the burgeoning folk song collecting movement. For example, the painter, antiquarian, and well-known folk song collector Frank Kidson contributed many articles on folk and popular songs to newspapers in the last decades of the nineteenth and early decades of the twentieth century.[12] In 1890 he executed one of his characteristic source-and-authenticity searches for words and music of a song, tracing the lineage of the music and words of a song called 'The King and the Countryman', which is found in the *Universal Songster*.[13] Kidson wrote that the song was popular around 1825–30 because it was often sung in the theatres at the time, and that similar versions appeared in other anthologies, but that all could be traced back to a black-letter ballad of 1640. Kidson, who generally argued that English song had begun to decline in the late eighteenth century with the rise of commercialized song, characteristically felt the 1640 version to be artistically superior on literary-critical grounds.

A few glimpses of the *Universal Songster* in late nineteenth- and early twentieth-century auction advertisements indicate that the book had also come to circulate in Scotland, probably for a number of reasons. It was a book of recognized antiquarian interest; it had Cruikshank illustrations; it could evoke a different world from that of urban and industrial modernity; it was entertaining in itself; and it had a section of Scots songs that were of interest in the context of the fabrication of a Romantic and post-Romantic Scotland. So the *Universal Songster* showed up in the 1895 auction of the library of a Mrs Henderson of Westbank House, Partick, Glasgow. She was likely a member, perhaps a widow, of the prominent Henderson family of marine engineers, shipbuilders, and shipping-line owners and operators. The Westbank books were decidedly Scottish in interest, including ballad and song collections, Burns and other Scots poets, Wilson's Border tales, Wilson's *Noctes Ambrosianae*, history and architecture of Glasgow, and *Proceedings of the Society of Antiquaries of Scotland* (of which John Henderson was a member). There were also standard histories of England, multiple volumes of prominent mid- to up-market periodicals, books on art and picturesque landscapes, Disraeli's novels, works of Rabelais, Montaigne's essays, modern British drama, 'Cruickshank's [*sic*] Universal Songster', 'and other well-known

---

12 Roy Palmer, 'Kidson's Collecting', *Folk Music Journal*, 5.2 (1986), 150–75.
13 *Leeds Mercury*, 10 May 1890, p. 1.

Authors in Literature' – 'Many of the Books are finely Bound and in good order, &c. &c.'[14]

A generation later, in 1916, on the other side of Scotland, a collection resembling the Scottish and literary parts of the Henderson sale, with more of the latter, and also including 'The Universal Songster, with Cruickshank's [sic] Illustrations', was auctioned over four nights in Aberdeen.[15] Again in Scotland, in 1924 the Conservative politician Sir John L. Baird, of Ury House, Aberdeenshire, auctioned books and other furnishings, presumably because he was setting off to become Governor-General of Australia. The books indicated strong Scottish as well as family interest. There were several volumes on Scottish clan tartans (a major example of the nineteenth-century invention of tradition). Baird's family, originally farmers from east of Glasgow, exploited local coal and ironstone resources to create a massive iron foundry at Gartsherrie, which by the 1840s was probably the largest producer of pig-iron in the world.[16] Characteristic of the way new industrial wealth felt impelled to re-identify as old landed wealth (and title), a Baird son acquired the Ury estate from its historic owners the Barclays (co-founders of Barclays Bank) in 1854, and promptly replaced the older house with a large mansion (now ruined) in the style of a Jacobean fortified house. Sir John may have wanted to affirm his status as laird and naturally invested in the new lore of clans and tartans – as Walter Scott, who was responsible for invention of the clan tartan, and others had done before. Predictably, then, the collection at new/old Ury House included a set of the Waverley novels and twelve volumes of the antiquarian Aberdeenshire-centred Spalding Club, as well as some standard sets of literary authors, and the *Universal Songster*, which sold for 27s.[17] Just before he left for Australia, Baird was created Viscount Stonehaven; the family had gone from iron-founders to nobility in three generations.

If the *Universal Songster*, one of Fairburn's largest productions, can be traced through and in relation to a century of British and imperial political, social, economic, and cultural change, one of Fairburn's humblest productions, apparently published ten or twenty years after the *Universal Songster*, discloses other uses of songs and print objects in this process of creating modernity. This was Fairburn's edition of *The*

---

[14] 'Choice Collection of Books', *Glasgow Herald*, 10 May 1895, p. 12.

[15] *Aberdeen Journal*, 21 February 1916, p. 2.

[16] Grace's Guide to British Industrial History https://www.gracesguide.co.uk/William_Baird_and_Co.

[17] 'Ury House Library Collection Sold at Stonehaven', *Dundee Courier*, 22 May 1924, p. 8.

Laughable Tale of the Farmer's Blunder.[18] It was published, undated and without a price, on cheap paper with blurry print from the Fairburn shop at No. 110, Minories, the address typically used for Fairburn's books for youngsters and certain kinds of prints, and the cover/title page declared that it was 'Sold by all Booksellers and Toy-shops in Town and Country' (*Figure 3*).

Figure 3. The Farmer's Blunder, Fairburn's Edition.

The only illustration, on the cover/title page, was a wood engraving of a kind of beehive known as a skep, formed of thick straw rope coiled into a rounded cone with a tuft atop. Rather than an illustration, this was more likely a symbol, with various possible meanings. It could symbolize diligent labour, orderly living, frugality, and cooperation, and thus could be used by organizations proclaiming these values, from worker's cooperatives and unions to clubs and institutions promoting 'sweetness' (honey, standing for sociability,

---

[18] *The Laughable Tale of the Farmer's Blunder*, Fairburn's Edition (London: J. Fairburn, 110, Minories; sold by all booksellers and toy-shops in town and country).

benevolence, social harmony) and 'light' (candle-wax, for education and enlightenment). In short, there could be a visual appeal to those with the kinds of social and political interests that much of Fairburn's print served. A related possibility is suggested by what serve as small printer's ornaments on the cover of the *Farmer's Blunder*: two sphinxes, two sphinx's heads on columns, and a satyr's head. These symbols point to Freemasonry, which would also account for the beehive.[19]

Certainly, Freemasons' songs were included as a category in the *Universal Songster*. Printers and booksellers were often found in Masonic lodge membership lists. Freemasons' Hall, headquarters of the Grand Lodge of England, was twenty minutes walk from Fairburn's Ludgate Broadway shop, and there were numerous lodges meeting at different venues near the Fairburns. As printers, the Fairburns would have relied on a wide range of jobbing printing, much of it occasional and ephemeral, for which Masons' lodges were likely customers. This was also the kind of work that George Cruikshank took on in order to fill gaps in his income. At this time, Freemasonry in England was emphasizing the usefulness and value of networking and trading with 'brethren', which was particularly important in the City of London but perhaps also for establishing provincial connections of the kind suggested by Russell's stock in Birmingham and Loraine's in Newcastle. The small fact that the *Farmer's Blunder* had no price on its cover, which was somewhat unusual for Fairburn, might indicate that the piece was a giveaway, sample, or donation, perhaps for a Masonic lodge dinner, where songs and readings of such matter would be part of the programme. Both politically and commercially, a Masonic connection would be useful for Fairburn.

Though Freemasonry as a movement at this time professed values that were broadly liberal, charitable, rationalist, loyalist, patriotic, and deistic, ideological discipline was elastic and individual lodges could differ significantly in religious and political engagements and commitments. In conservative loyalist circles, with their conspiracy theories and polemics, Freemasonry had come to be tainted with political disloyalty, religious scepticism and infidelity, immorality, and extreme commitment to 'innovation' – a kind of excessive and dangerous modernity, exemplified for many by the French

---

[19] See Albert Churchward, *The Arcana of Freemasonry* (London: George Allen and Unwin [1915]), chapters 9 and 10; also [John Entick], *The Free Masons Pocket Companion* (Glasgow: printed by Robert and Thomas Duncan, and sold at their shop, Pope's Head, Saltmarket, 1771).

Revolution, attributed to the influence of supposed Masonic organizations such as the 'Illuminati'. The Prince of Wales, at the time seen as a modernizer and sympathizer with reform, was Grand Master of the Grand Lodge of England from the mid-1790s, and even formed his own lodge along with certain cronies, but after he became Prince Regent in 1812 he turned to conservative and reactionary politicians for government and resigned as Grand Master in 1813. His estranged younger brother, the Duke of Sussex, known for his liberal and reformist sympathies, took his place. Furthermore, the City of London generally held a self-consciously independent perspective and tended to support the kinds of social, political, economic, patriotic, and imperialist commitments reflected in Fairburn's many publications. For example, the City sided with the Princess of Wales/Queen Caroline in her dispute with her husband the Prince Regent/George IV, especially during her trial for adultery during the crisis of 1820, which, many thought, brought Britain to the brink of revolution. Fairburn was prominent in publishing the numerous Hone–Cruikshank pamphlet collaborations that supported the queen in order to undermine the king and his government's increasingly reactionary and repressive policies, exemplified in the Peterloo Massacre of 1819, which sparked a paper war to which Fairburn contributed a substantial verse pamphlet, *The Field of Peterloo* (1819).

By the time Fairburn published *The Laughable Tale of the Farmer's Blunder* it had been around for the better part of a century. Sometimes titled *The Biters Bit; or, The Farmer's Blunder* ('A farmer once to London went'), it was printed in a range of media, from what seems to have been the first version in the *Gentleman's Magazine* in 1744, attributed to someone named Porter,[20] through street ballads, to anthologies of tales in prose and verse such as *The Agreeable Medley; or, Universal Entertainer* (1748) (*Figure 4*). There was also a different version of the same story with the same title ('A while but attend and a tale I'll relate').

In both versions, a farmer goes to London to pay his rent to the squire, who induces him to join a convivial party of gentry. Soon befuddled with drink and confused by genteel sociability, the farmer stands to deliver a speech, but as he sits down some of the party pull away his chair as a joke. As he falls, he drags the tablecloth and contents down, bespattering the ladies and gentlemen, to their dismay

---

[20] Emily Lorraine de Montluzin, 'Attributions of Authorship in the *Gentleman's Magazine*, 1741–45: A Supplement to the Union List', *ANQ: A Quarterly Journal of Short Articles, Notes and Reviews*, 24.3 (2011), 140–53.

and rage. They berate him and order him out, and he gladly leaves. In Fairburn's version the moral follows:

> This may teach rulers of a nation,
> Ne'er to place men above their station:
> And this may teach the wanton wit,
> That while he bites he may be bit.

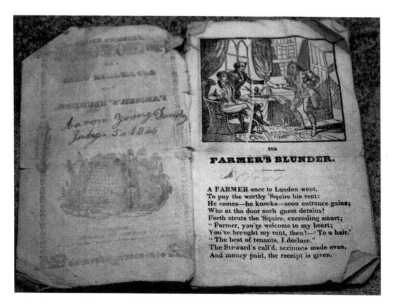

Figure 4. The Farmer's Blunder ('A farmer once to London went').

To fill out the pages, Fairburn's edition appends a sentimental poem entitled 'My Father' and 'An Alphabet for Beginners' comprising twenty-six practical proverbs, such as 'Out of debt out of danger'. *The Farmer's Blunder* sets town against country, urbane against rustic, artificial against authentic, and may be read to side with the latter, while hinting at the relation of social order and mutuality to national well-being and good governance.[21]

While not appearing as a traditional ballad, street ballad, or commercial new song, the verse tale published by Fairburn had already been adopted as a popular recitation piece at convivial adult gatherings, for school displays, and as a theatrical interlude. Through the nineteenth century it often appeared in programmes that included

---

[21] Gillian Williamson, *British Masculinity in the Gentleman's Magazine, 1731 to 1815* (London: Palgrave Macmillan, 2016), p. 92.

popular, commercial, and traditional songs, and various recitations in verse and prose. This was particularly the case from the 1850s with the rise of the Penny Readings movement. Notices of Penny Readings proliferate in the newspapers of the second half of the nineteenth century and indicate the ways in which they operated. *The Farmer's Blunder* often appears in these notices. Penny Readings were intentionally diverse programmes of recitations, songs, and other matter considered both entertaining and instructive, often and regularly mounted by local clergy, educators, and philanthropic organizations for a mixed, if not plebeian, audience. Admission was 1*d.*, apparently in order to control demand and probably on the view that what was free would not be valued. By and large, the Penny Readings seem to have been instigated, managed, and controlled by middle-class and clerical folk. Performers seem to have been largely amateurs early on, but were increasingly professionals as the movement grew in numbers but declined in cultural status.

By their heyday in the 1860s, the Penny Readings constituted an organized movement throughout the land and spread to the empire. They were part of the broader movement to displace customary and often carnivalesque plebeian entertainments, long associated by the propertied classes, clergy, and government with a mob culture of revel and riot, and more recently regarded as the seedbed of a distinctive plebeian culture and politics. Penny Readings were part of a culture that was meant to replace both the commercialized and the traditional popular culture of fun, just as the Religious Tract Society, the Society for the Diffusion of Useful Knowledge, the *Penny Magazine*, the *Penny Cyclopædia*, and similar print programmes were designed to replace the kinds of material provided by the likes of Fairburn in the burgeoning market for entertaining and political cheap print. Penny Readings continued to be commonplace throughout the second half of the century, but came to be considered by some to be outdated and vulgar, or corrupted by inclusion of unsuitable, and presumably more popular, material, as the performances became more commercialized.

This brief account of the social, cultural, commercial, and political lives of Fairburn's Editions of the *Universal Songster* and *The Farmer's Blunder* illustrates the principle underlying integrational linguistics, effective semiotics, and ethnomethodology, that meaning does not inhere in an object or practice – whether a multi-volume book or a pamphlet poem, a singing performance or a recitation, a sociable exchange or a solitary reading, a desultory read or a companionable anthology, an introduction to quotidian life or a reminder of good times out and about.[22] Rather, meaning is created by the user, practitioner, or audience, as a unique creative social action at a particular time and place – whether a commercial transaction, an act of composition, or process of production; a convivial gathering, a private reading, a moment of purchase, an act of collecting, part of an organized social programme, an encounter in a library; a collaboration in the life of an organization, a librarian's act of tagging a print object in a particular taxonomy, an instance of a scholar's application of knowledge, or of professionally recognized procedures of narration and practices of research reporting. Having sketched some of the different uses of these two Fairburn's Editions through a century – two centuries if we include my use of them here – it remains to set these two objects within the perspective of what we know about the extent and contents and possible uses of Fairburn's Editions as a print 'megatext' – a notional object created in and for the time and place of its production. 'Fairburn's Edition' was not only a brand, in the sense of a marketing device, a promise and invitation to the prospective purchaser and reader of familiar manner, matter, and utility. It was also a brand in the sense of marking and marking out a certain material, aesthetic, ideological, political, and cultural space.

Broadly, Fairburn's Editions and other prominent collections of cheap print at the time can be read as addressing the convergence of and contest between two plebeian cultures. One was a customary culture, imagined, expressed, and addressed for some generations in both oral and print discourse.[23] The other was a culture that was self-consciously modern and in important ways counter-customary.[24]

Elites were creating a literature imagining and promoting their modernity, from Romantic poetry, circulating library novels, expressive music, and memoirs, to modern, expert knowledge of the kind formalized, certified, professionalized, and commercialized in the

---

[22] Roy Harris, *The Language Myth* (London: Duckworth, 1981); Roy Harris, *After Epistemology* (Gamlingay: Authors OnLine, 2009); Alec McHoul, *Semiotic Investigations: Towards an Effective Semiotics* (Lincoln: University of Nebraska Press, 1996); Harold Garfinkel, *Studies in Ethnomethodology* (Englewood Cliffs: Prentice Hall, 1967).

[23] For example, Bob Bushaway, *By Rite: Custom, Ceremony and Community in England, 1700–1880* (London: Junction Books, 1982); E. P. Thompson, *The Making of the English Working Class* (London: Victor Gollancz, 1963); E. P. Thompson, *Customs in Common* (London: Merlin Press, 1991).

[24] Here I have adapted Anthony Giddens's structurationist sociology, as outlined in *The Consequences of Modernity* (Stanford: Stanford University Press, 1990); *Modernity and Self-identity: Self and Society in the Late Modern Age* (Cambridge: Polity Press, 1991); *The Transformation of Intimacy: Sexuality, Love and Eroticism in Modern Societies* (Cambridge: Polity Press, 1992).

disciplines of the humanities and sciences that are now enshrined in the academic-industrial complex. Such literature, arts, and sciences promoted new discourses of self-reflexive personal identity, or sovereign subjectivity; pure or disinterested social relations; intellectual and moral capital; and the consequent ability to negotiate accelerating and relentless change, enhanced relations of risk and trust, and new configurations and significations of space and time, and to transform historic abstract systems and proliferating new ones, from finance to law.

This form of modernity took two approaches to customary culture, whether practised by the common people or, in their interests, by elites: one was to extirpate it; the other was to museum-ize it as a necessarily if regrettably vanishing culture, be it in rural England, Highland Scotland, peasant Ireland, or the regions of empire, or even in the home (women and children). The massive financial, political, and cultural power of the elites could not effectively be resisted, let alone defeated, by practitioners of customs in common, who engaged in fashioning their own modernity from appropriated elements of elite culture, renovations of customary culture, and innovations of all kinds. They did so in their own interests, with the toleration, encouragement, and even participation of many of their betters, and assisted by their own intellectuals, artists, inventors, and entrepreneurs, exploiting the technologies and techniques of modernization and commercialization – as exemplified by Fairburn.

Fairburn's Editions, whether they bore that brand or not, seem designed to assist their audience in imagining, representing, and promoting a complex plebeian modernity in a wide variety of ways, implicitly and often explicitly resisting many aspects of elites' modernity and residual un-modernity. 'Old Corruption', for example, which was coming to stand for the entire un-modernized, unreformed edifice of state and church, of landed and financial interests, was comprehensively assailed in one of Fairburn's major successes, *The Black Book; or, Corruption Unmasked!* (1820, and augmented to 1829). This was a listing of state pensioners and beneficiaries of sinecures and ecclesiastical pluralism, with sarcastic commentary, by the reformist John Wade. Its revolutionary lineage was disclosed in the first version, published in 1819 as *The Black Book, hitherto Mis-named the Red Book*, which referred to a similar work with a similar purpose titled *Le Livre rouge*, published in several parts at Paris in 1790 during the early years of the French Revolution. In 1831, the *Black Book* was taken on by the firm of Effingham Wilson and augmented to boost the campaign for the Reform Bill of 1832. Wilson was a prominent free-speech advocate, promoter of new technologies, and publisher of leading political, economic, ecclesiastical, and social reformists and liberal Romantic writers in prose and verse. Fairburn's *Black Book* may be said, then, to connect French Revolutionary discourse of the 1790s with that of organized British middle- and lower-class reformism of the mid-nineteenth century. It may be said further, that Fairburn's Editions, considered as a megatext evolving over several crucial decades, provided a broad range of cheap materials for the creation by the target readership of a distinctive plebeian modernity.[25] The cultural, social, and political dimensions of this megatext can only briefly be indicated here.

There were, for example, republished and visually and materially modernized versions of classics from the generations-old repertoire of street literature – chapbooks embodying the historic plebeian lottery mentality of fatalism, opportunism, sociability, magic, and customs in common. These included dream and prophecy books, such as *The Instructing Gipsy* and *The Universal Fortune Teller*, accounts of shipwrecks and narrow escapes, criminal biographies, and accounts of oddities and marvels, such as the comet of 1811, the 'pig-faced lady', and the millenarian prophet Joanna Southcott's 'pregnancy'. Historically, many artisans and shopkeepers had lived in the same buildings they worked and traded in, but that was changing. Fairburn's Editions for this aspect of plebeian modernity included a cookery pamphlet, a modern *Frugal Housewife*, and a housekeeping manual, and a Valentine-writer and a letter-writer for personal and business use. There was a guide to the tax act. Both useful and entertaining for such citizens' private and business lives would be pamphlets exposing the tricks of tradesmen and swindlers. The modern culture of childhood and home education was served by a variety of books issued from the Minories shop, including an ABC, an introduction to useful modern knowledge, a natural history, fairy tales, and a historic religious anthology, Isaac Watts's *Divine Songs*, long circulated as a street literature chapbook.

Entertainments for the modern urban plebeian home were furnished by pamphlets on conjuring and card games, and jest-books and songsters, which would also be handy for sociability and which connected domestic and community life with public entertainers and entertainments, theatres, street culture, and shows. A contiguous body of print comprised pamphlet versions of burlesque and comic operas,

---

[25] Gary Kelly, 'Sixpenny State? Cheap Print and Cultural-Political Citizenship in the Onset of Modernity', *Lumen*, 26 (2017), 37–61 https://www.erudit.org/en/journals/lumen/2017-v36-lumen02702/1037853ar/.

and pamphlet tales mainly gothic, sentimental, and titillating, such as *Memoirs of a Modern Rake*, *Love Tales for Young Ladies*, *The Horrible Revenge*, *Allan the Freebooter*, and *Vincent and Arabella; or, The Reward of Virtue*. Alongside these versions of modern literature were drastically abbreviated novels old and new, prose and verse, such as Defoe's *Moll Flanders*, Scott's *St Ronan's Well*, and a novelized pamphlet version of Byron's *Don Juan*. These could be supplemented by engraved portraits of celebrity actors, suitable for home ornamentation with tinsel, and mezzotints of iconic sentimentalized images, such as allegories of the four main continents, mariners, and life events such as courtship and marriage. These were all potentially participatory ways of both living out and reflecting on a cultural modernity that subsumed and developed a popular print tradition.

Culturally continuous with cheap print addressing personal, domestic, and sociable aspects of plebeian modernity was print promoting a plebeian political and commercial modernity. Long popular cheap print concerning crime and criminals was continued by Fairburn, perhaps focusing more on the crimes and misconduct of the great, from royalty through nobility to the complacent bourgeoisie, especially titillating trials for 'crim. con.' (adultery), and often emphasizing plebeian victims of the elites and the lack of difference between the elites and the common people in these respects.

The outstanding examples of reformist politics through scandal literature in Fairburn's repertoire were the numerous pamphlets written by William Hone and illustrated by George Cruikshank during the Queen Caroline affair, but there were many others, and numerous graphic satires by the Cruikshank brothers and others on the government, monarchy, established church, and the establishment generally, along with verse satires by a 'Peter Pindar' (not the original, John Wolcot). There was a one-off burlesque of the government publication the *Gazette Extraordinary* called *The Quizzical Gazette Extraordinary* (1819), full of political, social, ethnic, anticlerical, and other kinds of satire, somewhat in the style of today's *Private Eye*. There were *Trials* of sensational murderers, illustrating the operation of the criminal justice system, and of celebrated dissidents and reformists, such as the Nore naval mutineers, the Cato Street conspirators, Sir Francis Burdett, Colonel Despard, and, of course, Queen Caroline, illustrating the repressive operation of the state apparatus. Fairburn also engaged in the kind of political education exemplified by writers such as Paine and Cobbett, with texts of reformist touchstones such as the Magna Charta and George Washington's will, and state documents such as the Treaty of Amiens.

Unlike many (or most) cheap print specialists, Fairburn eschewed popular religious and neo-puritan literature, though he did co-publish an edition of Bishop William Paley's *Moral and Political Philosophy*, which reformists read as deistic. National affairs included accounts of the assassination of prime minister Spencer Perceval, naval battles such as Copenhagen and Trafalgar, and a satirical verse account of Peterloo. Fairburn's maps included London and the new docks, as well as the Peninsular War and the *Scene of Operations in France* (1814). A less successful venture, one perhaps appealing to reformist Bonapartism, was a multi-volume life of Napoleon in numbers, which had to be handed off to another publisher before completion. At the other extreme were Fairburn's editions of tiny pocket-watch papers, such as a calendar and a map of the Peninsular War.

I conclude that Fairburn's Editions can be related to a broad and evolving, reformist and plebeian, urban and commercialized, popular culture of the early nineteenth century. This culture, I would argue, was in dynamic and conflicting relationship with the culture of the elites in a larger and continuing struggle to create and assert a modernity in their own image, imagination, and interests – a struggle that continues.

Children and Cheap Print in Europe: Towards a Transnational Account, 1700–1900

Elisa Marazzi

It is widely accepted that children have long been part of the audience for street literature. Nevertheless, their role in the cheap print trade remains obscure. As far as Britain is concerned, chapbooks specifically aimed at children have been the subject of different studies from the late 1960s onwards.[1] These studies show that, before the publishers of the early nineteenth century revamped street literature in order to lure an emerging juvenile audience with children's chapbooks, cheap print was already being enjoyed by younger audiences, sometimes as listeners.[2] The decision to issue children's chapbooks has therefore been interpreted as a consequence of the appreciation that young audiences showed for cheap print. The underlying idea is that popular literature satisfied children's need for entertainment better than the moral and educational tracts otherwise available to them.[3] One example of this is that of Elisabeth Wrather, who as a little girl in the

---

[1] See M. O. Grenby, 'Before Children's Literature: Children, Chapbooks and Popular Culture in Early Modern Britain', in *Popular Children's Literature in Britain*, ed. Julia Briggs, Dennis Butts, and M. O. Grenby (Farnham and Burlington, VT: Ashgate, 2008), pp. 25–46. For more recent research, see Jonathan Cooper, 'The Development of the Children's Chapbooks in London', in *Street Literature of the Long Nineteenth Century: Producers, Sellers, Consumers*, ed. David Atkinson and Steve Roud (Newcastle upon Tyne: Cambridge Scholars Publishing, 2017), pp. 217–37; Valentina Bold, 'Children's Chapbook Literature in the Nineteenth Century', in *The Land of Story-Books: Scottish Children's Literature in the Long Nineteenth Century*, ed. Sarah Dunnigan and Shu-Fang Lai (Glasgow: Scottish Literature International, 2019), pp. 42–61.

[2] M. O. Grenby, 'Chapbooks, Children, and Children's Literature', *The Library*, 7th ser., 8 (2007), 277–303; Grenby, 'Before Children's Literature' (which includes a discussion of definitions of chapbooks and chapbooks for children, pp. 27–33); Bold, 'Children's Chapbook Literature in the Nineteenth Century', p. 44.

[3] This idea is developed throughout Victor Neuburg's works on literacy and cheap print: Victor E. Neuburg, *The Penny Histories: A Study of Chapbooks for Young Readers over Two Centuries* (London: Oxford University Press, 1968); Victor E. Neuburg, *Popular Education in 18th Century England* (London: Woburn Press, 1971), esp. chapters 4–5; Victor E. Neuburg, *Popular Literature: A History and Guide, from the Beginning of Printing to the Year 1897* (Harmondsworth: Penguin, 1977).

1770s hid her treasure, a collection of seven chapbooks, in the chimney of her parents' house.[4]

Chapbooks continued to represent a reading option for children, especially those of limited means, *after* what is referred to as 'the birth of children's literature'.[5] This might have been very specific to England, or to Britain and Ireland,[6] but similar forms of street literature were also present across Europe.[7] Nonetheless, a trans-European study of cheap print for children is still lacking. The omission is regrettable because it is well known that the so-called *bibliothèque bleue*, cheap booklets printed first in Troyes and then in many other French provincial cities, included a wealth of educational texts, sometimes aimed directly at schoolchildren. Other kinds of cheap print were widespread across Europe; among the most interesting examples are almanacs for children and illustrated broadsides, the latter resembling modern comics.

The research in progress described here is intended to collect data on European cheap print explicitly aimed at children, and, in parallel, to gather evidence of children consuming cheap print that was not specifically addressed to them.[8] I shall therefore provide examples of

---

[4] Cooper, 'Development of the Children's Chapbooks in London', p. 217.

[5] Grenby, 'Chapbooks, Children, and Children's Literature'; Grenby, 'Before Children's Literature'.

[6] Although Scottish chapbooks were produced on a large scale, only recently has attention been paid to children as readers of chapbooks in Scotland. See Kirsteen Connor, 'Youth's Poison?: The Creation and Evolution of Children's Chapbooks in Scotland, 1800–1870' (unpublished MPhil thesis, University of Glasgow, 2010) http://theses.gla.ac.uk/1938. For Ireland, see Niall Ó Ciosáin, *Print and Popular Culture in Ireland, 1750–1850* (London: Palgrave Macmillan, 1997).

[7] The first transnational account was provided by Roger Chartier, 'Letture e lettori "popolari" dal Rinascimento al Settecento', in *Storia della lettura nel mondo occidentale* (Roma and Bari: Giuseppe Laterza & Figli, 1995), pp. 317–35 [English translation: 'Reading Matter and "Popular" Reading from the Renaissance to the Seventeenth Century', in *A History of Reading in the West*, ed. Guglielmo Cavallo and Roger Chartier (Cambridge: Polity Press, 1999), pp. 269–83]; followed by research on specific genres such as Hans-Jürgen Lüsebrink et al. (eds), *Les lectures du peuple en Europe et dans les Amériques (XVIIe–XXe siècle)* (Bruxelles: Complexe, 2002). More recently, the transnationality of cheap print has been the object of a new wave of studies, exemplified by David Atkinson and Steve Roud (eds), *Cheap Print and the People: European Perspectives on Popular Literature* (Newcastle upon Tyne: Cambridge Scholars Publishing, 2019); and Matthew Grenby, Elisa Marazzi, and Jeroen Salman (eds), *The European Dimension of Popular Print Culture: A Comparative Approach*, special issue of *Quaerendo* (forthcoming, 2021).

[8] The Children and Transnational Popular Print (1700–1900) (CaTPoP) project is funded by the EU-H2020 MSCA scheme grant agreement no. 838161. Prior to this, Matthew Grenby and I circulated a survey among European specialists in either

types of popular print that have been identified as specifically printed for children or read by them. This will be followed by a discussion of the different sources that allow us to assess the relevance of juvenile audiences to the history of cheap print.

Cheap print and children, defining the undefinable

Anyone acquainted with book history will know how problematic defining 'cheap print' is. The adjective 'popular' has also often been used to refer to what is at the core of my interest, but that, too, is a slippery adjective.[9] 'Popular culture' has become an historiographical category in the wake of Peter Burke's foundational work,[10] which provides an important acknowledgment that defining some cultural expressions as 'popular' does not mean that they were confined to the peasants or working classes at all.[11] The French adjective *populaire*, which implies low status, has ignited a particularly inflamed debate in France where the expression *culture populaire*, as in the title of Robert Mandrou's pioneering study of the *bibliothèque bleue*,[12] has been called into question for not reflecting the actual nature of the bibliographical corpus, which drew on a culture that was shared across different social classes until at least the sixteenth century. Moreover, it is now widely accepted that an interest in cheap print was shared by the whole of early modern society, in spite of contemporary (mainly post-seventeenth-century) judgements of value.[13]

---

popular print or children's literature and discussed the results at a workshop on Popular Children's Literature in Europe (1450–1900) held at the University of Milan in March 2018 and co-funded by the research network European Dimensions of Popular Printed Culture (EDPOP). I am grateful to all the participants for the fruitful discussions that have stimulated some of the reflections included in this article. In particular, I would like to thank Laura Carnelos and Emmanuelle Chapron for making me aware of some sources referenced in this paper.

[9] M. O. Grenby, 'Introduction', in *Popular Children's Literature in Britain*, ed. Julia Briggs, Dennis Butts, and M. O. Grenby (Farnham and Burlington, VT: Ashgate, 2008), pp. 1–20 (p. 1).

[10] Peter Burke, *Popular Culture in Early Modern Europe* (London: Temple Smith, 1978).

[11] For a discussion of the debate around this, see Jonathan Barry, 'Literacy and Literature in Popular Culture: Reading and Writing in Historical Perspective', in *Popular Culture in England, c.1500–1850*, ed. Tim Harris (Basingstoke: Macmillan, 1995), pp. 69–94. See also Steve Roud and David Atkinson, 'Introduction', in *Street Literature of the Long Nineteenth Century: Producers, Sellers, Consumers*, ed. David Atkinson and Steve Roud (Newcastle upon Tyne: Cambridge Scholars Publishing, 2017), pp. 1–6 (p. 4).

[12] Robert Mandrou, *De la culture populaire aux 17e et 18e siècles: La bibliothèque bleue de Troyes* (Paris : Stock, 1964).

[13] Roger Chartier 'Culture as Appropriation: Popular Cultural Uses in Early Modern France', in *Understanding Popular Culture: Europe from the Middle Ages to the Nineteenth*

Although such debates are far from over, focusing on materiality can allow us to overcome the historiographical conundrum. One could object that the adjective 'cheap' concerns the economic value, or, more trivially, the price, of a product, not its materiality. Indeed, it can be difficult to determine prices for these kinds of publications, although it is widely believed that chapbooks could be sold for 1*d.* or less.[14] In some cases prices are noted down in ledgers or included in book catalogues, but such documents are hard to find, especially for minor publishers. Consequently, in this sub-field of book history it is unlikely that prices can be compared across Europe.[15] There is, however, a shared knowledge among specialists on how to identify printed products that were cheaply produced, and consequently cheaply sold, based on production and dissemination.[16] So it is possible to take into account the various printed items that are recognized as having been cheaply published and widely circulated: chapbooks, under their different national descriptions (*bibliothèque bleue*, *pliegos sueltos*);[17] illustrated broadsides, in their transnational varieties (*aleluyas*, penny-prints, *imagerie d'Épinal*, *Bilderbogen*, *stampe popolari*);[18] ballads; songs; almanacs and calendars; books of secrets; religious tracts; catechisms; ABCs; primers; and so on.[19]

Century, ed. Steven L. Kaplan (Berlin and New York: Mouton, 1984), pp. 229–53. The debate is summarized by Niall Ó Ciosáin, 'Bibliothèque Bleue, Verte Erin: Some Aspects of Popular Printed Literature in France and Ireland in the 18th and 19th Centuries', *Revue LISA/LISA e-journal*, 3.1 (2005) https://doi.org/10.4000/lisa.2519.

[14] Although children's chapbooks could cost 6*d.* or sometimes even more (Grenby, 'Chapbooks, Children, and Children's Literature', p. 278).

[15] The Evidence-Based Reconstruction of the Economic and Juridical Framework of the European Book Market (EMoBookTrade) project http://emobooktrade.unimi.it/ led by Angela Nuovo will undoubtedly provide new data and a tested methodology, but cheap print still remains elusive.

[16] Besides the works previously published by the editors of this volume, who give thorough definitions of the field in their introductory articles, useful accounts are provided by Laura Carnelos, 'Popular Print under the Press: Strategies, Practices and Materials', and Jeroen Salman, 'The Dissemination of European Popular Print: Exploring Comparative Approaches', in *The European Dimension of Popular Print Culture: A Comparative Approach*, ed. Matthew Grenby, Elisa Marazzi, and Jeroen Salman, special issue of *Quaerendo* (forthcoming, 2021).

[17] A preliminary typology of different European varieties of widely circulated print is provided by Chartier, 'Letture e lettori "popolari" dal Rinascimento al Settecento'.

[18] It is important to note that in different languages the terms used differ between what such publications were actually called when they were in circulation (e.g. *Bilderbogen*), and what collectors or scholars have later called them (e.g. *imagerie d'Épinal*, or just 'Epinals' in English). In France the label *imagerie populaire* was printed on the sheets, whereas in Italy *stampe popolari* is a later term. Illustrated single sheets printed across Europe are briefly catalogued in Juan Gomis and Jereon Salman, 'Tall

What is the current project searching for within this corpus? The aim is to gather evidence about items that were intentionally targeted at children, and about those that were in different ways handled, looked at, read, listened to, or sometimes just overheard by children. This implies spending some words on a second rather undefinable concept, that of childhood. It is not possible here to give an account of the historiographical and pedagogical debate that has followed Philippe Ariès's work on the evolution of adult attitudes to children as a result of social and cultural changes during the early modern period.[20] It is now widely recognized that the eighteenth century was a watershed, when the earlier stages of life came to be perceived as a phase during which individuals needed to be disciplined and instructed. At the same time, it is increasingly accepted that children have probably always read, even before books started to be offered to them by educators and publishers.[21] Young people must therefore have shared their reading materials with adults, and the simplest and most attractive reading materials that the early modern world could offer them lay in the fictional narratives published in chapbooks and cognate cheap publications across Europe.[22] It can be objected that children needed to be literate in order to do so, which reflects their social status as well as many other variables that could differ from one region to another. Nonetheless, cheap print is also known to have circulated widely by oral means: for instance, through collective

---

Tales for a Mass Audience: Dutch Penny Prints and Spanish Aleluyas in Comparative Perspective', in *The European Dimension of Popular Print Culture: A Comparative Approach*, ed. Matthew Grenby, Elisa Marazzi, and Jeroen Salman, special issue of *Quaerendo* (forthcoming, 2021).

[19] It is not possible to cite here the wealth of studies published on such topics in recent decades, but extremely valuable for their comparative approach are Atkinson and Roud (eds), *Cheap Print and the People*, and Massimo Rospocher, Jeroen Salman, and Hannu Salmi (eds), *Crossing Borders, Crossing Cultures: Popular Print in Europe (1450–1900)* (Berlin and Boston: De Gruyter Oldenbourg, 2019).

[20] Philippe Ariès, *Centuries of Childhood: A Social History of Family Life* (London: J. Cape, 1973 [Paris: Plon, 1960]).

[21] Seth Lerer, *Children's Literature: A Reader's History, from Aesop to Harry Potter* (Chicago and London: University of Chicago Press, 2008), p. 1; Grenby, 'Before Children's Literature', p. 25.

[22] See, for example, Francesco Montorsi, '"Un fatras de livres a quoy l'enfance s'amuse": Lectures de jeunesse et romans de chevalerie au XVIe siècle', *Camenulae*, no. 4 (février 2010) https://lettres.sorbonne-universite.fr/sites/default/files/media/2020-06/montorsi.pdf; Marina Roggero, 'Des enfants et des livres: Remarques sur des souvenirs d'enfance du monde anglo-saxon', *Études de lettres*, 1–2 (2016) https://doi.org/10.4000/edl.878.

readings or performances by street-sellers and artists.[23] It is likely, therefore, that non-literate and pre-literate individuals, including children, were very much acquainted with the materials of cheap print.

In consequence, historians are largely agreed that the development of children's literature can be traced back to the eighteenth century, although this observation is not globally valid and entails a wealth of specificities.[24] Once pedagogues became keen on disciplining the behaviour of individuals from the early stages of their lives specific books began to be targeted at young readers. In parallel, awareness grew among printers and authors that the young could represent a new, profitable audience.[25] Fostered by publishers for commercial reasons, children's literature was thenceforth perceived as a tool in the hands of educators and parents to keep children off the streets.

This process also included the production of chapbooks *for* children. The relationship between cheap print and children's literature has been widely discussed, resulting sometimes in totally opposed arguments – from the death of chapbooks to the need for educational works to include a pinch of popular culture in order to make them more attractive.[26] As research advances, it seems more likely that, in Grenby's words, 'the rational and moral children's literature of the later eighteenth century actually fostered the chapbook, at least in this new, nineteenth-century, specially-for-children form, rather than contributing to its demise'.[27] This might be true for Britain, although (as we will see) different kinds of chapbooks that were not specifically aimed at an audience of children continued to proliferate. In the rest of the Europe, however, there is no evidence (thus far) of anything comparable. The market for children's books

---

[23] For an account of oral encounters with literature, especially romances, in early modern Italy, see Marina Roggero, *Le carte piene di sogni* (Bologna: il Mulino, 2006), pp. 121–208.

[24] The timing of the implementation of mass education, for example, had an effect on the earlier or later development of juvenile audiences in some areas of western Europe. See Laura Carnelos and Elisa Marazzi, 'Children and Cheap Print from a Transnational Perspective (1500–1900)', in *The European Dimension of Popular Print Culture: A Comparative Approach*, ed. Matthew Grenby, Elisa Marazzi, and Jeroen Salman, special issue of *Quaerendo* (forthcoming, 2021).

[25] Brian Alderson and Felix De Marez Oyens, *Be Merry and Wise: Origins of Children's Book Publishing in England* (New Castle, DE: Oak Knoll Press; London: British Library, 2006), pp. xi–xii. Similar patterns are traced for the Netherlands by Jeroen Salman, 'Children's Books as a Commodity: The Rise of a New Literary Subsystem in the Eighteenth-Century Dutch Republic', *Poetics*, 28 (2001), pp. 399–421.

[26] See Grenby, 'Chapbooks, Children, and Children's Literature'.

[27] Grenby, 'Chapbooks, Children, and Children's Literature', p. 303.

was often limited, at least in the eighteenth century, to the more affluent sections of society. The majority of children, on the other hand, were likely to have been acquainted with the cheaply printed products that were sold, read, sung, and retold in the streets.

The boundaries of the juvenile audience can be very blurred, with upper-class children reading predominantly, though not exclusively, instructional and educational works from a young age, and lower-class children sticking to fictional and often coarse publications, potentially for their whole lives. Moreover, the conventional age ranges for childhood, adolescence, adulthood, and so forth are in constant evolution. It is therefore not possible to select a particular age range as defining juvenile readers. Instead, juvenile readership will be treated here in a pragmatic way and will also include the 'marriageable youth' towards which a wealth of cheaply printed products were directed.

Establishing the corpus

When attempting to infer from their contents, or even from their paratexts, which cheaply printed products might have been enjoyed by children, pitfalls are almost unavoidable.[28] Reading is a volatile practice, a 'mystery', as Robert Darnton puts it, and 'our relation to [. . .] texts cannot be the same as that of readers in the past'.[29] Moreover, historians have stressed how the intended audience of a work or collection hardly corresponds to its actual audience.

Nevertheless, it is tempting to point to a couple of early prints that, to the modern reader, appear to have been conceived with a young audience in mind. One is an eighteenth-century piece called *The Parents Pious Gift; or, A Choice Present for Children*, which takes the form of a dialogue between a religious father and an extravagant son, 'containing a dispute about bad company, or evil communication, pride, drunkenness, riotous living, and all the vanities of a vicious course of life'.[30] With a happy ending in which the son takes control of himself and rejects his bad habits, it was meant to present 'an

---

[28] For example, Grenby, 'Chapbooks, Children, and Children's Literature', p. 282, observes that Margaret Spufford was prone to deducing the readership of chapbooks from their contents.
[29] Robert Darnton, 'First Steps Towards a History of Reading', *Australian Journal of French Studies*, 51 (2014), 152–77 (p. 154). Darnton's seminal essay was first published in *Australian Journal of French Studies*, 23 (1986), 5–30; reprinted in Robert Darnton, *The Kiss of Lamourette: Reflections in Cultural History* (New York: W. W. Norton, 1990), pp. 154–87.
[30] *The Parents Pious Gift; or, A Choice Present for Children* (printed in the year 1704) [ESTC T55106] (subtitle text from a later printing).

excellent pattern for all young persons to set before them in these present sinfull times'. The second example is an early seventeenth-century ballad titled *A Table of Good Nurture*, 'wherin is contained a schoole-masters admonition to his schollers to learne good manners: the father to his children to learne vertue: and the hous-houlder to his seruants to learne godlinesse'.[31] Also found in early modern ballads is the topos of the mother on her deathbed providing her children with advice for their future lives.[32] Although the warnings were applicable to the whole of society, it is not unlikely that juvenile audiences might have been in the writer's mind.

In the same direction, texts instructing young women and men about the joys and sorrows of marriage occur frequently in eighteenth- and early nineteenth-century printed collections of popular songs. These songs seem addressed to young people, offering them an educational moral regarding their future steps in life, warning them, for example, not to break their vows, sometimes by means of gruesome stories, as in *The Perjur'd Maid Who Foreswore Herself for Riches*.[33] This kind of instruction was not limited to songs and can be found in chapbooks like *Mother Bunch's Closet Newly Broke Open*, in print since the late seventeenth century, which contained 'rare secrets of art & nature, tried and experienced by learned philosophers, and recommended to all ingenious young men and maids, teaching them, in a natural way, how to get good wives and husbands'.[34] This kind of text was so common that it was parodied in a misogynistic chapbook called *John Thompson's Man; or, A Short Survey of the Difficulties and Disturbances that May Attend a Married Life*.[35] Unsurprisingly, advice on how to behave in life, and in marriage, is found in literature for young adults across the centuries.

Another example from the British tradition of street literature can be drawn from the so-called gallows literature, which, in general, has little to do with children.[36] Nevertheless, the educational interest for

[31] *A Table of Good Nurture* (printed at London, for H. G.) [ESTC R215850].

[32] For example, *A Hundred Godly Lessons* (printed for F. Coles, T. Vere, J. Wright, and J. Clarke) [ESTC R178307].

[33] *The Perjur'd Maid Who Foreswore Herself for Riches* [. . .] *to which are added, Willy's Lovely Vocie; O Sweet Sleep; Sweet and Smart* (Glasgow: printed by J. & M. Robertson, 1800) [ESTC T123740].

[34] *Mother Bunch's Closet Newly Broke Open* (printed and sold in Aldermary Churchyard, London) [ESTC T67116].

[35] *John Thompson's Man; or, A Short Survey of the Difficulties and Disturbances that May Attend a Married Life* (licensed and enter'd according to order) [ESTC T27872].

[36] See Hans-Jürgen Lüsebrink, 'La letteratura del patibolo: Continuità e transformazioni tra '600 e '800', *Quaderni Storici*, 49 (1982), 285–301; also Una

an audience that included children is apparent in a gallows story like that of John Harris, a young man executed for murdering his father, mother, and maidservant, and robbing and setting fire to the house, which includes a 'dying exhortation to all young people'.[37] Nevertheless, we cannot be sure that children took an interest in publications like these, and we cannot take them as evidence that early modern writers of street literature specifically intended to address children. They merely confirm the general assumption that cheap print was meant for an audience that comprised people with a 'rudimentary literacy', including children.[38]

Conversely, there is evidence that chapbooks *for* children were widely published in Britain in the first decades of the nineteenth century. Bibliographies and studies have been devoted to those issued in Banbury and York,[39] but printers in Derby, Gainsborough, Wellington, Alnwick, Edinburgh, and Glasgow also put much effort in printing chapbooks for children. For a long time publishers in London were left out of this picture until the recent work by Jonathan Cooper who traces chapbooks for children printed in the capital from 1795, although with the warning that before 1800 there were perhaps fewer than ten titles available in London.[40]

Earlier items printed in Britain and Ireland are likely to emerge. The Cotsen Children's Library holds a book of riddles published in Dublin in 1785, 'adorned with 59 beautiful cuts' (dab-coloured in the exemplar viewed), and explicitly intended 'for the entertainment of youth'.[41] A similar chronology can be traced for Scotland, as shown by Kirsteen Connor who has tracked down a few titles available in the very late 1790s, although (unlike the collections printed in York and Banbury) it is not always possible to ascertain from Scottish examples

---

McIlvenna, Siv Gøril Brandtzæg, and Juan Gomis, 'Singing the News of Punishment: The Execution Ballad in Europe, 1550–1900', in *The European Dimension of Popular Print Culture: A Comparative Approach*, ed. Matthew Grenby, Elisa Marazzi, and Jeroen Salman, special issue of *Quaerendo* (forthcoming, 2021).

[37] *A Dreadful Warning to Disobedient Children* (licensed and entered, 1800)[ESTC T165734].

[38] Grenby, 'Before Children's Literature', p. 33. Grenby's argument concerning chapbooks can easily be extended to cheap print at large.

[39] Roger Davis, *Kendrew of York and his Chapbooks for Children* (Collingham: Elmete Press, 1988); Leo John De Freitas, *The Banbury Chapbooks* (Banbury: Banbury Historical Society, 2014).

[40] Cooper, 'Development of the Children's Chapbooks in London', p. 222.

[41] *The Most Diverting Riddle Book* [...] (Dublin: B. Cocoran, 1785) [Princeton, NJ, Cotsen Children's Library, Eng 18 26395].

whether a chapbook was specifically meant for children.[42] Some publishers neither specialized in the juvenile market nor issued dedicated collections, but advertised different kinds of popular printed products, including educational items, which showed an interest in the new juvenile audience.

This pattern seems also to have been followed south of the border, where the Angus firm in Newcastle issued a considerable number of narrative chapbooks c.1800–10. They included romances, folktales, fairy tales, and jests from the traditional chapbook repertoire. Some of their imprints include text advertising the firm's premises, 'where is always kept on sale a choice and extensive assortment of histories, songs, children's story books, school books, &c. &c.' Although not specifically directed at children, some of their chapbooks do make mention on the title page of either a juvenile audience or an educational intent. *The Merry and Entertaining Jokes of George Buchanan*, for instance, were offered 'for the entertainment of youth'.[43] The principle of combining instruction and delight emerges from the rhyming title page of *The History of Valentine and Orson*:

> Reader, you'll find this little book contains,
> Enough to answer thy Expence and Pains;
> And if with Caution thou wilt read it through,
> 'Twill both instruct thee, and delight thee too.[44]

It is well established that Newcastle chapbooks were also sold north of the border.[45] Research on how chapbook texts and woodcuts migrated across Britain and Ireland would require extraordinary effort but could shed further light on the patterns of cheap print. For instance, some of the Newcastle chapbooks have a title-page woodcut depicting what looks like a family group of three singers, two adults and a child, offering for sale a broadside or chapbook, and a very similar (not identical) title-page image is found with chapbooks published by the Glasgow firm of J. and M. Robertson.[46]

---

[42] Connor, 'Youth's Poison?'.

[43] *The Merry and Entertaining Jokes of George Buchanan* [. . .] Number I (Newcastle: printed by M. Angus and Son) [ESTC T39265] (includes Numbers II and III).

[44] *The History of Valentine and Orson* (Newcastle: printed by M. Angus & Son, in the Side; where is always kept on sale a choice and extensive assortment of histories, songs, children's story books, school books, &c. &c.) [ESTC T36563].

[45] John Feather, *The Provincial Book Trade in Eighteenth-Century England* (Cambridge: Cambridge University Press, 1985), p. 107.

[46] Compare, for example, *A Garland of New Songs, containing 1. Abraham Newland; 2. Crazy Jane; 3. The Ghost of Crazy Jane; 4. The Adventurous Sailor; 5. The Soldier's Cloak*

Nonetheless, these chapbooks circulating in northern England and Scotland remain hybrids, although they winked at children by means of the paratextual elements mentioned above. Was investing fully in a juvenile audience a less profitable choice in this area, or at this time? At this stage it is impossible to say, but these hybrids not only demonstrate the capacity of cheap print for evolution and adaptation, but show this process in the making.[47]

In search of new audiences?

Recent analyses have highlighted how the corpus of cheap print was broadly the same across different areas of western Europe, stressing the transnationality of some narratives (one of the possible examples is the aforementioned *Valentine and Orson*, which is known to refer to the French tradition).[48] A study of how transnational was the progressive adaptation of cheap print to children still needs to be undertaken and is one of the aims of the research in progress. Is it possible to trace a similar tendency in the French chapbooks? This is difficult to argue at present, but previous scholarship has shown that popular books for educational purposes represented a part of the *bibliothèque bleue*. In Troyes, the 1789 inventory of the Garnier family, printers of French chapbooks, shows that about 5 per cent of their production consisted of ABCs, primers, conduct books, and arithmetic, and 12.7 per cent comprised religious education, partly for children.[49] These are the only statistics available so far, but other relevant data are likely to be found in the catalogue of the *veuve* (widow) Oudot, in whose Paris shop chapbooks produced in the provinces were sold; dating from *c*.1720, this was the first catalogue devoted to didactic publications.[50]

([colophon] Angus, printer) [London, British Library, 11606.aa.23.(14.)], and *The Crafty Miller; or, The Mistaken Batchelor; to which are added, Farewel to Spring; Thundering Roaring Guns; Beautiful Nancy; A Favourite Hunting Song* (Glasgow: printed by J. & M. Robertson, Saltmarket, 1802) [London, British Library, 11606.aa.23.(95.)]. On Robertson's publications for children, see Connor, 'Youth's Poison?', pp. 60–68.

[47] Grenby, 'Introduction', p. 19.

[48] Rita Schlusemann and Krystyna Wierzbicka-Trwoga, 'Narrative Fiction in Early Modern Europe: A Comparative Study of Genre Classifications' in *The European Dimension of Popular Print Culture: A Comparative Approach*, ed. Matthew Grenby, Elisa Marazzi, and Jeroen Salman, special issue of *Quaerendo* (forthcoming, 2021).

[49] Henri-Jean Martin, 'Culture écrite et culture orale: Culture savante et culture populaire dans la France d'Ancien Régime', *Journal des savants*, 3 (1975), 225–82.

[50] I owe this information to Emmanuelle Chapron, whom I also thank for the previous reference and for fruitful discussions on this topic.

Indeed, in many of the countries involved in the project children came into contact with cheap print through booklets conceived for use in school or informal education.[51] The main tools used for learning to read in the romance-language countries are extraordinarily similar. The *cartilla* in Spain, *croisette* in France, and *salterio* or *salteriolo* in Italy consisted of a book of prayers/catechism, preceded by the alphabet, preceded by the sign of the cross. These have been studied and discussed by historians across Europe,[52] but their production and distribution through the traditional channels of cheap print need to be further analysed.

In Protestant countries, the so-called *hanebok* ('rooster primer'), an ABC fronted by a woodcut depicting a rooster, was the standard means for learning the alphabet (there are also occasional Catholic examples of such books).[53] How and why did this tradition develop in areas that shared the same linguistic and/or confessional roots? Was the rooster a popular symbol, or a sort of commercial ploy, that enabled illiterate people immediately to recognize an ABC book when they met with a pedlar? Another fascinating aspect of the history of cheap print is the reuse and copying of woodcuts, which can provide further knowledge on transnational contacts in the early modern world.[54]

If the religious implications of what we can loosely describe as catechism primers are self-evident, religious education was also pursued in England by means of tracts, which were supposed to keep people away from less elevated reading, mainly in the form of chapbooks.[55] Surprisingly, tracts published from the late eighteenth century in the wake of the Evangelical movement also circulated in

---

[51] Cf. Carnelos and Marazzi, 'Children and Cheap Print from a Transnational Perspective'.

[52] For a transnational account, Carnelos and Marazzi, 'Children and Cheap Print from a Transnational Perspective'. Recently, a dedicated research group has focused on the trans-European history of catechism primers, leading to the publication of B. Juska-Bacher, W. Sroka, and T. Laine (eds), *Catechism Primers in Europe* (forthcoming). For Spain, see also Antonio Castillo Gómez, 'Apprendere a leggere e a scrivere nella Spagna della prima età moderna', in *Maestri e pratiche educative dalla Riforma alla Rivoluzione francese: Contributi per una storia della didattica* (forthcoming).

[53] Juska-Bacher, Sroka, and Laine (eds), *Catechism Primers in Europe*.

[54] On this topic, see Philippe Kaenel and Rolf Reichardt (eds), *Interkulturelle Kommunikation in der europäischen Druckgraphik im 18. und 19. Jahrhundert* (Hildesheim and New York: Olms, 2007); Alberto Milano (ed.), *Commercio delle stampe e diffusione delle immagini nei secoli XVIII e XIX* (Rovereto: Via della terra, 2008).

[55] On 'voices [. . .] raised against chapbooks', see Neuburg, *Penny Histories*. On religious tracts, see also Neuburg, *Popular Literature*, pp. 249–64.

Catholic countries.[56] Alice Colombo has tracked down at least twenty-four translations of Evangelical tracts in English translated into Italian and printed in the peninsula in the early nineteenth century.[57] In order to allay the suspicions of the Roman Catholic church, these tracts were presented as educational books for English or Protestant children living in Italy. Similar research is needed into publications of the French evangelical society in order to investigate possible links with tracts issued in Britain.[58]

Educational cheap print, although also used by adults, can readily be included in a corpus of cheap print for children. This is less evidently the case when it comes to the almanac, probably the most globally successful genre of cheap print.[59] Almanacs were, broadly speaking, annual publications containing a calendar, prognostications for the year to come, and a variety of instructional and/or entertaining short texts. They were also transnational. Not only was the same format used in different countries, and almanacs were among the first printed items to be exported along the routes of colonization,[60] but titles and contents were often shared across geographical and cultural

---

[56] Susan Pedersen, 'Hannah More Meets Simple Simon: Tracts, Chapbooks, and Popular Culture in Late Eighteenth-Century England', *Journal of British Studies*, 25 (1986), pp. 84–113; Dennis Butts and Pat Garret (eds), *From the Dairyman's Daughter to Worrals of the WAAF: The Religious Tract Society, Lutterworth Press and Children's Literature* (Cambridge: Lutterworth Press, 2006).

[57] Alice Colombo, 'The Translational Dimension of Street Literature: The Nineteenth-Century Italian Repertoire', in *Crossing Borders, Crossing Cultures: Popular Print in Europe (1450–1900)*, ed. Massimo Rospocher, Jeroen Salman, and Hannu Salmi (Berlin and Boston: De Gruyter Oldenbourg, 2019), pp. 143–58 (p. 155). A specific Anglo-Italian tract is analysed in Alice Colombo, 'Translation, Book History and the Transnational Life of "Street Literature"', *Translation Studies*, 12 (2019), 288–307.

[58] An almanac addressed to families and children was printed by the French evangelical society from the 1820s to the twentieth century under the title *Almanach des bons conseils, pour la famille et la jeunesse* (some issues are preserved in Marseille, Centre de conservation et de ressources du MuCEM, 1.pr.57.3). From the 1820s the society published educational texts for all audiences. Analysis of the tracts might open new perspectives on the transnational circulation of confessional cheap print.

[59] Almanacs probably represent the most widespread kind of cheap print across Europe, and show many similarities across borders. Following the foundational work on French almanacs by Geneviève Bollème, *Les almanachs populaires aux XVII et XVIII siècles: Essai d'histoire sociale* (Paris and La Haye: Mouton, 1969), scholars have investigated a wealth of publications, enabling transnational comparisons.

[60] The best-known examples were in northern America; see Lüsebrink et al. (eds), *Les lectures du peuple en Europe et dans les Amériques*. An almanac was also printed by the Danish mission in Tranquebar, discussed in a paper presented by Niklas Thode Jensen at the Medical Knowledge and Publication Strategies in European Perspective (1500–1800) conference, Prague, November 2016.

borders.[61] Another peculiarity of almanacs was their ability to evolve over time, often in order to enhance their status and satisfy the interests of wealthier, urban readers, in the form of city guides, court almanacs, almanacs for ladies, and so on. Rural almanacs continued to be printed, however, and were increasingly adapted to educational purposes, such as fostering new agricultural techniques or supporting public health and temperance movements. Given this ability to evolve, when publishers started to consider children as an audience it was natural that they should introduce juvenile versions of almanacs.

Almanacs were cheap; they had readers even in the most remote villages of the countryside, where they were sold by pedlars; and they were accessible to the semi-literate, thanks to the use of symbols. More importantly, almost anyone in the early modern world would recognize an almanac and agree upon its usefulness. Juvenile versions of almanacs started to appear as early as the 1750s, such as the British *Youth's Entertaining and Instructive Calendar for the Jubilee Year 1750*.[62] Almanacs for children were also issued in the Netherlands and in Germany before the end of the eighteenth century.[63]

Leafing through early children's almanacs it is sometimes difficult to identify the elements that, in the minds of the publishers, transformed them into juvenile booklets. Some Dutch examples show that ordinary almanacs were simply collated with new pages containing educational stories. Perhaps this was initially a commercial strategy to increase the opportunities for selling cheaply assembled products aimed at the new juvenile audience.[64] With time, the calendar part was combined with (coloured) woodcuts or even engravings, and the contents were progressively adapted to suit what were understood to be the needs of children (alphabets, short stories, moral tales, riddles, fairy tales). This happened, for instance, with the German

---

[61] See Lüsebrink et al. (eds), *Les lectures du peuple en Europe et dans les Amériques*.

[62] *Youth's Entertaining and Instructive Calendar for the Jubilee Year 1750* (printed for W. Owen, ncar Temple Bar; and sold by R. Goadby, at Sherborne; B. Hickey and J. Palmer, at Bristol; J. Hildyard, at York; and by all other booksellers in town and country) [ESTC T146012].

[63] So far, I have examined *Prentjes almanach voor kinderen vor het jaar 1799* [Princeton, NJ, Cotsen Children's Library, Euro 18 3466]. There are records of this title from 1794 to 1839, with some issues held in Dutch libraries accessible online. On Dutch almanacs for children, see J. Salman, '"Die ze niet hebben wil mag het laaten": Kinderalmanakken in de achttiende eeuw', *Literatuur*, 17 (2000), 76–84.

[64] Elisa Marazzi, 'Almanacs for Children: The Transnational Evolution of a Classic of Popular Print', in *Transnational Books for Children: Producers, Consumers, Encounters (1750–1900)*, ed. Charlotte Appel, Nina Christensen, Matthew O. Grenby, and Andrea Immel (Amsterdam: John Benjamins, forthcoming).

Taschenkalender zur belehrenden Unterhaltung für die Jugend und ihre Freunde (*c*.1795), which combined the traditional format of the almanac (including the genealogy of major royal families) with short stories for children and educational content.[65] In many instances, this revamp meant a rise in the cultural and social status of children's almanacs, leading to very refined products being issued in the late nineteenth century. Examples include *Mère Gigogne: Almanac des petits enfants*, printed in Paris from 1850 for at least four decades, and *Barbadoro, figlio di Barbanera: Lunario per ragazzi*, printed in Florence in 1902.

Illustrated broadsides for all

Anyone living in the twenty-first century would associate children's literature with coloured illustrations. This was not the case for the vast majority of the items mentioned so far. But there were some printed products that circulated widely in the early modern world and that relied more on images (sometimes coloured) than on texts – illustrated broadsides. Scholars have suggested that in many different countries they represented a 'popular mass medium' for both the old and the young.[66] Across Europe the kind of illustrated broadside known as a (catch)penny print had a standardized appearance: printed on one side of a single sheet, it consisted of four to eight rows of woodcuts with captions, which when read together narrated a story. These broadsides had different names according to geography and chronology; *pliegos de aleluyas* (or just *aleluyas*) in Spain and *centsprenten* in Dutch-speaking areas constitute probably the earliest examples (beginning, roughly, in the seventeenth century). The use of lithography, and later chromolithography, in the nineteenth century extended their reach into France, where they were known as *imagerie populaire*,[67] Germany, where they were known as *Bilderbogen*, mainly printed in Neuruppin,[68]

---

[65] *Taschenkalender zur belehrenden unterhaltung für die Jugend und ihre Freunde* (Bayreuth: [1795]) [Princeton, NJ, Cotsen Children's Library, Euro 18 46214].

[66] Jeroen Salman, 'An Early Modern Mass Medium: The Adventures of Cartouche in Dutch Penny Prints (1700–1900)', *Cultural History*, 7 (2018), 20–47. See also Gomis and Salman, 'Tall Tales for a Mass Audience'.

[67] Now known as *imagerie d'Épinal* after the name of the town where the printer Pellerin first developed these kinds of sheets. Before the nineteenth century illustrated broadsides by Pellerin had a different format, with a central figure surrounded by columns of text, more like earlier religious prints. A good account is provided by Jean Mistler, François Blaudez, and André Jacquemin, *Épinal et l'imagerie populaire* (Paris: Hachette, 1961).

[68] See Heimatmuseum Neuruppin, *'Was ist der Ruhm der Times gegen die zivilisatorische Aufgabe des Ruppiner Bilderbogens?': Die Bilderbogensammlung Dietrich Hecht* (Berlin: Kulturstiftung der Länder, Stadt Neuruppin, Land Brandenburg, 1995).

and later also Belgium and Italy.[69] Their spread was often driven by family networks, and partnerships (which still need to be investigated) enabled their export to the Scandinavian market,[70] and across the Atlantic.[71]

A wide range of topics travelled across borders by these means: retellings of popular romances and tales, historical events, professions and costumes from around the world, religion and devotion, proverbs, amusing stories that circulated widely through popular print, such as 'the world upside down' and 'the henpecked husband'. Their format – heavily illustrated (often hand- or dab-coloured), relying on the images more than the captions – suggests they might have been particularly enjoyed by children. Moreover, the border with play was quite blurred. Especially in Spain, this material was tightly intertwined with lottery games, where the broadsides were cut into as many pictures as there were printed illustrations, which were then used to play the lottery.[72]

With the development of a juvenile audience, publishers of sheets of images (which in France were commonly known as *feuilles d'images*) started to address themselves to children, gradually changing their repertoires and adapting the sharper elements of some of the folk tales to what was perceived at the time to be more suited to the juvenile sensibility.[73] The adoption of lithography in the nineteenth century further expanded the possibilities for printers, who added to their stocks cheap board games or paper toys. With the latter, the principle was that the purchaser could paste the sheet on to thick paper or cardboard and then cut out and fold the images in order to build theatres, characters, and other objects. Henry Mayhew recorded

[69] Alberto Milano, in collaboration with Sergio Ruzzier (eds), *Fabbrica d'immagini: Gioco e litografia nei fogli della raccolta Bertarelli* (Milano: Vangelista, 1993), pp. 13–21.

[70] German *Bilderbogen* for the Danish market are mentioned in Konrad Vanja, 'Themen des europaeischen Bilderbogens in der Sammlung Hecht', in *'Was ist der Ruhm der Times gegen die zivilisatorische Aufgabe des Ruppiner Bilderbogens?': Die Bilderbogen-Sammlung Dietrich Hecht* (Berlin: Kulturstiftung der Länder, Stadt Neuruppin, Land Brandenburg, 1995), pp. 16–57.

[71] A set of Épinal broadsides printed in Kansas City and preserved at Princeton, NJ, Cotsen Children's Library, French Popular Print 149986 (Box 1), contains exactly the same illustrations as corresponding French broadsides, but the captions are printed in English. The colophon mentions both the Humoristic Publishing Co. and *Imagerie d'Épinal*, perhaps indicating a transatlantic partnership.

[72] Pedro Cerrillo and Jesús Maria Martínez González, *Aleluyas: Juegos y literatura infantil en los pliegos de aleluyas españoles y europeos del siglo XIX* (Cuenca: Universidad de Castilla La Mancha, 2012).

[73] François Blaudez, 'L'histoire de l'imagerie d'Épinal', in Jean Mistler, François Blaudez, and André Jacquemin, *Épinal et l'imagerie populaire* (Paris: Hachette, 1961), pp. 69–138 (p. 113).

that this also happened in nineteenth-century London, where similar illustrated sheets of engravings sold in the streets provided 'the winter-evenings' amusements of the children of the working-classes. The principal street customers for these penny papers were mechanics, who bought them on their way home for the amusement of their families. Boys, however, bought almost as many.'[74] This was the era of Victorian movable picture books and paper theatres, and these printed sheets extended the market for ludic products to less affluent audiences.[75]

In search of the readers

Although debate around Mayhew's work has shown the limits of his account, his pages on the street book trade in London are part of the wealth of evidence available on the dynamics of cheap print in nineteenth-century Britain.[76] Other kinds of evidence include fiction, autobiography, essays, and critical exchanges about education and literature – which, unfortunately, were in many cases 'circumstantial, subjective and tendentious', as Matthew Grenby has observed, with accounts tailored in favour of chapbooks (by the Romantics) or against them (by religious pamphleteers).[77] Historians are agreed that autobiographical writings can be problematic in their representations of reality. Nevertheless, while we do not always know what the writers wanted to show about themselves, from the list of chapbooks purchased by the young Samuel Bamford, which roughly corresponds to the core repertoire of English chapbooks,[78] to the penny-dreadfuls

---

[74] Henry Mayhew, *London Labour and the London Poor*, 4 vols (London: Griffin, Bohn, 1861–62), I, 287.

[75] See Hannah Field, *Playing with the Book: Victorian Movable Picture Books and the Child Reader* (Minneapolis: University of Minnesota Press, 2019).

[76] Richard Maxwell, 'Henry Mayhew and the Life of the Streets', *Journal of British Studies*, 17.2 (1978), 87–105; Paul Thomas Murphy, 'The Voices of the Poor?: Dialogue in Henry Mayhew's London Labour and the London Poor', *Nineteenth-Century Prose*, 25 (1998), 24–44. Despite criticisms of his methods, data collected by Mayhew can be used profitably, as shown by Isabel Corfe, 'Sensation and Song: Street Ballad Consumption in Nineteenth-Century England', in *Media and Print Culture Consumption in Nineteenth-Century Britain*, ed. Paul R. Rooney and Anna Gasperini (London: Palgrave Macmillan, 2016), pp. 131–45.

[77] Grenby, 'Before Children's Literature', p. 34; also Grenby, 'Chapbooks, Children, and Children's Literature'.

[78] Samuel Bamford, *Passages in the Life of a Radical and Early Days*, ed. Henry Dunckley, 2 vols (London: T. F. Unwin, 1893), I, 87. Chapbooks mentioned by Bamford are *Jack the Giant Killer, Saint George and the Dragon, Tom Hickathrift, Jack and the Beanstalk, The Seven Champions of Christendom, Fair Rosamond, History of Friar Bacon, Account of the*

read in shop windows by Robert Louis Stevenson,[79] we do learn that chapbooks were an important part of children's experience.[80]

At the same time, such narratives are scarcely representative in terms of gender, ethnicity, or social status. This is true for other European countries, too. Consider Valentin Jamerey-Duval, born in 1695. Raised as a shepherd in Lorraine, he studied as an autodidact and later became librarian of the Grand Duchy of Tuscany. In his memoir he describes how he taught himself to read through volumes of the *bibliothèque bleue*, in particular Aesop's Fables and French *chansons de gestes*.[81] Knowing by heart some of the stories, which he had heard at communal gatherings, once he had the book in his hands he was able to match the words with the stories he already knew. It is known that schoolmasters and priests also exploited the intersection between learning by heart and learning to read: for example, learning to read by means of prayers and catechisms.[82] At the same time, we should bear in mind that autobiographical accounts have a tendency to exaggerate the author's vicissitudes.[83]

A cautious attitude towards the sources does not mean that this wealth of evidence is to be totally discarded. Some historians observe that fiction, although intrinsically untrue, is still based on the

---

Lancashire Witches, The Witches of the Woodlands, Robin Hood's Songs, The Ballad of Chevy Chase.

[79] Marie Léger-St-Jean, 'Serialization and Story-Telling Illustrations: R. L. Stevenson Window-Shopping for Penny Dreadfuls', in *Media and Print Culture Consumption in Nineteenth-Century Britain*, ed. Paul R. Rooney and Anna Gasperini (London: Palgrave Macmillan, 2016), pp. 111–29.

[80] On nineteenth-century autobiographies, see David Vincent, *Bread, Knowledge and Freedom: A Study of Nineteenth Century Working Class Autobiography* (London: Methuen, 1981). See also Roggero, 'Des enfants et des livres'.

[81] Jean Hébrard, 'Comment Jamerey-Duval apprit-il à lire ? L'autodidaxie exemplaire', in *Pratiques de la lecture*, ed. Roger Chartier (Paris and Marseille: Éditions Payot and Rivages, 1993 [1985]), pp. 29–76. Aesop's Fables were also the jewel in the collection of James Raine, born in Yorkshire at the end of the eighteenth century. See Margaret Spufford, 'Women Teaching Reading to Poor Children in the Sixteenth and Seventeenth Centuries', in *Opening the Nursery Door: Reading, Writing and Childhood 1600–1900*, ed. Mary Hilton, Morag Styles, and Victor Watson (London: Routledge, 1997), pp. 47–62; also David Whitley, *Samuel Richardson's Aesop*, in *Opening the Nursery Door: Reading, Writing and Childhood 1600–1900*, ed. Mary Hilton, Morag Styles, and Victor Watson (London: Routledge, 1997), pp. 65–79.

[82] Cf. Darnton, 'First Steps Towards a History of Reading', p. 168.

[83] See Fabian Brändle, 'Pitfalls in Reading Popular Self-Narratives', in *Mapping the 'I': Research on Self-Narratives in Germany and Switzerland*, ed. Claudia Ulbrich, Kaspar von Greyerz, and Lorenz Heiligensetzer (Leiden: Brill, 2015), pp. 190–205.

experience of its authors.[84] The same is true of iconography, which can deliver depictions of reading scenes, albeit influenced by the tastes and manners of a given period.[85] For instance, an eighteenth-century Venetian painting shows a young girl in a coffee shop holding in her hand an illustrated broadsheet which she is using as a fan (*fogli per ventola*).[86] The scene comes from a relatively affluent milieu, showing that upper-class children could facilitate the circulation of cheap print between social classes.[87]

It is arguable, therefore, that literary and pictorial evidence provides potentially useful data, if analysed in the right context.[88] Context can be provided by official sources, for example, which are inherently less subjective. Remaining in Venice, we can trust the schoolmasters who reluctantly declared that they made use of abridged chivalric poems as textbooks because these were the books the children brought to school; this happened in the sixteenth century, but a later Venetian inquiry confirms that this practice was still going on in the eighteenth century.[89] Similarly, Niall Ó Ciosáin has found evidence that in the early nineteenth century the majority of books used in Irish schools were chapbooks.[90]

The French situation is less clear. There is evidence that in Angers, as early as 1678, bishops banned from schools the use of 'Les livres de fables, les romans et toutes sortes de livres profanes dont on se sert pour commencer à leur [les élèves] apprendre à lire' ('tales, romances

---

[84] Antonio Castillo Gómez, *Leggere nella Spagna moderna: Erudizione, religiosità, e svago* (Bologna: Pàtron, 2013), p. 15, and his own use of literary sources, pp. 106–08. See also Roggero, *Le carte piene di sogni*, p. 8.

[85] This is widely discussed, as far as pictorial representations of reading women are concerned, in Tiziana Plebani, *Il 'genere' dei libri: Storie e rappresentazioni della lettura al femminile e al maschile tra Medioevo e età moderna* (Milano: FrancoAngeli, 2001), pp. 154–63. On reading represented in printed illustrations, see Jean-François Botrel, 'Les images et l'évolution de la lecture (France, Espagne, XIXe siècle)', in *Lire en Europe: Textes, formes, lectures (XVIIe–XXIe siècle)*, ed. Lodovica Braida and Brigitte Ouvry-Vial (Rennes: PUR, 2020), pp. 45–76.

[86] The painting, *La bottega del caffè*, by a follower of Pietro Longhi, is preserved in Vicenza, Palazzo Leoni Montanari https://progettocultura.intesasanpaolo.com/patrimonio-artistico/opere/la-bottega-del-caffe/.

[87] Roggero, *Le carte piene di sogni*, pp. 67–68.

[88] See Amelia Yeates, 'Space and Place in Nineteenth-Century Images of Women Readers', in *The Edinburgh History of Reading: Common Readers*, ed. Jonathan Rose (Edinburgh: Edinburgh University Press, 2020), pp. 96–115.

[89] Roggero, *Le carte piene di sogni*, p. 85; Laura Carnelos, *'Con libri alla mano': Editoria di larga diffusione a Venezia tra '6 e '700* (Milano: Unicopli, 2012), pp. 30–32.

[90] Ó Ciosáin, *Print and Popular Culture in Ireland*, p. 50.

and all kinds of secular books used to teach [pupils] to read').[91] No similar bans have been found so far concerning other areas of France, and (unlike other countries) the titles of the banned texts were not listed. In this case it could be argued that the official source is nonetheless contentious, forbidding something that might have not been in actual use. This appears more likely when we examine the Rapport Grégoire, a survey conducted by Henri Jean-Baptiste Grégoire into linguistic uses in the French countryside of the 1790s. Grégoire sent his correspondents, among other things, some questions about the texts that were used in the schools of their provinces, but no books other than ABCs, catechisms, and devotional books were ever reported.[92] Did correspondents lie for some obscure reason, or did French children from the countryside encounter cheap print only at home, where any family would own devotional books but also at least an almanac and sometimes 'Quelques mauvais contes de près de deux cents ans d'impression' ('some bad tales that had been in print for nearly two hundred years')?[93]

There are several possible answers to this question. First, according to Emmanuelle Chapron, there could have been an implicitly shared school culture which rejected secular books in the name of a supposed decency; even so, informal education might have been completely bypassed by a survey such as that conducted by Grégoire.[94] A second hypothesis is that, unlike the reluctant teachers who admitted they had to use romances as primers, Grégoire's correspondents (who were notables and religious living in the areas covered by the inquiry) might have wanted to conceal what they thought to be bad practices in the schools in their region. Thirdly, instead of making an accurate survey of what people actually read and learned, correspondents might have written down their own ideas about rural schools and homes without ever visiting them.

---

[91] Helwi Blom, 'Vieux romans' et 'Grand Siècle': Éditions et réceptions de la littérature chevaleresque médiévale dans la France du dix-septième siècle (unpublished doctoral thesis, Utrecht University, 2012). I am grateful to Helwi Blom for bringing this to my attention.
[92] The documents of the inquiry are published in Augustin Louis Grazier (ed.), Lettres à Grégoire sur les patois de France, 1790–1794 (Paris: A. Durand and Pedone-Lauriel, 1880). See also Michel de Certeau, Dominique Julia, and Jacques Revel, Une Politique de la langue: La Révolution française et les patois, l'enquête de Grégoire (Paris: Gallimard, 1975).
[93] Grazier (ed.), Lettres à Gregoire sur les patois de France, p. 245, from a correspondent in St Calais, Sarthe.
[94] A point made by Chapron at the workshop on Popular Children's Literature in Europe (1450–1900), Milan, 2018.

In the end, the average French child living in the countryside might have had fewer opportunities to read secular cheap print. Evidence about young peasants' ownership of books from eighteenth-century police reports usually concerns psalters or books of hours. Officials would discover booklets on small corpses lying by the roadside, or in the pockets of children caught out in small thefts or left to drive their herds in the fields, and rural officers would sometimes seize these books as security in order to force children to comply with court orders.[95] Irrespective of the absence of secular cheap books from young French peasants' reading matter, these documents provide evidence that encounters between cheap print and children were manifold.

Conclusions

Since the 1960s, studies of cheap print have proliferated, allowing deeper insights into the kinds of printed items that circulated across Europe. Much has been done from the point of view of production and distribution, less from the point of view of reception, which presents a real challenge, especially when dealing with 'common readers', in particular the younger ones.[96] Nevertheless, recalling the possible methods proposed by Robert Darnton, and thanks to further advances in scholarship,[97] we are now in a position to collect, catalogue, and discuss the different types of cheaply printed products that were likely to be handled, looked at, read, listened to, and even overheard, by young people in different areas of western Europe in the eighteenth and nineteenth centuries. Research into rural life, education, and literacy has provided information on children's encounters with cheap print, showing that they took place in similar ways in different places (and although the research presented here is limited to Europe, a wealth of cheap print travelled further as a

---

[95] Françoise Bayard, 'Au cœur de l'intime: Les poches des cadavres, Lyon, Lyonnais, Beaujolais, XVIIe–XVIIIe siècle', *Bulletin du centre d'histoire économique et sociale de la région lyonnaise*, 2 (1989), 5–41; Philippe Martin, *Une religion des livres (1640–1850)* (Paris: Éditions du Cerf, 2003). Once more I am grateful to Emmanuelle Chapron for drawing my attention to this evidence, which is also discussed in Carnelos and Marazzi, 'Children and Cheap Print from a Transnational Perspective'.

[96] See Sasha Roberts, 'Reading in Early Modern England: Contexts and Problems', *Critical Survey*, 12.2 (2000), 1–16 (pp. 5–6).

[97] There are some encouraging examples of how research into the cultural life of people who have left scarce written records is possible, such as Jonathan Rose, *The Intellectual Life of the British Working Classes*, 2nd edn (New Haven and London: Yale University Press, 2010). See also Jonathan Rose (ed.), *The Edinburgh History of Reading: Common Readers* (Edinburgh: Edinburgh University Press, 2020).

consequence of colonization).[98] Further research should make it possible to assess whether a shared culture existed across Europe, with children consuming similar materials with similar stories in different parts of the continent.

Some important issues need to be kept in mind. First, there is the divergence between intended and actual use. Just as children read products that were not specifically intended for them, such as eighteenth-century chapbooks, it was not always the case that works for encouraging literacy or moral tales were intended to be read by a juvenile audience. In some Mediterranean areas, for instance, the category of learners might include adults and older people.[99] Similarly, if children were mentioned on the title page of a booklet, this did not necessarily mean that it was actually read by children; some tracts intended for the education of the common people may never have been read at all. This may be apparent from survival rates; survival is often a poor guide to commercial success and items that survive in large numbers may well have been unsold, commercially unsuccessful, products. In contrast, the pamphlets and broadsides that were read the most were likely to have been passed from one generation to the next and consequently worn, torn, and destroyed.

The variety and diversity of sources does not allow for comprehensive accounts of all the different geographical areas. Some of the sources pose particular problems: for example, the unreliability and unrepresentative nature of autobiography; the difficulty in evaluating fiction and iconography as historical evidence; the scattered nature of legal and official sources; the possible biases in surveys and analyses produced in the past. The difficulty of finding documents about the lives and businesses of key figures from the cheap print trade, such as publishers and settled or itinerant sellers, does not leave much space for adding to what is already known (in contrast to other sectors of the print trade, such as textbooks or highbrow children's literature).[100]

---

[98] I think, for instance, of the transatlantic travels of *cartillas*, or the *New England Primer*, but there is much more work to be done on a global perspective. Matthew Grenby discussed this in his paper 'Going Global: Transnational Networks and the Spread of Cheap Print for Children', presented at the Books for Children: Transnational Encounters, 1750–1850 conference, Princeton, NJ, Cotsen Children's Library, 31 October–2 November 2019.

[99] Carnelos and Marazzi, 'Children and Cheap Print from a Transnational Perspective'.

[100] Cf. Salman, 'Children's Books as a Commodity'; Alderson and De Marez Oyens, *Be Merry and Wise*. Cf. also the work of Jean-Yves Mollier in France and Giorgio Chiosso in Italy.

Combining different approaches – from social history to the history of publishing, from the history of education to research into the commercial networks of the past – can reduce the scope for error and allow a deeper understanding of printing in the early modern world. For instance, new light can be shed on informal education processes, which often involved individuals less likely to have left written records. It may be that in some regions, especially where literacy rates were lower, cheap print was the only reading and teaching material that circulated among the young before the later nineteenth or even the twentieth century. Collecting information about the juvenile use of cheaply printed products is also likely to provide further knowledge about issues related to production and distribution, such as the trade in and reuse of woodblocks and lithographic stones, publishing partnerships, and transnational commercial networks, as in the case of the *Épinals* and *Bilderbogen*.

This preliminary survey, albeit limited and not systematic, leads us to argue that juvenile audiences played a role in the reception of street literature, something that has not been the specific object of research so far. Reassessing the part played by juvenile audiences in the cheap print trade therefore allows us to reconsider the importance of popular print within the publishing trade and, more ambitiously, in early modern society.

'Hawkie' and his Audiences

David Atkinson

Historically, when someone in the street started singing a ballad, or relating a criminal's last dying speech, or recounting an old chapbook tale, a crowd would gather and would buy, or not buy, the printed sheets that they were selling. It is reasonable to infer that this audience would influence the repertoire of street-criers and ballad singers, although they were constrained, too, by what the printers had to offer. Street-criers and ballad singers did usually need to sell printed sheets in order to make a living. The audience itself was, of course, intrinsically fluid. An individual would probably only buy a particular chapbook or ballad on one occasion, but they might have wanted to hear it more than once. Nevertheless, the sales of printed sheets offer an opportunity to chart something of the audience response to the ubiquitous characters who hawked cheap print in the towns and cities of eighteenth-century Britain (and also in the countryside, although in that regard the records are generally poorer).

A considerable amount of scholarly work has been done on vendors of street literature, but even so the audience remains a shadowy, shifting presence.[1] In response, this short study seeks to

---

[1] For example: Sue Allan, 'Penurious Poets and Ballad-Mongers: Some Nineteenth-Century Ballad Singers in Cumberland and Westmorland', in *Street Literature and the Circulation of Songs*, ed. David Atkinson and Steve Roud (London: Ballad Partners, 2019), pp. 17–33; Iain Beavan, 'The Decline and Fall of the Scottish Chapbook', in *Street Literature of the Long Nineteenth Century: Producers, Sellers, Consumers*, ed. David Atkinson and Steve Roud (Newcastle upon Tyne: Cambridge Scholars Publishing, 2017), pp. 154–92; Oskar Cox Jensen, 'The *Travels* of John Magee: Tracing the Geographies of Britain's Itinerant Print-Sellers, 1789–1815', *Cultural and Social History*, 11 (2014), 195–216; Vic Gammon, 'Street Ballad Sellers in the Nineteenth Century', in *Street Literature of the Long Nineteenth Century: Producers, Sellers, Consumers*, ed. David Atkinson and Steve Roud (Newcastle upon Tyne: Cambridge Scholars Publishing, 2017), pp. 119–51; Michael Harris, 'A Few Shillings for Small Books: The Experiences of a Flying Stationer in the 18th Century', in *Spreading the Word: The Distribution Networks of Print, 1550–1850*, ed. Robin Myers and Michael Harris (Winchester: St Paul's Bibliographies; New Castle, DE: Oak Knoll Press, 1998 [1990]), pp. 83–108; Barry McKay, 'Some Lake Counties Chapmen and their Wares', *Quadrat*, no. 25 (2013); John Morris, 'The Scottish Chapman', in *Fairs, Markets and the Itinerant Book*

interrogate the autobiographical memoir of the Scottish hawker and street-crier William Cameron (*c*.1787–1851), known as 'Hawkie', for the light that it can shed on his interactions with various kinds of audiences, and also with the printers who supplied him.[2] Hawkie wrote his *Autobiography of a Gangrel* while he was a winter inmate of the Glasgow Town's Hospital during the period 1840–50 for his publisher friend David Robertson, probably as a way of earning some money, although it was only published, in edited form, well after his death. Its chronology is somewhat confusing and the memoir is cast, as is quite typical of labouring-class autobiographies of the time, in part as a moral exemplum. Others have written more about Hawkie in the round, and about the trade in cheap print in Scotland and in Glasgow, the city with which he was most strongly associated.[3] Writers on Glasgow's past have regularly included anecdotes about Hawkie, some of which have an apocryphal air to them, but which generally tend to corroborate his own account.[4] Despite some caveats, therefore, the moments when Hawkie was interacting with his audiences have the capacity to expose some recurrent patterns in the street literature trade at the beginning of the nineteenth century.

Hawkie travelled in Scotland and England during the early decades of the century. At various times the occupations he pursued included journeyman tailor, itinerant preacher, schoolteacher, strolling player, toy-maker, china-mender, street-seller, speech-crier (a term used to

---

Trade, ed. Robin Myers, Michael Harris, and Giles Mandelbrote (New Castle, DE: Oak Knoll Press; London: British Library, 2007), pp. 159–86.

[2] [William Cameron], *Hawkie: The Autobiography of a Gangrel*, ed. John Strathesk (Glasgow: David Robertson & Co., 1888). See further David M. Hopkin, 'Cameron, William [*nicknamed* Hawkie] (*c*.1787–1851)', *ODNB* https://doi.org/10.1093/ref: odnb/94320.

[3] Beavan, 'Decline and Fall'; Edward J. Cowan and Mike Patterson, *Folk in Print: Scotland's Chapbook Heritage, 1750–1850* (Edinburgh: John Donald, 2007); William Harvey, *Scottish Chapbook Literature* (Paisley: Alexander Gardner, 1903); Adam McNaughtan, 'A Century of Saltmarket Literature, 1790–1890', in *Six Centuries of the Provincial Book Trade in Britain*, ed. Peter Isaac (Winchester: St Paul's Bibliographies, 1990), pp. 165–80.

[4] *The Laird of Logan; or, Anecdotes and Tales, Illustrative of the Wit and Humour of Scotland* (Glasgow: David Robertson, 1841); [William Finlay], 'Street Oratory', in *Whistle-Binkie; or, The Piper of the Party*, ed. Alexander Rodger, 2nd series (Glasgow: David Robertson, 1842), pp. 61–71; Peter Mackenzie, *Reminiscences of Glasgow and the West of Scotland*, 3 vols (Glasgow: John Tweed, 1865–68), III, 75–116; Robert Ford, *Thistledown: A Book of Scotch Humour, Character, Folk-Lore, Story, and Anecdote* (Paisley: Alexander Gardner, 1891), pp. 294–315; Robert Alison, *The Anecdotage of Glasgow* (Glasgow: Thomas D. Morison; London: Simpkin, Marshall, & Co., 1892), pp. 248–59; John Urie, *Reminiscences of Eighty Years* (Paisley: Alexander Gardner, 1908).

describe a street vendor of speeches, particularly one who hawked the 'last dying speeches' of criminals),[5] trickster, and cadger or beggar. Sometimes he worked in company with another speech-crier known as Jamie Blue (James M'Indoe).[6] He was crippled early in life and subsequently apprenticed to the tailoring trade, which did not suit his disposition, although he did acknowledge that it rendered him independent of his father. He travelled to Glasgow as a journeyman tailor, where one Sunday he heard a field preacher addressing a large audience on Glasgow Green.[7] He did not think much of the preaching, but was impressed with the money the preacher could make, and declared that he could do better himself. To his surprise, his fellow tailors took him at his word and persuaded him to preach on the following Sunday. Fortunately, he had had some elocution lessons as a child, and his parents had taken pleasure in the sermons of Ralph Erskine of Dunfermline,[8] so he was able to deliver one of Erskine's sermons, and the money came in so quickly there was scarcely any need to pass round the hat. This experience, which comes early on in the autobiography, seems to have introduced Hawkie to the opportunities available from playing an audience in one way or another. After this, he returned briefly to the tailoring trade, kept a school, and spent some time with a company of strolling players.

The early part of the autobiography concentrates rather heavily on cadging and trickery. In Paisley, for example, where the bookseller George Caldwell had retired from the business, Hawkie bought some newspapers from (an unknowing) Mrs Caldwell, went out into the street, told a long tale, and made 4s. by selling the papers.[9] No one complained at the time, but afterwards a young woman objected that she had been cheated out of ½d. Selling old newspapers in the guise of chapbooks was a trick Hawkie tried more than once. In Auchterarder, where he could not find a stationer's or obtain any books for sale, his companions encouraged him to 'tell a good tale on

---

[5] *SND*, speech, *n*. Sc. usages: 1 Combs. †(1) speech-crier; *OED*, speech, *n.1* C2. speech-crier *n*.

[6] Described by Hawkie's editor as a disgraced soldier, dealer in hardware, leeches, spurious pepper and blue (for laundering clothes), also a ballad singer and speech-crier, one of the ne'er-do-weels of Glasgow, who died in 1837 (*Hawkie*, p. 90 n.).

[7] *Hawkie*, pp. 13–15.

[8] David C. Lachman, 'Erskine, Ralph (1686–1752)', *ODNB* https://doi.org/10.1093/ref:odnb/8871.

[9] *Hawkie*, pp. 35–36. George Caldwell (*Hawkie*, pp. 35, 96), bookseller, stationer, and proprietor of a circulating library, was in business in Paisley, 1774–1825, and was succeeded by his son, also George (SBTI).

an old newspaper', out of which he made 3*s*., although this time he felt ashamed of the deceit.[10]

In Dunfermline he went to a bookseller's named Miller and asked for ballads or histories (prose chapbooks), but he had nothing but tracts.[11] He bought four dozen of them, went into the street, and began a long story, which soon gathered an audience who relished the tale and many of whom bought his books. One of the buyers, however, complained that he had been fobbed off with 'John Covey', a religious tract, instead of the story Hawkie had been telling, and demanded his halfpenny back.[12] The disgruntled customer told the town-keeper (an official acting as a kind of constable whose chief duty was to keep order in the streets and deal with beggars and other troublesome persons) and Hawkie was arrested and ordered out of town.[13] Hawkie, it seems, knew what his audience would prefer – ballads or histories – but he also sensed that the street performance could carry enough weight with most of them and he was able to adapt to the circumstances despite the bookseller's limited stock.

Hawkie's proper induction into the trade of speech-crier came, according to his own account, when he returned to Glasgow from England in 1818 (although this chronology does not entirely tally with the earlier account of his time in Northumberland).[14] He did not wish to cadge in a city where he was so well known, and having seen an old man in the street (who turned out to be Jamie Blue) 'calling' an eight-page chapbook, which was selling tolerably well, he had the idea that he, too, could make a living in this way:

> At this time I knew nothing about books, nor where I could get them. I went up the Saltmarket, into a bookseller's shop of the name of Hutcheson, and asked 'if he had any eight-page books for crying in the street?' He told me that 'he had eight-page ballads, but no books'. I asked the price, and he told me 'twopence a dozen'. I bought a dozen, and had laid out my little all, with only one penny behind. What was to be done? They were ballads, and I could not sing.[15]

---

[10] *Hawkie*, p. 59.
[11] *Hawkie*, pp. 57–58. John Miller (1780–1852), printer and bookseller in Dunfermline, issued chapbooks including a series titled 'Cheap Tracts' in the 1820s–30s (SBTI).
[12] The story of John (or James) Covey, a seaman who lost his legs at the battle of Camperdown in 1797, was printed by religious tract societies in Gaelic and Welsh as well as English (Beavan, 'Decline and Fall', p. 159).
[13] *SND*, toun, *n.*, *v.* I *n.* 1 †(18) toun(s)-keeper.
[14] *Hawkie*, pp. 90–91.
[15] Robert Hutcheson, bookseller and printer, active in Glasgow's Saltmarket, 1796–1831, published numerous chapbooks in verse and prose, and also chapbooks for

But it was Saturday night and there was no time for deliberation, so he set to work, at first rather diffidently, not making eye contact with the audience lest he should see anyone he knew:

> What the ballads were I never knew, but at that time I had a grand voice, and gathered a crowd. I told them a long tale, as I found them totally in my hand. I held out the book, and in a few minutes I had sold the dozen.

He then purchased another three dozen, which he sold in half an hour, another two quires, sold in another half-hour, and finally yet another two quires. A quire was normally twenty-four sheets and we can assume that each sheet was folded to make an eight-page chapbook.[16] Thus he sold a total of 144 copies (one dozen, plus three dozen, plus four quires). The figure also provides a clue to the number of auditors a successful street-crier could attract, in under two hours if Hawkie is to be believed. According to his own account, from his initial 2d. he brought home upwards of 6s., for a net profit of around 4s.[17]

Hawkie wrote: 'This was the first of my crying "specs"; I have continued at the trade ever since, and for long I spurned the name of a cadger. For many years this was a money-making business.'[18] The profits he recorded from street-selling were mostly in the region of a few shillings at a time. The autobiography offers some scattered points of comparison with other ways of making a living, especially begging, where the sorts of sums to be earned were in the region of a few shillings per day. The estimated annual cost of support for a vagrant in Yorkshire was £25, roughly 1s. 4½d. per day.[19] In the three parishes of Johnstone, Kilbarchan, and Houston, west of Glasgow, a selection of beggars, match-dealers, petty thieves, tinkers, and ballad singers could expect to take 2s. per day, although on account of his lameness Hawkie could earn only about half that sum.[20] When he was

---

children (McNaughtan, 'A Century of Saltmarket Literature', p. 169; SBTI). The eight-page chapbook was a standard format for ballads and songs in Scotland and northern England at this time.

[16] *SND*, quair, *n.* 1; *OED*, quire, *n.* 2.a. There is a slight complication in that elsewhere Hawkie refers to a Scots quire as comprising ninety-four sheets (*Hawkie*, p. 41), but that does not readily fit with what he says here about his takings in Glasgow.

[17] At 2d. per dozen, 144 copies cost him 2s. Sold on the street at ½d. each they would bring in a total of 6s., leaving a net profit of 4s. for the evening's work.

[18] *Hawkie*, p. 91.

[19] *Hawkie*, p. 20.

[20] *Hawkie*, pp. 84–85.

with the strolling players they made 1*s*. 2*d*. each for a night's work.[21] In contrast, at one time he was with a female companion who some days could make 20*s*. at tin-smithing.[22] These figures can be compared with the daily wages of workers in Glasgow recorded in Cleland's statistical tables for the city, which remained more or less flat across the period 1810–19 and never rose above 4*s*. per day.[23]

The autobiography also gives an idea of the cost of some necessities. When he kept a rural school, he boarded in a house at 10*s*. per week.[24] Later, he recorded the cost of a shared bed in a lodging-house for vagrants at around 2*d*. or 3*d*. per night, or 5*d*. per night in a more respectable lodging.[25] On one occasion he paid 3*d*. for a sheep's head.[26] Whisky sold at 6*d*. per gill (a variable measure, but probably around a quarter to half a pint).[27] On balance, street-crying probably was more of a 'money-making business' than begging, but one suspects that for Hawkie the real difference lay in the sense of a profession that it gave him, the interaction with the audience in the streets, the creativity of being both performer and writer. The last chapter of the autobiography turns against begging as a way of life, which might be little more than a conventional way of structuring such a memoir, but does at least chime with his documented career and with the way he was remembered by other Glasgow writers.[28]

Hawkie's career began uncertainly, with trial and error, but he soon became acquainted with the Glasgow booksellers catering for the chapbook trade and acquired a feeling for the titles 'most likely to take the market'.[29] The Glasgow photographer John Urie (1820–1910) claimed to have been on friendly terms with him at one time, and wrote:

---

[21] *Hawkie*, p. 17.

[22] *Hawkie*, p. 20.

[23] James Cleland, *Statistical and Population Tables Relative to the City of Glasgow*, 3rd edn (Glasgow: John Smith & Son, 1828), p. 132.

[24] *Hawkie*, p. 15.

[25] *Hawkie*, pp. 33, 60, 70, 73, 107.

[26] *Hawkie*, p. 29.

[27] *Hawkie*, p. 25. See *SND*, gill *n*.¹, *v*. I *n*. 1; *OED*, gill *n*.2; Cleland, *Statistical and Population Tables*, pp. 69–71. Alison, *Anecdotage of Glasgow*, p. 253, has Hawkie saying it cost 15*d*. (1*s*. 3*d*.) to make him decently drunk.

[28] *Hawkie*, pp. 108–10.

[29] *Hawkie*, p. 92. Some other Glasgow booksellers whom Hawkie frequented were Thomas Duncan, Ebenezer Millar, and John Muir (*Hawkie*, pp. 91–95). See McNaughtan, 'A Century of Saltmarket Literature', pp. 167–69; Morris, 'Scottish Chapman', pp. 179–80; SBTI.

Before the advent of the penny newspaper these chapbooks and leaflets were very popular. 'Hawkie' had considerable gifts as an elocutionist, having a fine clear voice and almost perfect articulation. This, with his witty descriptions of the contents of his pamphlets, made him the most successful speech-crier in Glasgow. If a public execution were to take place, 'Hawkie' was sure to be on the streets loaded with a huge bundle of the 'Speech and Last Dying Confession' of the unhappy felon. These he quickly disposed of at a halfpenny each.

But executions did not occur every day, and, failing such a stirring event, 'Hawkie' retailed broadsheets of all kinds, some with crude and often coarse tales, some with political or personal lampoons in verse, some with old legends or stories. The titles of a few that 'Hawkie' used to sell will give an idea of their contents. 'Watty and Meg – A Cure for Ill Wives', 'Janet Clinker's Oration on the wit of the Old Wives and the Pride of the Young Women', 'The Trial and Burning of Maggie Lang, the Cardonald Witch', etc.[30]

Some of the titles that Hawkie himself describes as being among 'the *best* old standard books of the "flying stationer" order in Scotland' – *Willie Lawson's Courtship of Bess Gibb*, *The History of the Haveral Wives*, *John Thomson's Man*, *Janet Clinker's Oration*, *The Misfortunes of Simple John*, *Grannie M'Nab's Lectures on the Women* – can be identified with chapbooks printed by booksellers in centres such as Glasgow, Edinburgh, and Stirling.[31] Hawkie wrote that he had sold a number of reams of *Willie Lawson's Courtship* and cleaned out the shop, but had 'never seen it since, and it is a small loss to the public', although there are in fact a couple of extant editions.[32]

It was when pattering *The History of the Haveral Wives*, a satirical dialogue between two garrulous old wives (though not without some historical interest), that Hawkie found 'the women first marked me out as their enemy'.[33] Nevertheless, it still sold in great numbers. Another heavily gendered piece was *Watty and Meg; or, The Wife Reformed*, a version of the battle of the sexes by the Paisley poet Alexander Wilson (1766–1813), first published in 1792, which

---

[30] Urie, *Reminiscences of Eighty Years*, pp. 49–50.

[31] *Hawkie*, p. 92; Beavan, 'Decline and Fall', p. 166 n. 40.

[32] *The Fraserburgh-Wedding!* (entered according to order) [ESTC T225242]; *The Art of Courtship* (Stirling, printed in this present year) [ESTC T186407].

[33] *Hawkie*, p. 92. See Cowan and Patterson, *Folk in Print*, pp. 101–11; Harvey, *Scottish Chapbook Literature*, pp. 48–51.

allegedly sold 100,000 copies.[34] Hawkie knew it by heart from childhood and, in competition with Jamie Blue, cried it in Glasgow 'in the character of "A Cure for Ill Wives"', presumably elaborating around the subject in the course of telling the tale.[35] Despite (or because of) the subject matter, *Watty and Meg* was a very successful title; on occasion he could raise the price from ½*d*. to 1*d*. and it would still sell well. In Hamilton, where he made upwards of 7*s*., he told his audience 'it was a cure for ill wives', adding, 'and I suppose the men *knew* that they needed it'.[36] Around Crieff he sold a quire and a half at 1*d*. per copy.[37] In Stranraer he took upwards of 5*s*. in less than an hour and eventually sold nigh on three quires.[38] In Glasgow, after raising the price to 1*d*., he took around 16*s*., which suggests he sold a little short of two hundred copies.[39]

Of a different nature were *The Life and Transactions with the Trial and Burning of Maggie Lang, the Cardonald Witch*, and *The Life and Transactions with the Trial and Burning of Maggie Osborne, the Ayrshire Witch*, both left over from George Caldwell's business in Paisley, of which Hawkie managed to sell several reams in Paisley and Ayr.[40] 'Last dying speeches', such as those of two men condemned to be hanged on Leith Sands for piracy and murder at sea, were written in advance: 'The night *before* the execution, the criers were supplied with the last speeches of the condemned men.'[41] Another case concerned a man called Robertson, sentenced to death for housebreaking and theft but rumoured to be expecting a reprieve, so when Hawkie and Jamie Blue found a tract called *A Reprieve from the Punishment of Death* in a bookseller's shop they each took four dozen copies, priced at 1½*d*. each, and they sold well.[42] On the day of execution further sales in Glasgow were banned by the police, so the printer, Thomas Duncan, offered Hawkie half a ream if he would go and sell them in Paisley, but he managed to sell them all before he had even left Glasgow. The audience was evidently not concerned that the tract had nothing to do with the criminal of the day. Hawkie wrote that he only ever cried two

---

[34] Cowan and Patterson, *Folk in Print*, p. 30; Harvey, *Scottish Chapbook Literature*, pp. 65–66; Frank N. Egerton, 'Wilson, Alexander (1766–1813)', *ODNB* https://doi.org/10.1093/ref:odnb/29634.

[35] *Hawkie*, p. 99.

[36] *Hawkie*, p. 23.

[37] *Hawkie*, p. 60.

[38] *Hawkie*, p. 74.

[39] *Hawkie*, p. 99.

[40] *Hawkie*, p. 96.

[41] *Hawkie*, p. 101.

[42] *Hawkie*, pp. 93–5.

last dying speeches, but others recalled that he was regularly present at executions in this capacity.[43] Perhaps the moral framework of the autobiography required some distancing from the practice.

Hawkie wrote that he had considerable success with pamphlets of his own composition, although there is little surviving trace of them. In Morpeth, in Northumberland, he drew up an account of a conscience-stricken murderer in Glasgow who confessed to a murder he had committed twenty years before, which brought in nearly 18s.[44] In Edinburgh he wrote an account of a man who had disguised himself as the devil in order to rob the house of a maiden lady, under the title of *Hairie's Counterfeit*, and the printer, Robert Menzies, sold six reams in one night and kept his press working on it for three weeks.[45] Also printed by Menzies was an account of *Ancient King Crispin*, written in twelve pages of six-line verse for the occasion of the Edinburgh shoemakers' procession, which sold rapidly at 2d. per copy until the other speech-criers got hold of it.[46] Hawkie had requested the printer not to include his imprint so that this would not happen, and so they fell out for a while, but eventually they came to an understanding and Menzies also printed Hawkie's *Adventures of a Temperance Gentleman from Edinburgh to Lasswade on his Horse 'Glanders', being a Coffee-Drinking Excursion*, running to forty-eight pages, which sold well until friends of the gentleman concerned paid Hawkie to put a stop to it.[47]

On a suggestion of Jamie Blue, he wrote up a story about a drunken exciseman whom a group of colliers had taken down the pit with them so that when he woke up he thought he had gone to hell, under the title of *The Gauger's Journey to the Land of Darkness*, but they made little profit out of it because it was taken up by other speech-criers.[48] In Newcastle the story drew such a crowd that it landed him in the House of Correction.[49] Also in Newcastle, he found a copy that had been turned into a song and sung by a blind ballad singer.[50] It is

[43] *Hawkie*, p. 101; Urie, *Reminiscences of Eighty Years*, pp. 49–50; Mackenzie, *Reminiscences of Glasgow*, III, 80–81.
[44] *Hawkie*, p. 42.
[45] *Hawkie*, pp. 99–100. Robert Menzies printed and published slip songs, catchpennies, and occasional chapbooks in Edinburgh, 1810–45 (Morris, 'Scottish Chapman', p. 179; SBTI). A ream would normally be twenty quires or 480 sheets, so six reams would be a little short of three thousand sheets (*OED*, ream, *n.3* 1.a.).
[46] *Hawkie*, p. 100.
[47] *Hawkie*, p. 100.
[48] *Hawkie*, p. 93.
[49] *Hawkie*, p. 42.
[50] *Hawkie*, pp. 93–94.

perhaps the only one of Hawkie's compositions that has definitely survived in print, in a copy in the British Library.[51]

The Expiring Groans, Death, and Funeral Procession of the Beacon Newspaper was written on behalf of the newspaper office, printed on a large sheet, and sold well at 6*d.* per copy, with one customer buying a dozen.[52] Another commission was from the masons, wrights, and plasterers of Edinburgh who approached Hawkie to write something promoting their cause when they were in dispute with their masters who had reduced their wages in 1826/7.[53] According to a ballad printed by the Glasgow Poet's Box in 1851, the year of Hawkie's death, his political sympathies were with the Whigs and the Chartists and against the Tories, and he was a scourge of Catholics.[54] From the titles cited in the autobiography, he does not seem to have imposed his political views on his audiences. He did, however, write *The Prophecies of 'Hawkie', a Cow*, a spoof on one Ross, a weaver by trade, who went by the name of the 'Glasgow Prophet'.[55] While the Glasgow audiences understood the point of the satire, in Edinburgh they did not, and that is where Hawkie acquired his nickname, after the book. Some, he said, bought it for fun, others out of contempt for the Prophet, but Ross himself attacked Hawkie and he had to be rescued by the people in the street.

Hawkie makes brief mention, later in his autobiography, of a new system of 'straw-selling', where he would say: 'This is a most particular book, but I daurna' cry the book; 'deed, I daurna' either name the book, nor sell the book, but I will sell ony o' ye a *straw*, an' gie ye the book into the bargain.'[56] The implication is that the purchasers would be getting something surreptitious, perhaps rather racy. The book he was selling in this way in Edinburgh is named as *Gilderoy, the Scotch Robber* and Hawkie claims he sold nearly twenty reams (which sounds a very high figure), but it is difficult to know exactly what this was and

---

[51] *A Gauger's Journey to the Land of Darkness! with a Particular Description of the Country, the Inhabitants, and the Treatment They Give Gaugers Who Go Yonder!* [London, British Library, 1875.b.30.(56.)].

[52] *Hawkie*, p. 101.

[53] *Hawkie*, p. 101.

[54] *Hawkie*, second edition since 3d May 1851 (Glasgow, Poet's Box, Saturday, 10th May 1851). On the other hand, *The Laird of Logan*, p. 150, records Hawkie as saying, 'I am neither [. . .] a Tory nor a Radical; I like middle courses – gang ayont that, either up or doun, it disna matter – it's a wreck ony way ye tak it.'

[55] *Hawkie*, pp. 92–93.

[56] *Hawkie*, p. 101.

whether this example of straw-selling would have counted as trickery or mere novelty.[57]

Most, though not all, of the surviving titles named in Hawkie's autobiography are in prose (*Watty and Meg* is an obvious exception), but he successfully sold ballads even though, according to his own account, he did not sing them. Urie refers to lampoons in verse (quoted above). Mackenzie provides some examples of verses.[58] Probably, he made little distinction between prose and verse, and he was certainly familiar with songs. Mackenzie records him telling the story of 'The Scotch Servant Lassie Stealing the Milk' to the women washing clothes on Glasgow Green, and winding up with the sentence: 'Fair fa' the limmer, they say "she's o'er the border and awa' wi' Jock o' Hazeldean".'[59] Hawkie was quoting from Walter Scott's song of 'Jock o' Hazeldean' and, Mackenzie observes, he 'could sometimes twist the prettiest songs in our language to his advantage, in the passing scene'.[60]

In Aberdeenshire he teamed up with a roguish piper and when they came to the Earl of Aboyne's residence had him play the Jacobite tune 'Johnnie Cope'.[61] The song 'Johnnie Cope' ridicules the army commander whose tactical retreat at Prestonpans in 1745 made him a scapegoat and turned him, quite undeservedly from a military point of view, into a figure of ridicule.[62] The Countess of Aboyne was the daughter of Sir John Cope (though the piper did not know this) and eventually someone opened the window and threw them half a crown (2*s.* 6*d.*) to go away and never return.

At Wooler Fair, in Northumberland, Hawkie had no success and complained about a man and woman who were selling 'the most

---

[57] 'Gilderoy' is best known as an old song ('Gilderoy was a bonny boy'), but there was a melodrama called *Gilderoy; or, The Bonnie Boy* by William Barrymore and perhaps Hawkie was selling this without permission.

[58] Mackenzie, *Reminiscences of Glasgow*, III, 83–88.

[59] Mackenzie, *Reminiscences of Glasgow*, III, 108.

[60] 'Jock o' Hazeldean' was written by Walter Scott for Alexander Campbell's *Albyn's Anthology* (1816), with the first stanza based on an old ballad. See Robert Ford, *Song Histories* (Glasgow and Edinburgh: William Hodge & Company, 1900), pp. 282–85.

[61] *Hawkie*, pp. 67–68.

[62] Stephen Brumwell, 'Cope, Sir John [Jonathan] (1690–1760)', *ODNB* https://doi.org/10.1093/ref:odnb/6254. The song 'Johnnie Cope' was composed by one Adam Skirving (1719–1803) around the time of the battle, according to Ford, *Song Histories*, pp. 227–32. Most Jacobite songs were actually written around the last decades of the century, however, and William Donaldson, *The Jacobite Song: Political Myth and National Identity* (Aberdeen: Aberdeen University Press, 1988), p. 4, is duly circumspect.

infamous and abominable songs that can be picked from the works of the lowest poets that ever wrote'.[63] They sold, he said, seventeen quires of ballads and made a profit of about £3 7s.[64] He observed grumpily, 'I have had the cheek, *when I was drunk*, to sing such songs; but, at my worst, I would not take £5 and sing one of them in the presence of a female.' This sounds rather like sour grapes; it is likely to have been a holiday crowd at the fair, probably fuelled by alcohol, and Hawkie seems to have misjudged the mood of the audience on this occasion.

While he was in England, Hawkie observed the distress of unemployed tradesmen and also the imposture of beggars impersonating them so as to receive charity, and intriguingly he made singing in the street a sign of distinction between the two groups: 'did they [the charitable public] think that a respectable tradesman would bemean himself to sing on the street? I have known them, by strong necessity, make known their wants to a fellow-creature, but to *sing* on the street requires a person who is a stranger to shame.'[65] Possibly Hawkie regarded the trade of speech-crier as superior to that of ballad singer. Henry Mayhew found that in London in the mid-nineteenth century the 'patterers' (more or less equivalent to speech-criers) regarded themselves as the aristocracy of the streets on account of their education and the exercise of intellect involved in their performances: 'People don't pay us for what we gives 'em, but only to hear us talk.'[66]

Urie and others testify to Hawkie's elocution, clarity of delivery, inventiveness and wit, and there is no doubt that he could draw a crowd. Under the heading of 'Street Oratory', the Paisley poet William Finlay gave a reconstructed example of Hawkie's street repartee and exchanges with his audience which shows he was well able to handle interruptions. Where Hawkie gives an idea of the numbers of printed copies he sold, the figures also give an idea of the numbers of people he could attract, allowing for the fact that they were probably not all present at the same time and that others may have stopped to listen but did not make a purchase. Glasgow itself was a city of some

---

[63] *Hawkie*, p. 41.

[64] This is where Hawkie specifies the Scots quire containing ninety-four sheets. I have not been able to verify this quantity, but Beavan, 'Decline and Fall', p. 163 n. 30, calculates a profit of about ½d. per copy on 1,598 copies if they sold at 1d. each.

[65] *Hawkie*, p. 36.

[66] Henry Mayhew, *London Labour and the London Poor*, 4 vols (London: Griffin, Bohn, 1861–62), I, 213.

147,000 inhabitants by 1821.[67] Hawkie's comments about gender indicate that his audiences included both men and women. According to Mackenzie, the women washing on Glasgow Green rewarded him for his story with a shower of copper money. Those who bought his wares must have had a halfpenny or a penny to spare, so probably not the poorest of the poor – although they, too, might have been in the crowd. Mackenzie also makes the point that ballad singers and street-criers made news accessible to the common people for a halfpenny at a time when a Glasgow newspaper cost 7½d.[68] Referring to Hawkie's readiness in repartee, Finlay wrote, 'woe betide any of our whiskered-cigar-smokers who attempt to break a lance with him!', so perhaps on occasion he could draw some more sophisticated listeners.[69]

Besides the street oratory, people paid Hawkie for the chapbooks he was selling, and their expenditure provides a measure of commercial success which distinguishes these exchanges from mere begging. There are, therefore, several elements to these audience interactions:

(a) *Familiarity*: What Hawkie called 'the *best* old standard books of the "flying stationer" order', titles that are well known to scholars from surviving printed copies, stood him in good stead with the paying audience.

(b) *Topicality*: On the other hand, his own compositions on different topics also sold well, such as last dying speeches and pieces written for particular events or groups of people, and Hawkie took some pains to protect his ownership of such works.

(c) *Inventiveness*: Hawkie was remembered for the fluency of his street performances and his ability to improvise even around the set topics of the chapbooks, as well as his trickery, which mostly seems to have paid off, with only the occasional complaint recorded.

(d) *Exchange*: On the other hand, his cash-paying audience did expect to receive something in print in return for their halfpenny or penny.

These elements were evidently fluid, and they can appear contradictory, but it is also not difficult to see how the twin imperatives of commerce and entertainment mean that there is a logic running through them. In principle, it did not matter to either the street-seller or the printer what the audience actually did with the chapbooks they bought. Nevertheless, although Hawkie could be

---

[67] Cleland, *Statistical and Population Tables*, p. 9.
[68] Mackenzie, *Reminiscences of Glasgow*, III, 79.
[69] Finlay, 'Street Oratory', p. 65.

quite cynical on occasion, mostly he seems to have recited something fairly close to the stories he was selling. Both printer and street-crier wanted the audience to come back for more, so we can infer a degree of feedback, although at this hit-and-miss, cheap end of the trade one might not want to posit a fully self-sufficient network in the manner of Robert Darnton's 'communications circuit'.[70]

The whole of Hawkie's autobiography has, of course, to be approached with caution. Like all such productions, it is a construct of the author's and the editor's imagination.[71] There is as much, if not more, about begging and whisky as about audiences and street-selling. Nevertheless, it is consistent both with what we know of the itinerant street trade and with the recollections of other writers about Glasgow's past. For all its possible pitfalls, Hawkie's account does have a demonstrable historical basis.

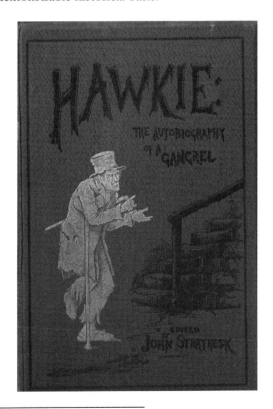

---

[70] Robert Darnton, 'What Is the History of Books?', *Daedalus*, 111.3 (1982), 65–83; reprinted in Robert Darnton, *The Kiss of Lamourette: Reflections in Cultural History* (New York: W. W. Norton, 1990), pp. 107–35.
[71] Cf. Harris, 'A Few Shillings for Small Books', p. 102.

'Griddling' Tramps (1879)

By an Ex-Mendicity Officer

Introduction by Steve Roud

The piece reprinted here was one chapter in a weekly series about tramps and vagrants under the general title of 'The Doings & Dodges of our Social Wastrels' written by an 'Ex-Mendicity Officer' and published in the *South Wales Daily News* in 1878–79 (and reprinted elsewhere). This piece on '"Griddling" Tramps' was published in two parts on 9 and 16 January 1879.

'Griddling' was a contemporary term for singing in the streets as a beggar; the first citation recorded in the *Oxford English Dictionary* is from Henry Mayhew's *London Labour and the London Poor* (1851). The 'ex-mendicity officer' who wrote the articles was a former employee of one of the organizations established during the nineteenth century for the alleviation or suppression of begging (mendicity). He had started work in London but had later transferred to Wales and many of the details he provides are from these two areas, but in this case he was writing mostly about the north-west of England. He clearly knew a great deal about the subject, and he quotes extensively from official and local publications as well as from his own experience.

There was evidently something of a social panic concerning vagrancy at this period. The author starts the series on 28 November 1878 by referring to the 'outrages which have been committed by tramps during the last few months, culminating in the terrible tragedy enacted at Llangibby', which refers to the brutal murder of William and Elizabeth Watkins and their three children by Joseph Garcia, a Spanish sailor, in July 1878. Garcia was consistently described in the newspaper coverage of the murders as a tramp.

The main thrust of this series on 'wastrels' is that many (probably most) tramps and beggars had chosen that course of life, or had fallen into it by misfortune and then decided to stay there, and that 'trades' such as broadside singing and selling (in some of the other articles the author refers to people singing in the street apparently without selling anything) were just one of the many dodges and tricks adopted by them. Just as the broadside printers themselves were highly attuned to the latest murder or disaster, so, too, were the general cadgers and tramps. The 'cotton famine' is mentioned here as being on its way out as a valid reason for begging, but the article published on 5 June 1879 refers to a 'Dinas widow' – that is, someone who, dressed in shabby black clothes, pretended to be the widow of one of the sixty-three miners killed in an explosion at the Dinas colliery in the Rhondda not long before – 'nothing to beat that just now', commented one of the vagrants, 'It'll soon be stale, but while it lasts [. . .] Joe says he won't mend umbrellas any more, he'll just follow the explosions over the country.'

Many of the contemporary descriptions of street sellers of ballads and other kinds of cheap print, such as Mayhew, concentrate on the 'professionals' (as do the autobiographical accounts of street-criers and ballad singers like John Magee, David Love, 'Hawkie', and others). The nature of the business, however, made it open to 'casuals' – people down on their luck or destitute – as well as professional beggars and those with criminal intent. Coupled with the fear of ballad sellers spreading sedition and immorality through their songs, this side of the trade explains in part why so many 'respectable' people treated the whole business with such distaste and were so vehement in their condemnation. As with many social commentators of the day, this anonymous officer provides a wealth of detail that we would not get otherwise, and he would probably be surprised that it is his descriptions of the 'griddlers', rather than his own moral standpoint, that so interests us nowadays.[1]

'Griddling' Tramps

'Griddling' in lodging-house, or tramp lingo, signifies street-singing, whether accompanied by any musical instrument or not. 'Griddlers' are divided into many classes, from the poor woe-begone creature whose quavering voice is not heard till you come close upon her, to the shabby-genteel, bearded and moustached individual who ensconces himself in the porch of the best hotel, and gives the latest new song from the latest opera. Between these two extremes there are many means, and I purpose not only, as far as possible, to furnish illustrations of the most common types of 'griddlers', but to give specimens of some of their songs. Real 'griddlers', or street-singers, first attracted my notice during the Lancashire cotton famine, when

---

[1] A small number of minor typographical errors have been silently corrected in the transcription from the newspapers.

the starving operatives left their native county and perambulated the country in droves, sometimes eight or ten in a gang, singing

We're all the way from Manchester, &c.

But some of them were more select in the choice of their ditties, and sang various old songs, such as 'Be kind to thy father', 'Come whoam to thy childer an' me', 'Tay an' Rum ditty, Rum', and other songs in the Lancashire dialect, the composition of the well-known Edwin Waugh, almost invariably including in their catalogue the pathetic song, commencing with

Let us pause with life's pleasures, and count its many tears
While we all sup sorrow with the poor;
It's a song that will linger for ever in our ears,
Oh! Hard times come again no more.[2]

This really touching ballad, the music of which is in full sympathy with the words, never failed of its desired effect in drawing the coppers from the pockets of the bystanders. But there was one song, though I only heard it once, which must have brought a golden harvest to the three who sang it – two men and a woman, in the streets of Kendal, in Westmoreland, on a Saturday night. The words were written in rather doggerel form, and were originally, I believe, composed in the corn famine year, 1847, but were so appropriate to the then condition of things in Lancashire, that the singers might be excused for altering the word 'corn' to 'cotton'. The song runs thus: –

One cold winter's morning, as the day was a-dawning,
A voice came so hollow and shrill,
The cold winds did whistle, and the snow it was fast falling,
As a stranger came over the hill.
The clothing he was wearing was tattered and torn,
He seemed all despairing and wandering forlorn,
Lamenting for pleasures that never will return.
Oh! Old England! What have you come to?

The first part of the next verse might very appropriately be sung now
–

---

[2] 'Hard Times Come Again No More' was not in fact by Waugh but by the popular American songwriter Stephen Foster.

'Griddling' Tramps (1879)

He said, 'Oh I sigh for those hearts so undeserving,
In their own native land led astray,
For in the midst of plenty some thousands are starving,
Neither house, food, nor clothing have they.
The cotton is kept up, and our trade is gone away,' &c.

The air to this mournful ditty is in the minor key, and the trio I heard singing it were evidently bent on making enough that Saturday to keep them all the following week. They had the song to sell, and scrupled not to tell their listeners they had sold three reams of it, – 1,440 that day; it was then only about 4 o'clock. These, at a penny each, gave them £6, or five guineas profit, sheet songs being only 2s 6d a ream of 480, or 2d a quire of 24 by retail. By far the best specimen of 'griddling' during the Lancashire cotton famine, however, was that of a man who always appeared in the streets alone, and sang to an air I have never since been able to procure or to recognise, that grand poem of Gerald Massey's,

THE CRY OF THE UNEMPLOYED.

'T is hard, 't is hard to wander on through this bright world of ours,
Beneath a sky of smiling blue, on velvet paths of flowers,
With music in the woods, as there were nought but joyaunce known,
Or Angels walkt earth's solitudes, and yet with want to groan,
To see no beauty in the stars, nor in God's radiant smile,
To wail and wander misery-curst! willing, but cannot toil.
There's burning sickness at my heart, I sink down famished!
God of the wretched, hear my prayer: I would that I were dead!

Heaven droppeth down with manna still in many a golden show'r,
And feeds the leaves with fragrant breath, with silver dew the flow'r.
There's honeyed fruit for bee and bird, with bloom laughs out the
    tree,
And food for all God's happy things; but none gives food to me.
Earth, deckt with Plenty's garland-crown, smiles on my aching eye,
The purse-proud – swathed in luxury – disdainful pass me by:
I've eager hands, and earnest heart – but may not work for bread!
God of the wretched, hear my prayer: I would that I were dead!

Gold, art thou not a blessed thing – a charm above all other,
To shut up hearts to Nature's cry, when brother pleads with brother?
Hast thou a music sweeter than the voice of loving-kindness?
No! curse thee, thou'rt a mist 'twixt God and men in outer blindness.
'Father, come back!' my children cry; their voices once so sweet,
Now quiver lance-like in my bleeding heart! I cannot meet

The looks that make the brain go mad, for dear ones asking bread –
God of the wretched, hear my prayer: I would that I were dead!

Lord! what right have the poor to wed? Love's for the gilded great,
Are they not form'd of nobler clay, who dine off golden plate?
'T is the worst curse of poverty to have a feeling heart,
Why can I not, with iron-grasp, tear out the tender part!
I cannot slave in yon Bastille! ah no, 't were the bitterest pain,
To wear the Pauper's iron within, than drag the Convict's chain.
I'd work but cannot, starve I may, but will not beg for bread:
God of the wretched, hear my prayer: I would that I were dead!

Gerald Massey knew from bitter experience the miseries of the poor. His father was a canal boatman, whose wages amounted to the handsome sum of 10s a week! Gerald was born at Tring, in Hertfordshire; and his father often was out of work, and there was no bread in the cupboard. At eight years of age the boy went to work in a silk mill, and in after years thus referred to it: –

Still all the day the iron wheels go onward,
Grinding life down from its mark;
And the children's souls, which God is calling onward,
Spin on blindly in the dark!

Can we wonder that Gerald Massey, the poet, should be eloquent on the miseries of the lower classes? The poem above cited is only one among many written by him to illustrate the terrible privations the poor are subjected to in such times as the present.

The words of his beautiful poem are so very appropriate to present circumstances in this country, that I have ventured to give them in full. The man I heard singing these noble lines was no ordinary 'griddler'. His whole appearance – whether studied or natural I cannot tell – accorded so well with the words he sang, that crowds used to gather round him, and the money given him – for he never asked, or went round with his hat – must have amounted to a considerable sum in the course of an evening. It was rumoured that he was a genuine factory operative, a man of some note in his native place, and secretary to the Local Spinners' Association. He had a splendid baritone voice, and sang with an expression that proved him to be no novice. I think, indeed, it was generally believed that the man had set the words to his own music. Whether this be so or not, there could not be found a more appropriate *finale* than the way in which the pitiful words, 'God of the wretched, hear my prayer: I would that I were dead!' was sung.

'Griddling' has sadly degenerated from what it was twenty or thirty years ago. There have always been two classes of street-singers, whether respectable or miserable; viz., those who try to move our pity by their wretchedness, and those [who] profess to give us something in return for our coppers. When the present generation were children it was common enough to hear a couple of broken-down sailors singing not inharmoniously some of Dibdin's well known sea-songs; and even the poorest attempts at street-singing then were a hundred times better than now The style of songs composed now are only suitable for music halls; the old songs are mostly forgotten or ignored by 'griddlers', and it thus happens that we so often hear a wretched parody of Moody and Sankey, the tune being barely recognisable. Street-singers, who sing hymns or sacred songs, are 'dodgers' in the truest sense of the word. They adopt the hymn with a view to gain the sympathies of the religious public, but are, without exception, the most depraved of the 'griddling' fraternity; far worse than the bawling fellow who grinds out of his capacious lungs, in stentorian tones, the last hours of the last executed murderer. By the way, it will interest my readers to know how street songs are brought out so soon after a murder, a great shipwreck, explosion, &c., takes place. There are well-known street-song printers, who strike off the 'flimsy' songs by tens of thousands; indeed, a striking song, after a national calamity, will sell by hundreds of thousands. No sooner does a 'diabolical' murder, a 'terrific' explosion, or a 'horrible' catastrophe of any description take place, than the song-printer receives MSS. songs on the subject from men who gain a precarious livelihood by writing such stuff. For stuff it is, as everyone who has heard these 'halfpenny awfuls' in the song line must acknowledge. The song publisher does not affect to choose the best MS. from a literary standpoint; he takes the one most graphic and startling, no matter whether the rhyme and rhythm be correct or not. Such songs 'run' about ten days or a fortnight in towns, and perhaps a month in the country, and when murders sufficiently awful and accidents sufficiently terrible are scarce, the sensation griddler falls back upon 'Where does the wages go?' 'The coming taxes', or some other ever-popular comic ditty.

But in order that my readers may have a true insight into the mysteries of 'griddling', I will give in my next chapter a few scenes I have witnessed, and stories I have heard, amongst the 'griddlers' of the metropolis.

(*Continued*) 'Griddling' does not need a very long apprenticeship. Given a sufficiency of assurance, or as it is termed by the tramps, 'cheek', and the ability to sing in some fashion, if it is only one song, the 'griddler' may start work forthwith. If his voice is of the costermonger's order, more bawl than melody, he need not despair, for he will probably obtain a few coppers 'to go into the next street', if he does not get any for the pleasure (?) he gives his hearers. I once heard a big lout of fellow telling another 'cadger' that he 'griddled' seven streets and got nothing, and that in the eighth a lady came out and gave him a shilling to move on, for she had a sick child, whom his voice awakened, when it was absolutely necessary the child should sleep. In Chapter II., on 'Kite Flyers', I mentioned that I had been sent up into Cumberland to identify the 'Parson', a well-known member of the tramp swell mob. During the few days the 'Parson' was on remand, I had an opportunity, and turned it to good account, of seeing some phases of tramp life in a part of the country where many of the primitive habits and customs of English life a hundred years ago are still in force. Cumberland is a beautiful country, as all tourists know who have traversed it, and as it was early in the month of September, Nature had not yet put off her summer garb, and the Cumberland hills were purple with heather, the lakes unruffled by the storms that rage on their surface in winter, and thus the few days I spent there, both before and after the 'Parson's' committal, were very pleasant ones. I started from Hawkshead on a short pedestrian tour, by way of Broughton, Ravenglass, Gosforth, Egremont, Whitehaven, Workington, Maryport, Cockermouth, and back to Keswick and Ambleside. At Broughton I scraped acquaintance with a couple of 'griddlers', old hands apparently, for one of them played an old battered concertina, and the other carried a bundle of songs. The instrumentalist made no secret of the fact that he had been at that game since the cotton famine some seven or eight years before, and meant to follow it as long as he could live as he did then. He became quite confidential over a pint of beer with which I provided him, desiring to obtain some information as to his 'lay' in that part of the country. 'No, I did not get on very well at first. A gentleman in Ulverstone gave me five shillings, and as begging by Lancashire chaps was just then becoming too common, I bought a cheap concertina, got a few quires of mixed songs, and started "griddling". But I found it was no use without a mate. I wanted a chum to sell the songs in the "publics", and to knock at the doors, and go into the shops. Jerry, the clock dresser, what keeps a lodging-house in Ulverstone, recommended me to one, and a capital mate he seemed to be, till I found out that for every penny he shared with me he put another in his own pocket on the quiet. So I "jacked him up", and "pal'd in" with an old fellow about 50. He *could* sing, and no mistake. Hardly a song could be asked for in the public-houses, but he knew it. But he was troubled with some queer-named complaint, and I had to leave him in Newcastle workhouse. No, I never goes out of Cumberland, Westmoreland, and Northumberland. It don't pay to go into Lancashire, or Yorkshire either. Yes, you may look at my songs.' I found that his stock-in-trade consisted mostly of old songs, some of them local, but the greater part long ago forgotten, except in such primitive parts as the one we were then in. 'The Farmer's Boy', 'The Dark-eyed Sailor', 'The Lively Flea', 'The Cork Leg', 'Brennan on the Moor', were largely represented in his *repertoire*; whilst another bundle, specially kept for business in Irish neighbourhoods, contained 'The harp that once', 'The Minstrel Boy', 'The Exile of Erin', and 'The Irish Emigrant'. At Broughton I parted from the 'griddling' couple; they were going to Ravenglass, I to Gosforth. But on my arrival at Cockermouth a week later, I found it was Cockermouth fair, and the town was full of tramps of all descriptions. Here was an opportunity of becoming acquainted with North-country tramp life which I should not probably have presented to me again. So I asked a policeman which was the largest and most popular lodging-house in the town. 'Blind Peggy's,' said he, 'but you will not be able to get a bed there, I know, Old Peggy is full up at fair time, and I have no doubt there will be plenty of "travellers" sitting by the kitchen fire to-night They will be quite as well off as those in bed, for there will be too much of a row for any of them to get sleep.' I provided myself with a few things necessary to enable me to pass as a traveller, and found my way into 'Blind Peggy's' kitchen. It was a long room, with two long tables and forms, and a fire-place at each end. The room was full of tramps, or as they style themselves, travellers, of all sorts and descriptions, but the 'griddling' element apparently predominated. My Broughton acquaintance was there having tea at the end of one of the long tables, with a rather pretty-looking young girl whom he introduced to me as his wife. He afterwards told me that he had met her in a lodging-house in Whitehaven, where she had been living for some years; her father having been transported for stabbing a rival pedlar in a drunken quarrel. She had got tired of life in a lodging-house, and having become only too well initiated into the depraved nature of such a mode of living, had finally accepted the 'griddler's' offer to go 'on the road' with him. 'My other mate? Oh! I told him we must part, and as I gave him more than half of our "flimsies" he could not grumble. Yes,

Polly can sing first rate; I did not take her for her pretty face; though a
wife does make a fellow more comfortable.' 'Why don't you marry
her, then?' asked I. 'Well, I don't know, but I might, if I could afford
it. But may-be she wouldn't marry me.' I took the first opportunity I
had of asking her the same question, and she said she would be only
too glad. 'Even among this sort of people,' she said, 'a woman who
can show her "lines" is thought much better of than one that can't.
Yes, Joe is reckoned a good fellow. I have seen him off and on at Mrs
Maguire's, where I was a "slavey", for a long time, and never heard a
bad word of Joe.' I went to the Vicar of Cockermouth, represented
the case to him, and he readily consented to marry the couple. I had
the satisfaction of giving away the bride, and the kind-hearted
clergyman not only gave her half a sovereign, but so interested his lady
on the girl's behalf that a bundle of good clothes was sent to 'Old
Peggy's' for the young wife, now a wife in reality, and not in name
only. The other 'griddlers' in the house were of the ordinary stamp. A
couple of 'latest sensation' singers; an Italian with a monkey, and a
singing English wife; a boy singer, accompanied by his father, who
lazily lived on his child's earnings; and an execrable German band,
consisting of a father and four sons, comprised the lot. Later in the
evening 'Lanky Joe', as the concertina player was called, came and
whispered in my ear that a wedding was coming off that night. I had
not then been fortunate enough to witness a 'broomstick' wedding,
and although I had previously resolved upon shifting my quarters ere
bed-time, the chance of witnessing this now rather rare occurrence
made me stay. It appeared that a jewellery hawker, fifty years of age if
he was a day, had fallen in love with a ladies' cap hawker, who could
not have been more than twenty. He dazzled the girl by a promise to
keep her 'like a lady', and so the wedding was to take place that night.
A curious affair it was. One of the 'sensation singers' offered his
services as parson, the bridegroom's best white shirt doing duty as a
surplice. The impromptu parson read the marriage service out of the
Prayer Book, after which the couple, hand in hand, jumped over a
broomstick held about a foot from the floor by two of the company. I
noticed that the Germans emptied their glasses very often, and I was
not, it appeared, the only one to notice it, for somebody played them a
scurvy trick near the end of the fun, which would, I think, effectually
cure them of 'swigging' so heavily 'on the cheap'.

There used to be in Wales a race of Welsh 'Griddlers' who sang
old Welsh songs, and not long ago I saw an antiquated specimen of
this class in Cardiff. About 15 years ago, when the Pembroke and
Tenby Railway was being constructed, a 'griddling' young Welsh girl's

coquetry led to her 'husband' being transported. 'Billy Jemmy' was a clever, keen pick-pocket, and well-known to the Merthyr police. He and his 'girl' were travelling the country, ostensibly getting a living by the girl's 'griddling' in the streets, but he was following *his* avocation wherever an opportunity presented itself. At Haverfordwest fair a lot of the navvies from Pembroke were drinking, and one of them, said to be a handsome young fellow, fell in love with 'Billy Jimmy's' wife. The girl must have given him some encouragement, for he followed the pair from Pembrokeshire into Glamorganshire, where a watch, stolen by James, his real name, was seen in the hands of the navvy, who had obtained it from James's wife. This led to James's conviction and sentence of seven years' penal servitude, the girl afterwards marrying the navvy. He turned out a scamp of a husband, however, for he compelled his young wife to go out singing in the streets with her baby in all kinds of weather, in order that he might have the means of 'fuddling' all day long.

A curious form of begging, closely allied to 'griddling', and styled 'pattering', must have a brief notice ere I conclude this chapter. The 'patterer' walks slowly down the middle of the street, and in a loud voice makes known his woes to the world in monotonous tones, or in a sing-song kind of way that is far more trying to the nerves and patience of those who are compelled to listen to him. Even now, as I write, the only 'patterer' I have heard for some years past is giving vent to his woes beneath my window. 'I'm a poor blind soldier' is all I can catch of his reiterated and certainly lugubrious 'patter', whilst his wife, a poor half-starved looking creature, is knocking at the doors as he goes slowly along. The 'patterer', however, is almost extinct. It used to be a successful method of obtaining a living, if one could judge by the shower of coppers that would be thrown out of the windows to a first-rate hand at 'pattering'. A decent-looking working man, dressed like a mechanic in monkey jacket and moleskin trousers, accompanied by a tidily-dressed wife, and clean children, such as I used to see some twenty or twenty-five years ago, would no doubt find 'pattering' a lucrative game. Even 'griddling', like 'pattering', is fast declining. We very seldom now-a-days hear a really good singer in the streets; the music-halls now catch them up. In my native town, when I was a boy, we often had visits from street-singers whose vocal abilities would not have disgraced a music-hall, but the race, has, apparently, died out.

My next chapter, on 'Thieving Tramps', will show the close alliance there exists between Vagrancy and Crime.